Gender and Educational Leadership in Greece

Educational Leadership: Innovative, Critical and Interdisciplinary Perspectives

Series Editors: Jeffrey S. Brooks, Alan J. Daly, Yi-Hwa Liou, Chen Schechter and Victoria Showunmi

The Educational Leadership series provides a forum for books that push the conceptual boundaries of educational leadership and that introduce novel perspectives with the promise of improving, challenging, and reconceptualizing the field of study and informing practice. Books in the series take a global, interdisciplinary focus and cover educational phases ranging from early years to higher education. They aspire to be field-leading innovations that advance new theories, topics, and methodologies. The series will be of interest to those working across disciplines such as educational leadership, school leadership, teacher education, sociology, anthropology, economics, psychology, political science, philosophy, and public policy.

Also available in the series:
Educational Leadership and Critical Theory, edited by Charles L. Lowery, Chetanath Gautam, Robert White and Michael E. Hess
The Relational Leader, edited by Yi-Hwa Liou and Alan J. Daly
Women Navigating Educational Research, Jana L. Carlisle
Islam, Education, and Freedom, Melanie C. Brooks and Miriam D. Ezzani

Forthcoming in the series:
Leadership for Society, Rima'a Da'as and Chen Schechter
Equity and Influence in the Funding of Schools, Matthew P. Sinclair
Socialisation of School Leaders in Sub-Saharan Africa, Pontso Moorosi and Callie Grant

Gender and Educational Leadership in Greece

Emmy Papanastasiou

BLOOMSBURY ACADEMIC
LONDON • NEW YORK • OXFORD • NEW DELHI • SYDNEY

BLOOMSBURY ACADEMIC

Bloomsbury Publishing Plc, 50 Bedford Square, London, WC1B 3DP, UK
Bloomsbury Publishing Inc, 1359 Broadway, New York, NY 10018, USA
Bloomsbury Publishing Ireland, 29 Earlsfort Terrace, Dublin 2, D02 AY28, Ireland

BLOOMSBURY, BLOOMSBURY ACADEMIC and the Diana logo are
trademarks of Bloomsbury Publishing Plc

First published in Great Britain 2024
This paperback edition published in 2025

Copyright © Emmy Papanastasiou, 2024

Emmy Papanastasiou has asserted her right under the Copyright,
Designs and Patents Act, 1988, to be identified as Author of this work.

Series design by Tjaša Krivec
Cover image © MirageC / Getty Images

All rights reserved. No part of this publication may be: i) reproduced or transmitted in any form, electronic or mechanical, including photocopying, recording or by means of any information storage or retrieval system without prior permission in writing from the publishers; or ii) used or reproduced in any way for the training, development or operation of artificial intelligence (AI) technologies, including generative AI technologies. The rights holders expressly reserve this publication from the text and data mining exception as per Article 4(3) of the Digital Single Market Directive (EU) 2019/790.

Bloomsbury Publishing Plc does not have any control over, or responsibility for, any third-party websites referred to or in this book. All internet addresses given in this book were correct at the time of going to press. The author and publisher regret any inconvenience caused if addresses have changed or sites have ceased to exist, but can accept no responsibility for any such changes.

A catalogue record for this book is available from the British Library.

A catalog record for this book is available from the Library of Congress.

Library of Congress Control Number: 2024933288

ISBN:	HB:	978-1-3503-9982-2
	PB:	978-1-3503-9985-3
	ePDF:	978-1-3503-9983-9
	eBook:	978-1-3503-9984-6

Series: Educational Leadership: Innovative, Critical and Interdisciplinary Perspectives

Typeset by Integra Software Services Pvt. Ltd.

For product safety related questions contact productsafety@bloomsbury.com.

To find out more about our authors and books visit www.bloomsbury.com
and sign up for our newsletters.

To Stavros and Elena
My first teachers

Contents

List of Tables	viii
Series Editors' Foreword	ix
Preface	xii
1 Introduction	1
2 Women in Educational Leadership: Global and National Context	15
3 Constructions of Becoming a Head Teacher	37
4 Constructions of Being a Head Teacher	71
5 Constructing Change	101
6 Conclusions	129
Notes	134
References	135
Index	169

Tables

1	Proportion of women teachers in OECD and EU countries (all phases of education)	16
2	Number of teachers in Greek primary schools (2013–2020)	28
3	Percentage of women teachers and head teachers in primary education	30

Series Editors' Foreword

Jeffrey S. Brooks, Curtin University School of Education, Australia
Chen Schechter, Bar-Ilan University, Israel
Alan J. Daly, UC-San Diego, USA
Victoria Showunmi, UCL Institute of Education, England
Yi-Hwa Liou, National Taipei University of Education, Taiwan

The history of thought and practice in educational leadership can be conceived as a punctuated equilibrium (English 2008). The arc of the field's history is a steady evolution of traditional ideas centered around management, administration, efficiency, rational decision-making, authority, and power (Beck and Murphy 1993). Heavily influenced by business administration and management literature, the field is also shaped by sociology, anthropology, economics, psychology, political science, philosophy, and public policy. As an applied field, scholarship in educational leadership shapes—and is shaped by—developments in schools, universities, policy-making processes, and in other formal and informal education settings (Brooks and Miles 2006). This has meant that there is space in the field for both highly theoretical work and for research grounded in a specific context. Of course, quite a lot of scholarship in the field seeks these aims at the same time as a way of generating relevant knowledge *in situ* while also advancing thought and practice throughout the world (Gunter 2016).

Occasionally, ideas are introduced that compel scholars and practitioners to reconsider the foundations of "what they know" and adopt new ways of thinking about and practicing their work. Among intellectual movements that upset educational leadership's orthodoxy were postmodernism, critical theory, feminist theories, social justice, culturally relevant school leadership, distributed leadership, and more purposeful studies of the relationship between leadership and learning (Brooks and Normore 2017). Each of these domains of inquiry produced novel perspectives on educational leadership (to be sure there are others—we do not pretend this is an exhaustive list) that inform contemporary conceptual and empirical research. Additionally, each of these intellectual movements initiated a paradigmatic shift in the way people engage in the practice of educational leadership, think about their work, and conduct themselves as leaders and followers in formal and informal education settings.

For all this innovation, the arc toward improvement has been slow, and often the emphasis on the traditional has subdued the exploration of the radical. This book series seeks to establish a space for research that (a) explores promising concepts at the edges of the field, (b) encourages the publication of new ideas, and (c) critiques contemporary assumptions about educational leadership. Our hope is that the series may play some role in prompting future conceptual and empirical revolutions that will move the field forward via emergent scientific and artistic revolutions.

New perspectives are emerging from across the field and other disciplines that have great potential to influence (and be influenced by) educational leadership scholarship and practice. Among these are exciting developments related to sustainability and climate change, social networking, religion and spirituality, immigration and globalization, student-centered leadership, and innovative contributions to traditional topics such as community-school relations, gender, race, ethnicity, sexuality, diversity, intercultural/cross-cultural studies, globalization, early childhood and adult education, student voice, and activism. To be sure, there are others. While it is easy to point to individual articles or small groups of scholars working in these areas, there is no clear publication outlet for deeper, focused, and nuanced works that explore and challenge such ideas in the detail afforded by a full-length book or highly focused edited volume. Reaching out beyond the field of educational leadership, there are developments in sociology, anthropology, political science, policy studies, psychology, curriculum studies, brain-based research, environmental science, creativity studies, medicine, law, and other fields that have yet to be deeply explored or understood in terms of their possible applicability to educational leadership. We see the series as a place where such disciplines, ideas, and lines of inquiry can come into dialogue and create innovation. We see this book series as a forum for interdisciplinary, innovative, creative, and indeed controversial work.

In addition to providing a forum for such exciting ideas, we aim for this series to also include a diversity of authors and contexts underrepresented in many extant book series. This means diversity of author, geographical context, and perspective. As this is a series of research books, we anticipate the primary audience being academics, but we also anticipate that the topics will be of interest to practicing school leaders, teachers, policy-makers, and scholars working across disciplines such as educational leadership, school leadership, teacher education, sociology, anthropology, economics, psychology, political science, philosophy, and public policy. We invite you to join us in the conversation—to share your work and your insights as we explore and extend the field of educational leadership.

References

Beck, L. G. and J. Murphy (1993), *Understanding the Principalship: Metaphorical Themes, 1920s–1990s*, New York: Teachers College Press.

Brooks, J. S. and A. H. Normore (2010), "Educational Leadership and Globalization: Literacy for a Glocal Perspective," *Educational Policy*, 24 (1): 52–82. doi:10.1177/0895904809354070

Brooks, J. S. and A. H. Normore (2017), *Foundations of Educational Leadership: Developing Excellent and Equitable Schools*, Routledge: New York.

Brooks, J. S. and M. T. Miles (2006), "From Scientific Management to Social Justice … and Back Again? Pedagogical Shifts in Educational Leadership," *International Electronic Journal for Leadership in Learning*, 4 (1): 2–15.

English, F. W. (2008), *Anatomy of Professional Practice: Promising Research Perspectives on Educational Leadership. Rowman & Littlefield Education*, Lanham, Md: Rowman & Littlefield Education.

Gunter, H. (2016), *An Intellectual History of School Leadership Practice and Research*, London: Bloomsbury.

Jackson, L. L., N. Lopoukhine and D. Hillyard (1995), "Ecological Restoration: A Definition and Comments," *Restoration Ecology*, 3 (2): 71–5.

Kensler, L. A. W. and C. L. Uline (2017), *Leadership for Green Schools: Sustainability for Our Children, Our Communities, and Our Planet*, New York: Routledge, Taylor & Francis Group.

Kensler, L. A. W. and C. L. Uline (2019), "Educational Restoration: A Foundational Model Inspired by Ecological Restoration," *International Journal of Educational Management*, 33 (6): 1198–218. doi:10.1108/ijem-03-2018-0095

Senge, P. M., N. Cambron-McCabe, T. Lucas, B. Smith and J. Dutton (2012), *Schools That Learn (Updated and Revised): A Fifth Discipline Fieldbook for Educators, Parents, and Everyone Who Cares about Education*, Crown Business.

Stafford-Smith, M., D. Griggs, O. Gaffney, F. Ullah, B. Reyers, N. Kanie, … D. O'Connell (2017), "Integration: The Key to Implementing the Sustainable Development Goals," *Sustainability Science*, 12 (6): 911–19. doi:10.1007/s11625-016-0383-3

Preface

Worldwide women constitute the majority of the teaching force, but men are more likely to achieve headship. The situation is similar in Greece, where women are represented in educational leadership in disproportionately low numbers.

Using a feminist social constructionist framework the research presented in this book seeks to identify the reasons for this underrepresentation, to explore the career progression of women and discuss the challenges that women educational leaders face in performing their duties.

The underrepresentation of women in educational leadership in Greece has received little attention in the mainstream media or even the public. It is only in the past few years that this issue has begun to gain attention in the Greek academic arena, with some studies being published and conferences held. Research on the subject has therefore been limited in Greece and most of that which has been conducted focuses mainly on the differences between the way women and men lead. Also, most of the studies have been in Greek, so they cannot be widely distributed, because of the language barrier.

The study utilizes a theoretical approach that can be defined as feminist social constructionism. This is to say it is primarily concerned with examining how certain constructions draw upon dominant positions and how these relate to wider relations of power. Feminist social constructionism is deeply concerned with social constructions that appear in the form of concepts, practices, entities, and attributes that constitute oppression against women (Friedman 2006). So, this study presents the male and female teachers' and head teachers' views on a specific and largely ignored situation in Greece. Women's underrepresentation in educational management is not only a numerical reality but a social construct, as well. Hence, as it is a product of social relationships that are presumably under human control and are not stable and fixed; whatever is oppressive to women can be made better by humans acting differently.

This project has been influenced by a number of scholars working internationally within sociology and the sociology of education, who have focused on the continued influence of gender on the shaping of identity and choices in relation to leadership, work, and home (for example, Coleman 1996, 2002, 2005a in the UK, Blackmore 1999 in Australia, Hall 1996 in the UK, Reay and Ball 2000 in the UK, Fuller and Harford 2016 and Showunmi et al. 2022 for more international perspectives). This scholarship has critically investigated the extent and impact of gender and leadership in the construction of identities. This book intends to continue this work by examining how gender informs women's and men's ability to access and perform leadership duties in primary schools in Greece, a country where research on this subject is scarce and what exists is mainly based on secondary data.

1

Introduction

One of my earliest memories at a school setting was when I was just three years old. My mother, who was working as a secondary teacher, took me to crèche because there was nowhere else to leave me. There was a female child-minder there and she also had administrative duties. I remember her when she was in her office struggling with papers and with fifteen children at the same time.

At the same period, I remember my mother at home, buried in her books every afternoon, preparing her lesson for the next morning. At the same time, taking care of me. I am an only child and I was quite naughty seeking constant attention. But lesson preparations and me were not her only "duties." She had to care for the household, cook, do the laundry etc. while my father was at work.

A few years later, when I started primary school I remember female teachers and male head teachers. In my six years in primary school, I never had a female head teacher. Especially at the lower classes (six- to eight-year-old children) the teachers were all women, too. So, my early school years were full with women.

Later on, when I entered high school at thirteen, the teachers were mixed gender, but women were teaching mainly theoretical subjects, like history, Greek language, philosophy etc., and the men were in the sciences (i.e., Math, physics, chemistry etc.). Of course, the head teachers were all males.

This, along with the fact that my mother (who recently retired after thirty-two years as a teacher) never wanted to be a head teacher, nor did her female friends and colleagues, piqued my interest. Another factor contributing to that interest quite early in my life was that when I was young, my mother took me with her when there were school meetings (because there was nowhere where she could leave me) and there I saw only male head teachers.

Later on, when I graduated and started work as a teacher myself, I was surrounded by female teachers. Of course, this could easily be explained as I was working in pre-primary education (four to five years old), a field where men were not allowed to study or work until 1987. Hence, the great majority of teachers are females, especially in urban areas (where I worked) as they tend to be older and appointed well before 1987. When I was transferred to my last post before joining academia (assessor of children with special educational needs) in 2004 I needed to be in regular contact with children's schools, I saw that the great majority of head teachers in the area of my responsibility were still males and the teachers were mainly females.

But, it was not until the mid-2000s that I became more interested in the experiences of women educational leaders. At that time I was studying for an MBA in Educational Management at a UK university and during one of the modules I came across the issue of women's under-representation in educational management. All my experiences came back to me and I realized that this was an international issue and not simply a Greek one. I conducted a literature search and discovered that it had not been adequately researched in Greece and especially in the area of primary education. This opened up a whole new area for me that was stimulating, exciting, and challenging. I wanted to work toward taking the issue of the underrepresentation of women in leadership positions in education further. As I thought back to those earlier times, who would have thought that twenty-five years later the situation would have actually been similar to that of my early childhood experiences? So, I decided to pursue my PhD on this subject. And from that PhD came this book, because I believe that there is a need for these issues to be known and for research to be disseminated.

In the following sections, I make a brief reference to gender and educational leadership, as this will be analyzed in Chapter 2 (*Women in Educational Leadership: Global and National Context*) in more depth. I also identify and expand the major theoretical discussion by tracing a movement from theories of essentialism, which still tend to underpin common understandings of gender, toward social constructionism. I unpack claims that underpin these discussions and explore their effects on women and men in educational leadership. I introduce the concepts of "femininities" and "masculinities" along with the concepts of "power" and "patriarchy" and their relationship to the construction of identities. And finally, I give an overview of the structure of this book.

Gender and Educational Leadership: A Brief History

It's been quite a lot of years since the debate on gender and educational leadership has started in many parts of the world among researchers, policy-makers, the media, the school workforce, and the wider public. The first scholarship emerged in the 1980s (i.e., Biklen and Brannigan 1981, Berman 1982, Marland 1982). The work of Shakeshaft (1989) was one of the first who brought to the forefront issues of gender and educational leadership. Her study can be considered as groundbreaking because it was one of the first scholarly texts based on a woman-centered approach and it reframed the study of women throwing light on gendered approaches to educational leadership. The same time, Blackmore (1989), contrary to Shakeshaft whose work was characterized by the distinctive aspect of female presence in educational leadership, focused on a feminist critique of educational leadership. Her critique calls for a paradigm shift in theory and not simply for a change in the focus of research. For Blackmore a reconstruction of the concept of educational leadership, involving a move away from notions of power and control over others toward a reconceptualization of leadership as acting with others, is necessary. In the mid-1990s several studies were published emphasizing the issue of the underrepresentation of women in educational leadership (i.e., Coleman 1996, Hall 1996, Gold 1996). In the 2000s, feminist scholarship on the issue of educational leadership increased. In this period, as Fuller (2021) notes, the issues that mostly concern the research are educational leadership and social justice, diversity leadership drawing mostly on Black feminist perspectives.

At a time when the debate about gender and educational leadership is still on, this book critically engages with it. Drawing on a range of primary and secondary sources, it investigates through a theoretical lens informed by a feminist social constructionism framework the various constructions of the issue in a range of institutional, national, and international contexts. This book also explores the experiences of men and women who hold a leadership post (or plan their careers), looking at the way. Gender and other power relationships frame their careers and private lives. Finally, it explores the ways in which female and male teachers construct head teachers.

Claims the women are underrepresented in educational leadership can be found in international literature (for example, Coleman 1996, 2002, 2005b in the UK, Blackmore 1999 in Australia, Hall 1996 in the UK, Reay and Ball 2000 in the UK, Fuller and Harford 2016, and Showunmi et al. 2022 for more international perspectives). Internationally, the term "leadership" is often seen as synonymous with "management" and "administration." The usage of these terms varies at different times and in different countries. In the UK, as Coleman (2005a) notes, "'leadership' tends to be seen as the most important of these concepts, 'management' tends to relate to more operational matters and 'administration' to relate to tasks which are a routine" (p. 6). In North America, Canada, and Australia the term "administration" has more or less the same meaning as "leadership" in the UK (Bush 2011). However, there are significant differences as leadership is seen as an aspect of management. Bush (1998) links leadership to value or purpose, while he relates management to implementation or technical issues. In the Greek school context, the head teacher can be classified as an "administrator" as the Greek educational system is characterized by centralization and bureaucracy and the head teacher can be seen as a person who implements laws and ministerial policies. So, as the main body of the literature comes from different countries where the head's role is different, I take care not to draw upon the literature unproblematically. I will use the terminology used in the countries the literature refers to; however, in my data I will use the term "leadership" and I will be referring to the process of providing directions to individuals and exercising influence on others in order to achieve the core work of schools and school systems.

Similarly, "gender" understandings have changed over time, from just being associated with biological characteristics acquired at birth, to broader constructions of sense of self, culturally conditioned or subjective identities (Butler 1990). In Greek the word "*fylo*" is used. This word in Greek has several meanings, such as gender in a grammatical sense (female, male, and neutral nouns and adjectives); race or tribe (as in the ancient Greek tribes/races),[1] and sex as well as gender.[2] The meaning each time is assumed by the context in which is used. So, in this book, I translated the word either as "sex" or "gender" depending on the way it was used in oral or written speech.

Although I come back to these terms in great depth in a following section, it is essential to note that they are being taken into consideration when discussing the issue of gender and educational leadership in the media, in policy-making, or among the educational workforce. They serve a regulatory purpose as they asset and re-asset gender binaries and they produce gender hierarchies.

Although the debate around gender and educational leadership is continuously going on, it is important to understand that it is not new, as mentioned earlier. Throughout history, various views on gender and educational leadership have appeared. With this in mind this book adopts a broad approach, focusing in current debates but also drawing on past research through a historical perspective, concentrating on specific national contexts and adopting a more international perspective, as well.

Theoretical Perspective

Social Constructionism

This book follows a social constructionist approach. So, knowledge is seen as a human construction and as such it cannot be an objective process (Burr 2003), but it is seen as local and specific to the people who participate in the research. This book is not intended to have objective "scientific" status. The truths sought by positivistic methods are not considered appropriate for constructionist studies like mine (Lincoln and Guba 2005). Social constructionist research is characterized by context (like historical and cultural influence), rich or thick explanations of events, participant inclusion, researcher reflexivity, and meaning generation (Gubrium and Holstein 2003). These characteristics differ from traditional positivistic research which focuses on objective knowledge captured via standardized procedures, which supposedly give access to the truths of the world (Hughes 1990).

Social constructionism is viewed as focusing on "attention to context, embedded meanings, acknowledgement of the contributions of the observer and the observed, utilization of tacit knowledge and preference for interactive modes of knowledge construction" (Hoshmand 1994, p. 27). These factors distinguish social constructionism from traditional positivistic science that fails to account for how people make sense of events and how they attribute meaning to situations.

In this book I involve critical engagement with the social and historical constructions of my own knowledge production, instead of claiming objectivity. In this way I seek to avoid "alienated knowledge" (Stanley 1990, p. 3) and an analysis that assumes what Haraway (2013) calls "the God trick" (p. 189), a gaze from nowhere which masks its own partialness by appearing to be completely neutral.

Both the researcher and participants are included as a part of the research outcomes. The process of conducting research is through dialogue, collaboration, and the co-constructed sharing of meanings and realities (Gubrium and Holstein 2003). Language is also very important. Meanings are thought to be created in the domain of language and therefore any attempt to understand the meaning making process would necessarily analyze the language used amongst people under study. Different social norms and values are carried through language usage in different societies, constructing specific realities.

So, in the present book which is based on a social constructionist framework, knowledge is co-constructed through the interview process from the participants and from me. I do not aim to generalize my conclusions, rather I want to explore the meanings and understandings of the participants in the research in this particular context and time.

The present study is grounded in a feminist research framework. This means in part, looking at the world from a woman's perspective, honoring the common experiences and histories of women in society, and at the same time respecting their different experiences. It also means recognizing gender power relationships, as well. It does not mean excluding or devaluing men. Any research that uses a feminist lens is research that is informed by the current and former status of women in society. Pritchard (1994) suggests that:

Feminist critique starts with "women" or "women's" issues but goes beyond to the impact of gender relations and gendered conditions of human development in all spheres of thought and action (p. 42).

This means that feminist research is concerned not only with gender inequality but it is more intersectional, as it looks into how gender intersects with other issues related to identities or race, ethnicity, class, sexual orientation, and physical ability (Fuller 2015, 2021) and how these intersections contribute for each woman (Crenshaw 1991). These intersections work together in producing injustice for women and were described as "interlocking systems of oppression" (Hill Collins 1990, p. 225). In this book I study the perceptions of men and women in relation to gender and school leadership in Greece. My research is feminist, as its aim is not just to conduct research about women and gender in educational management, but to produce research for women. It is research that "does not merely generate new knowledge about women for the sake of knowledge, but conducts research with the purpose of empowering women" (Langellier and Hall 1989, p. 195). It is my intention that this inquiry will produce knowledge that will assist other women and policy-makers in applying policies that raise awareness about and increase the participation of women in educational management in Greece.

Gender Identity

In international literature the debate between gender essentialism and gender social constructionism has been pivotal. Although the theoretical focus of this book is on gender social constructionism, I also engage in a discussion of the essentialist approaches to gender theory, as these still often underpin people's assumptions and the ongoing negotiations of gender (Sandilands 2004).

Public discourse and some literature tend to present differences in gender identities as representing a difference in nature, an innate difference reflecting an essentialist view followed by generalizations about women and men. So, an essentialist view argues that there are pervasive differences between men and women because of different biological and psychological dispositions. According to this view, sex is conceptualized in terms of binaries: male/female, man/women, masculine/feminine and gender is understood as being biological, depending on the body and its form or shape. So, unitary stereotypes tend to depict men as directive, bureaucratic and instrumental and women as collaborative, relational and organic (Ferguson 1984, Adler et al. 1993) because of different types of brain ("male" and "female") (Gurian et al. 2001, Baron-Cohen 2007). So, it can be assumed that women do not possess the qualities or abilities needed for leadership because of their brains.

One of the major critiques of the essentialist view of gender (and hence of leadership theory based on it) is that it ignores plausible social and local explanations because of the tendency to try to find evidence for the biological determination of differences between the sexes (Rose 2001). So, the proponents try to establish these differences as the root of differences in personality and of the leadership approaches of men and women. As Fine (2010) and Eliot (2009) note, given the recent research in neuroscience that suggests that biological differences between the sexes may be interpreted as minimal and that cultural context is the key, neurosexism may promote damaging, limiting, and potentially self-fulfilling stereotypes. Similarly, Jones (2002) argues that humanity is not only where men (and women I may add) are born, but also where they get unmade and unraveled by genetics, chemistry, history, culture, and ideology. More recently, he argued that human brains may be influenced by genes, but the environment and culture also play an important role in shaping gendered brains and abilities (Jones 2013). So, according to Jones, gender is socially rather than biologically constructed. Gender, therefore, should not be seen as two static categories, but rather "a set of socially constructed relationships which are produced and reproduced through people's actions" (Gerson and Peiss 1985, p. 327). It is constructed by dynamic relationships and it is something that "one does recurrently in interaction with the others" (West and Zimmerman 1987, p. 140). So, gender is viewed as a dynamic social process.

Court (1994) has also pointed out how cultural ideas developed within Western societies about appropriate ways to "be" "feminine" or "masculine" are associated with beliefs about the kind of work men and women are most suited to. In her view these beliefs have been particularly significant in the context of education where specific experiences are found to have shaped the way children see themselves as adults, such as when they take on a leadership position, like headship. These various experiences are likely to impact, not only on the construction of gender identities but on their leadership identities as well.

In this book gender identities are conceptualized as multiple, fluid, and ever-changing. In essence, these perceptions advocate the acceptance of multiplicity rather than consistency in each person's identity. This approach emphasizes the ways in which people may need to adopt multiple roles and construct multiple gender identities in order to negotiate meanings, status, security, and position in their everyday life (Burr 2003). People may have many identities at the same time, as parents, friends, husbands and wives, and as leaders. Each head teacher in this research is thus developing his/her own distinct leadership identity in a context where gender assumptions about leadership continue to prevail.

So, in contrast to essentialist, fixed conceptualizations of gender, therefore, social constructionism accounts for multiple configurations of gender, "masculinities" (Connell 1995) and "femininities" (Genz 2009). In contrast to widespread understandings in the West of "feminine" as naturally nurturing and caring, "femininity" is dynamic, various, and changing, and it is perhaps helpful to think in terms of multiple "femininities." As Laurie et al. (1999) argue, this recognition of a multiplicity of "femininities" suggests that dominant forms of "femininity" often draw on "natural" and "essential" associations between sex and gender. Also, in her research, Genz (2009) argues that there are multiple "femininities" that have power dynamics associated with them. So, while recognizing various forms of "femininity," it is important not to view them as stable and fixed but rather as related to context, position, and environment.

"Femininities" are best understood as being in process, constantly being made in different times and places. Many interrelated elements contribute to the construction of one's gender identity. Among the elements that may shape gender identity are age, social class, ethnicity, sexuality, and physical appearance. As Pyke (1996, p. 531) argues "hierarchies of social class, race and sexuality provide additional layers of compilation." They form the structural and cultural context in which gender is reproduced, reaffirmed, and challenged, in everyday life, thereby fragmenting gender into multiple "masculinities" and "femininities." Studies also show how other parameters, such as race or social structures affect the construction of "femininities" (Ware 1991). Mirza (1992), for example, reports that the construction of "femininities" among Black girls differs from the forms of "femininities" found among their white peers. The young Black women in her study made few distinctions between male and female abilities and qualities and perceived relationships between the sexes as more equitable than their white peers. Men and women therefore are not homogeneous groups. Rather, differences between women and between men exist according to, for example age, socioeconomic class, race, sexuality, and individual variation (hooks 2000, Reynolds 2002, Richardson 2008).

Despite this recognition, gender constructionism has been criticized for ignoring the interaction among gender, race, ethnicity, class, and other social categories (Hoff-Sommers 2000, Gurian et al. 2001). It is argued that the women who authorize and control most gender discourse are privileged white women, whose experience of gender is not similar to women who are marked differently within complex stories of gender, race, or class (hooks 1981, Sandoval 1990). In my research, all of the participants are white Greeks (this was not intentional, but reflects the demographics of the Greek primary school teaching force) and they represent various age groups, sexualities, and roles within the school. In this book, I acknowledge the differences that may exist between the participants in my research by drawing on a social constructionist framework throughout my study, rather than making assumptions about the way they construct gender.

There are also a number of studies from all around the world in which researchers have traced the construction of "masculinities" in particular time and place (Connell 2000). Connell (1995, 2002) has reached the conclusion that there is not one form of "masculinity," but "masculinities" (in plural). As Whitehead (2002) notes, "masculinities" are multiple and plural, differing over time, space, and context. They are also affected by variables such as race, ethnicity, class, and age and sometimes men learn to avoid behaviors that are considered as less "masculine" in order to avoid being stigmatized (Harris 1995). There seems to be a reconfiguration of power relations between different forms of "masculinity" where dominance is more fragmented and unpredictable and there is also an interplay between "masculinities" (Connell 1995, Ferguson 2001). As Christensen and Larsen (2008) note, "what in some contexts appears as marginalized masculinity may in other contexts be hegemonic" (p. 56).

Studying "masculinities" and "femininities" is not about more or less "masculine" or "feminine" characteristics, it is about patterns of social practice that construct and sustain a hierarchical relationship between men and women, "masculinities" and "femininities." This is of particular interest in my research, as I explore the relationships between male and female head teachers and teachers in the typically "masculine" arena of educational leadership in Greek primary schools.

Francis (2010) has identified a way to conceptualize the complexity and fluidity of gender as this is performed by women/girls or men/boys, as they are biologically sexed. She draws on Bakhtin's (1984) notions of monoglossia and heteroglossia in order to explore what it means to be a woman or a man. For Francis (2010), monoglossia describes the dominant definitions of gender— stereotypical notions of "masculinity" or "femininity." Heteroglossia, on the other hand, describes the transgression by women/girls in doing "masculine" behaviors or men/boys doing "feminine" behaviors. She argues that binary notions of "masculinity" and "femininity" and their interdependency with sexed bodies limit how we capture the fluidity of the everyday experiences of gender. For example, Francis (2010) cites a number of incidents where boys and girls take on "masculine"/"feminine" behaviors. In effect their behavior tends to be different from normative gender behaviors. It is of great interest that young children do not appear to take up counter identities in terms of "male femininities," rather there seems to be a complex arrangement of monoglossic and heteroglossic events, where the boys and girls she studied "did not conform to monological accounts of gender" (p. 486) rather they drew on accounts of gender depending on the situation. This conceptual division between gender monoglossia and gender heteroglossia enables her to locate behaviors that do not easily fit into traditional notions of "masculinity" and "femininity." In this study these theoretical discussions of gender identity are relevant, as if I am to pursue gender and educational leadership, the complex and often contradictory nature of gender needs to be grappled with. In a gender-sensitive stance I need to recognize and challenge the dominant constructions about gender identities, where assumptions and practices may serve to reify existing traditional constructions, while at the same time acknowledge that gender identities may be constructed in ways that are fluid and contradictory. As Francis (2010) argues:

> The conceptual tools of gender monoglossia and heteroglossia facilitate the marrying of these two positions: we may see patterns of gendered behaviours and inequalities as expressive of monoglossic gender practice, but within this be attuned to the complexity and contradiction at play (heteroglossia), both in the diversity of gender production and in our categorisation of it. It is this attunedness to heteroglossia that offers potential for disruption and the avoidance of the reification of gender norms, and the exposure of gender as discursively produced rather than inherent. (p. 488)

So, I believe that gender is conceptualized neither as something individuals are born with nor acquired solely through socialization, but as an active accomplishment that is done differently within specific social and cultural contexts (West and Zimmerman 1987, Connell 2002, Francis 2010, Messerschmidt 2011). Despite the dynamic and constantly changing gender construction, individuals are not entirely free to construct their gender identity, but they are restricted by social institutions which prescribe particular references of gender in specific contexts. So, I adopt a feminist social constructionist perspective of gender and leadership as the theoretical framework of my book.

Understanding Gender in Relation to Patriarchy and Power

Modern Greece is to a large degree a patriarchal society (Kantzara 2006). As Kaparou and Bush (2007) note: "in Greece, patriarchy ensures that society is based on a male model, where men are at the top and women at the lower level" (p. 229). But cultural constructions of Greek women are more complicated. Writing in a newspaper Karaiskaki (2006) comments that "the image of Greek women [is that they are] educated, economically independent and unafraid of taking their lives in their own hands. However this image does not account for the multiple roles of women, the dramatic changes they experience through their lives and the stereotypes which affect them."

Patriarchy is defined by Humm (1995) as "a system of male authority which oppresses women through its social, political and economic institutions" (Humm 1995, p. 200). Similarly, Walby (1990) defines patriarchy as a system of social structures and practices through which men dominate, oppress, and exploit women. Patriarchy involves gender relations that can be "understood as predicated on inequalities of power" (Jary and Jary 2000, p. 45).

Walby identifies six structures of patriarchy that, she claims, capture the depth and interconnectedness of women's subordination and allows for change over historical time. These six structures are: paid work, household production, culture, sexuality, violence, and the state, and a historical account of the shift from "private" to "public" forms of patriarchy. The last structure is maybe the most important, as "private patriarchy" is found in systems of household production and operates through the exclusion of women from the public realms of male power. In contrast, "public patriarchy" operates through the segregation and subordination of women within the public sphere of politics and culture. So, this structure is in relation to the position of women within the workforce and, in relation to the present study, within educational management.

Patriarchy is preserved firstly through a preparation process that starts with children's socialization in the family (the first agent of socialization) and is encouraged further by education, literature, and religion to such an extent that its values are adopted by men and women (Bryson 2003). However, this assumes that it is all-embracing, leaving no space for women (or men) who think differently.

A major critique of patriarchy is that it encourages a rather limited conceptualization of gender relations as occurring only between men and women, and does not acknowledge the full extent of gender relations and the fluid nature of gender (Ramazanoglou 1989).

As far as this critique is concerned, Walby's early work (1990) allows for change over historical time. Also, in her later work, Walby (1997) argues that in Britain although patriarchy still exists, it has altered in several respects. Especially, she argues, young women have made important gains compared with older women. So, older women may still be subject to private patriarchy whereas younger women are more likely to be subject to public patriarchy, by their subordination and segregation within the structures of paid employment as well as within the different cultures (i.e., there are differences between the ways women are being treated, are being raised etc.). As a result, women may not be excluded from the public sphere but they still are treated unequally to men (Walby 2007, 2009).

As Witz (1992) explains, patriarchy is "the way in which 'male' power is institutionalized within different sites of social relations in society" (p. 11). So, key to an understanding of gender is an understanding of gender and power relations. Bradley (1999) focused on power as a resource and related it to gender. This enabled her to demonstrate that there are variations in power since women and men can have control and access to different forms of power as a resource. In addition to this, she noted that there are differences in the amount of power as a resource that women and men can hold at different times. This means that power is not only complex but can also be flexible between and among women and men. This perspective enables the study to go beyond an analysis that conceptualizes gender power relations simply in terms of patriarchy that views men as power-holders and women as oppressed victims (Elson and Pearson 1984, Bradley 1999). It provides a point of view that power is a resource that can be acquired and used by both men and women and it can operate differently in the various sites of an organization. Men may be able to have more control over resources of an organization which has more institutionalized rules, but women may be able to find ways of controlling those in the household or vice versa. This perspective of power enables us to realize that there are "asymmetries of power" and with these, we realize who the "power-holders" are, what their "interests" are (Bradley 1999, p. 33), and what makes some women and men subjects and others objects of this power and sometimes even objects and subjects of power at the same time. Of course, this is fluid and can change over time (Bradley 1996). Although in my analysis I examine how workplace structures, cultures, identities, and practice can reflect and reproduce one another by revealing the dynamic and shifting nature of organizational and people's relations, I also want to retain Bradley's (1999) idea of power holders. Although it is, to some extent, in contradiction to my approach, it is also important, as I believe the underrepresentation of women in educational leadership has to do with structural factors that are produced and reproduced by individuals who exercise varying degrees of power attached to them because of their gender.

This approach seems to be useful, as it gives space for exploring how women may be empowered to resist dominations of gender, age, and sexuality and can identify power holders and their interests. This allows a serious engagement with the private and public sphere of the home and work which is central to understanding the underrepresentation of women in a patriarchal society like the Greek one.

However, patriarchy is still a useful concept to describe the situation in Greece, as it still extends through the society but I acknowledge that women can take power in different situations or particular contexts.

Structure of the Book

Although gender and educational leadership is a thriving research field internationally, there is limited research engaging with the issue in primary education in Greece. The existing research focuses either in other areas of education (secondary or pre-primary) (i.e., Lazaridou 2020 in pre-primary education, Hambidis 2012 in secondary education) or in one particular geographical area (i.e., Drosatos 2020 in Evia, Lazaridou 2020 in Pieria, Taki 2009 in Thessaloniki, Daraki 2007 in S. Greece). Some research also focuses on dominant constructions of gender which assume separate and distinct "feminine" and "masculine" characteristics and leadership styles (i.e., Brinia 2012) or only on women (i.e., Daraki 2007, Taki 2009, Lazaridou 2020). So, although the existent national literature provides a fertile ground for this book, it does not adopt a relational approach to gender and often focuses only on women, or it is limited in one geographical area or secondary and pre-primary education. So, there is a need for more contemporary research that focuses on gender and primary education leadership and on both men and women.

So, this book:

- Critically engages with contemporary discourses and debates about gender and educational leadership which can be found in a range of national and international literature.
- Explores the way these discourses contribute to female and male head teachers' professional and personal lives and considers the various ways in which the notion of gender is present in their experiences.

- Identifies the way the above discourses and debates are perceived and experienced by female and male teachers.
- Deconstructs the assumptions underpinning many contemporary discourses of gender and educational leadership and contributes to a more nuanced approach to gender and educational leadership.

Further to this introductory chapter, in the next chapter (*Women in Educational Leadership: Global and National Context*) I engage with the theoretical and empirical work that contributes to an understanding of gender and educational leadership within a global and Greek context. In the same chapter I present the local context, that is a historical perspective of gender issues and of the situation regarding gender and educational leadership in Greece.

The following three chapters mostly concentrate on original data collected through a research on female and male head teachers and teachers based in Greece. Chapter 3 (*Constructions of Becoming a Head Teacher*) after a brief presentation of the research methodology that was followed, explores which constructions of the patterns of careers men and women may follow and the process through which they decide to apply (or not) to become a head teacher. Chapter 4 (*Constructions of Being a Head Teacher*) is concerned with the approaches to leadership that female and male head teachers draw on and the extent to which these can be seen to fit (or not) with a construction of leadership as "feminine" or "masculine." In addition, conceptualizations of what constitutes an ideal head teacher and experiences of the potential difficulties of combining career with family are discussed. Chapter 5 (*Constructions of Change*) provides a critical examination of the participants' constructions of the future for women in educational leadership. Exploring their concerns and rationales, this analysis seeks to provide a stimulus for thinking about ways to change the current under-representation of women in leadership positions in primary education.

I conclude this book in Chapter 6 (*Conclusions*) with an overview of the key points of the book and I revisit the issue of gender and educational leadership in primary education in Greece in its various constructions.

2

Women in Educational Leadership: Global and National Context

As mentioned earlier, women have attracted considerable interest in academic studies as part of the politics of that time since the 1980s. Researchers in many fields have started using gender as a variable or focused directly on gender differences. This shift is characteristic of studies of leadership, including of educational leadership.

Research on women and leadership consistently implicates gender norms and gender expectations in the seemingly intractable "glass ceiling," in which women perceive a set of invisible restrains in reaching the top (the term is associated with Marilyn Loden in 1978, who is the one who introduced the term at a panel discussion about women's advancement), or a "glass cliff," which highlights the likelihood for women to be considered for leadership positions when an organization is in crisis rather than men (Ryan and Haslam 2005, Cook 2020). Both of these terms indicate the difficulties women have to face in order to get a leadership post. These difficulties include from getting informed of an open leadership position, to getting hired, or obtaining the experiences and opportunities that help build important skills, to being mentored and integrated into professional networks, to receiving equal salaries to men, to receiving support from colleagues and superiors.

Representation of Women in Leadership

"Women in educational leadership" is a topic widely explored. In particular there is a significant corpus of international scholarly literature focusing on women's underrepresentation in educational leadership. The underrepresentation persists despite the fact that teaching is a predominantly women-dominated profession (in 2019, on average across the OECD countries almost 70 percent of teachers were women and in the EU countries almost 73 percent (OECD 2019)). This has been an ongoing situation, as Table 1 shows. However, global accounts of the number of women in educational leadership are hard to come by. The available studies tend to be country-specific and tend to be limited to the Western countries as noted by Fuller (2021) and Arar et al. (2013). Of course, there are exceptions like Showunmi et al. (2022), McNae and Reilly (2018), and Reilly and Bauer (2015) where there is a global view. Also, there are some studies that focus on countries other than Western, like Malachias et al. (2020) in South America, Wilson (1997) and Macha and Bauer (2009) in non-English speaking European countries, Moorosi (2014) and Odhiambo (2011) in South Africa, Shah (2018) in Asia, Oplatka and Hertz-Lazarowitch (2006) in Middle East, and Arar et al. (2013) in Arabs in Israel. Nevertheless, the majority of the studies come from Western countries. But despite this fact, all the studies tend to agree on the existence women's underrepresentation and on the challenges they seem to face, offering an assumption of international patterns.

As Shakeshaft (2006) suggests the main reason for this global lack of data is that documentation reflects values. So, without global data to make comparisons between countries, it is difficult to know the extent of the underrepresentation and the possible changes over time. Several theorists argue that failure to report these data (or report it only in a few countries) may indicate resistance to addressing the underrepresentation of women in educational leadership.

Table 1 Proportion of women teachers in OECD and EU countries (all phases of education)

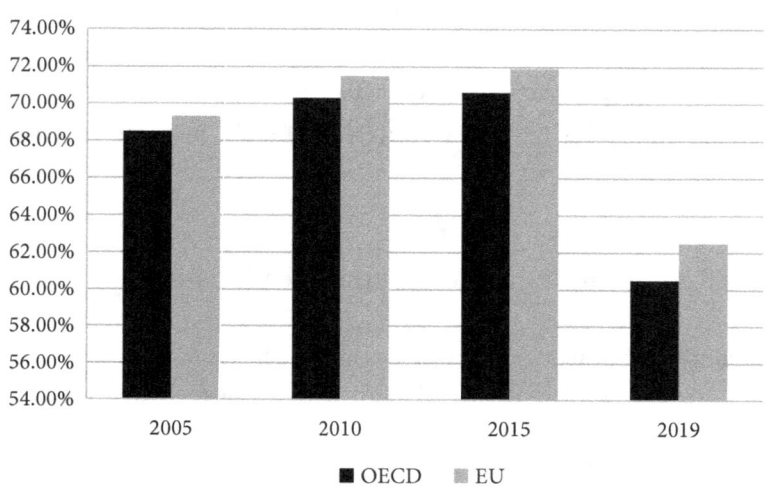

Source: OECD (2005–2019).

Earlier research from the late 1980s and early 1990s (e.g., Shakeshaft 1989, Ozga 1993) report findings indicating that women tended to adopt a different approach to leadership than men. The researchers concluded that to women leaders, relationships with others were central to their actions, teaching and learning were the major foci of their work, their style was more democratic and participatory, they were informal, more caring than men and the line they drew between the private and the professional was blurred. Also, these studies refer to research which indicates that women leaders tend to lead in a more democratic way than men, are more flexible, more intuitive than men, better at conflict solving and often more effective than men, and they call this "the traditional dichotomy of gender characteristics" (Ozga 1993, p. 111). Acker (1989) also notes that in earlier work on teachers' careers, gender differences were either ignored or tended to be explained in terms of women's differences.

More recently, several studies (Grogan and Shakeshaft 2011, Arar 2012) also came to the conclusion that that there seemed to be significant differences in the perceptions and beliefs of men and women head teachers. They agree with the earlier argument that there is a "feminine" approach to leadership in contrast to the traditional "masculine" approach.

Showunmi et al. (2016) argue that this may put women in a slightly compromised position as leadership is usually associated with power and women's way of leading does not seem to entail power in the masculinist/traditional notion. She also notes that in order to blend and restore the gender order that was disrupted by women's entrance in leadership, some women may adopt more "masculine" styles of leadership.

In contrast to these studies, Hall (1996) conducted a study of six women head teachers' experiences in the UK. These head teachers appeared to draw on leadership approaches that, according to the international literature, are not exclusive either to men or women. However, she acknowledges gender as a significant and pervasive feature of organizations which affects women's experiences and actions. She looked at the way women did the job without trying to draw comparisons with men and observed that the gender issue influenced both attaining headship and headship as a gendered identity, as well. While acknowledging that "[t]he problems in making comparisons are in knowing whether the differences are attributable to gender, the context or personalities" (p. 201), she came to the following conclusion:

> The women heads [...] represented one recurring interpretation in spite of differences in personality and context. In other words the similarities between them were greater than their differences. I have suggested that what they held

in common were the value systems underpinning their management and leadership behaviours, combined with the skills and competences they have developed throughout their careers. (p. 201)

Some of the abovementioned studies seem to be based on a theoretical framework that considers gender primarily in terms of a dichotomy between male and female. The women in the studies mentioned above tend to be considered as a distinct, homogeneous group, opposite to that of men, sharing the same or similar experiences, values, and approaches to leadership. Considering all women as similar to each other, without considering the many identities a person draws on, and understanding leadership as a product of gender dichotomy, as the determining factor of individual's experiences limits the understandings of the complexities of being an educational leader (Coleman 2022). This includes the risk of being an essentialist view, as each person, regardless of their gender, may draw on different identities in their leadership approach in a way that depends on the social, cultural, and educational context and on their own histories and experiences. So, the way gender is constructed may also affect leadership approaches, and women may sometimes be found in research to have different approaches from men because women have been seen to have more in common with other women.

Reay and Ball (2000) offer a different view on the way women shape their leadership in practice, by suggesting that leadership approaches adopted by women depend on the type of situation and culture of the school. So, they call for recognition of the diverse possibilities of multiple "femininities" by implying that there is a "femininity" more compatible with leadership. They argue that the roles that women undertake, as well as the context they work in, shape women's leadership in practice, not the other way around, or that at least it works both ways.

Other researchers (Oplatka 2001, Coleman 2022) have found less conclusive support for gender differences. It is suggested that an "either/or" and "male/female" dichotomy is too simplistic and called for a multidimensional approach that examines context, ethnicity, and other factors when conducting research on the issue of leadership approach.

Oplatka (2001) also notes that sometimes women head teachers may experience "cross-gender" (p. 291) transitions in their leadership approach. Those who began headship with a democratic leadership approach may have experienced a transition to a more directive approach. In particular, he suggests that women head teachers' mid-career may experience a change from "feminine" to "masculine" approaches. This reinforces the questioning of essentialist dualisms and suggests that gender may not be the only determining factor. In the case of Oplatka's study career stage may influence the particular approach adopted.

In conclusion, as individuals move between contexts, their experiences may lead to different and changing identity formations. This, in conjunction with the argument that the dominant constructions of leadership over time are "masculine," may lead to the assumption that the leadership identity of head teachers is therefore likely to change as they have experiences which may impact upon them in various ways. So, there may be differences between the way men and women approach leadership, as much research has shown, but these differences are not based on biology. Rather, these differences may be because of the different experiences of women and men, the different gender socialization, and their different cultural expectations.

Barriers to Career Progression for Women

After outlining the context of the underrepresentation of women in educational leadership in the previous section, in this section the documented obstacles and barriers women seem to encounter and are preventing them from getting leadership posts are discussed. A range of structural and cultural barriers have been recorded in the Anglo-Saxon countries and in the rest of the world. These include the traditional masculine culture that exists in some schools and the lack of supporting networks, the socially constructed beliefs about women, and the multiple identity conflicts they often face are going to be unpacked in this section.

Earlier literature on women in educational leadership often presumed "internal barriers" (i.e., lack of confidence, fear of failure, and lack of competitiveness) that were seen as the main reason for their low participation in educational leadership. This notion persists in some of the academic literature and in popular discourse today. But a number of studies have shown that women do not have lower aspirations or greater lack of confidence than men (i.e., Papanastasiou 2016). Furthermore, Shakeshaft (1989) denounces the presumed low aspirations and low self-esteem of women as a "blaming the victim" attitude and argues that "using internal barriers as an explanation for women's perceived lack of achievement is inadequate [...] It is not the women's psyche that is at fault and thus needs changing, but rather the social structure of society" (pp. 556–7).

Looking at women's underrepresentation in educational leadership, one of the greatest barriers to women's careers is the organizational culture in which they work. Appointing practices and sex discrimination for women who seek headship are part of this culture. There is a history of interview panels choosing men over women, along with the tendency that people have to hire those like themselves. Therefore, it is possible that white men tend to hire predominantly white men (Papanastasiou 2016, Showunmi 2018). Thus, women in the teaching profession face obstacles similar to those in other sectors, in terms of recruitment and promotion, as the accepted stereotype of what a leader looks like is associated with men.

Another barrier that can be perceived as one of the major external obstacles for women who may seek leadership positions is related to the organizational culture: it is the lack of support from colleagues, mentors, or other head teachers. The lack of support reported by women is significant and research shows that successful women usually had a superintendent or principal early in their careers who encouraged them to move from the classroom into headship. Coleman (2002) studied head teachers in England and Wales and drew the conclusion that 40 percent of the women and about 35 percent of the men appeared to have taken some action regarding encouraging other women to take the next step and move from the classroom into headship. Similarly, Moorosi (2022) stresses the importance of encouragement as a significant factor in women's career development.

Women seem to need more encouragement because of the additional stress they report as they enter leadership jobs in a male-dominated world. While both sexes are involved in presenting themselves as having an image of a successful manager, women seem to have to work harder to be seen as competent. Therefore, women have to do more work than men in order to legitimatize their presence in leadership. As a result, women leaders appear to be subject to a greater number of work-related pressures compared with their men counterparts (McNae 2022).

In order for women to enter leadership, networking is important, as inside information about leadership positions can be gained through networks, advice can be sought, and support can be found. Women often seem to be excluded from networking for career progression (Coleman 2002) in particular from "old boys" networks composed of men who hold power in the organization (Coleman 2002, 2005a). The exclusion of women from men's networks helps to perpetuate the more "masculine" customs and negative attitudes toward women leaders and this can block promotion, bring in discrimination and lower salaries, as women tend to remain in teaching posts that have lower salaries.

Knouse and Webb (2001) discussed the importance of networking and made recommendations for strengthening women's and minorities' networks in the United States. They suggest women's networks can provide a support group of people who have had similar experiences. However, Linehan (2001) argues that women in the corporate world in several EU countries (i.e., England, Belgium, France, Germany, and Ireland) are capable of forming networks, but their networks are less efficient because they are not integrated in organizations. Linehan (2001) also suggests that, although it is beneficial for women to be involved in these networks, there are still more benefits to be gained from networking in the established male-dominated groups, because power is still predominantly held by men in organizations.

Furthermore, because of stereotypical constructions of gender in society, there is a tendency to attribute occupational segregation (through which women tend to be subordinate to men and in caring/helping occupations) to personality differences. Thus it can be assumed that the way some women are constructed as inferior to men and in occupations that are considered more caring and nurturing may be due to traditional gender constructions (Coleman 2002).

One of the reasons for women's underrepresentation can be linked to the way some women perceive the constructions and expectations that others hold for them. So, if women are constructed as inferior to men, then they may act as such. On the other hand, research has shown that men and women teachers may possess the same level of aspirations for school leadership as they both may have advanced training in educational leadership at similar rates (Papanastasiou 2016), an indicator that they are interested in leadership, despite the fact women are not as likely to leave teaching. This may be happening because of the perception that teaching in a classroom is less demanding than a leadership position (Papanastasiou 2016).

Finally, women's underrepresentation in educational leadership may be due to the presumed difficulties of combining the multiple identities (head teacher, woman, wife, daughter, mother, etc.) that women draw on. In today's modern family, many women do not have practical support from other members of the extended family and they are assumed to take almost the entire responsibility for the household. This places pressure on women teachers to a greater extent than on men teachers. So, both private and professional identities may create pressure for women who seek headship.

Women have to juggle simultaneously different life components such as school, family, and social and personal areas. This multiplicity may present difficulties because of the assumed different demands of each identity. As women appear to hold the major responsibility for the family (Smith 2016), women have to adapt their careers in order to balance work and family, usually by prioritizing the family. As Wajcman (1998) indicated, in the late 1990s the average weekly hours of housework (defined as cooking, cleaning, laundry, shopping, and childcare) for the women was nineteen hours, whereas the average weekly total for men was ten hours. In Greece the situation is similar, as women appear to do more than 75 percent of household work (Mercarini and Sironi 2012). Women are still doing the majority of housework when living with a male partner in the UK (Moreau 2019, McMunn et al. 2020) and in other countries (Ferrant et al. 2014). Therefore, women do more housework than the men, while they perform the same number of hours of paid work as the men if they work full-time.

Faced with both social and household responsibilities, as well as career and family, the great majority of women try to make the best of both worlds. Most women are trying to balance a successful career and home and at the same time are attempting to establish identities that conform with social expectations (i.e., being a good mother, wife, daughter). An important feature of leadership work is the long hours that both men and women have to spend at work in order to gain recognition and eventual promotion. Women who desire both a family and a career often juggle heavy responsibilities in both domains. It can be practically impossible to reconcile the long hours of leadership work with the amount of time needed to care for a home and children. In this context, time is very much a gender issue.

All the above happened (and are still happening) globally. I believe that in order to understand gender and educational leadership in Greece today, it is important to reflect on the history of women's position in the country and then discuss the main construct. The following sections are presenting these.

An Historical Perspective on Gender Issues in Greece

While there is a significant corpus of international scholarly literature specifically focusing on women's subordinate status in society and their under-representation in educational leadership in particular (e.g., Shakeshaft 1989, Hall 1996, Coleman 2001, Moreau et al. 2007), the attempt to review the relevant local literature revealed in the most acute way the scarcity of pertinent literature and research in Greece. Deligianni and Ziogou (1993), in one of the few comprehensive texts, examine the position of Greek girls/women in society and education since the nineteenth century and explore the issues of women in education and gender differences. They provide evidence that the status of girls/women in Greece has been influenced by socio-cultural and religious norms.

Greek society of the nineteenth and the first half of the twentieth centuries was predominantly patriarchal with women viewed as physically and mentally subordinate to men and therefore economically and socially dependent on them (Deligianni and Ziogou 1993, Varikas 2004, Cassia and Bada 2006). Women tended to be stereotypically typecast as mothers, wives, and housekeepers and, to this end, they tended to be socialized accordingly. The fact that patriarchy dominated was displayed in various ways (Moussourou 1985a). For instance, girls/women were commonly physically and mentally oppressed by fathers, brothers, and/or husbands. It was imperative for a woman to retain virginity until marriage to avoid "traumatizing" the family's honor (Deligianni and Ziogou 1993). Young women were advised by their parents and relatives that it was "better to damage their eye than their name" (dignity) which is a traditional saying, and this is illustrative. Up until 1929, naming girls-only schools as "virgins" schools (*parthenagogia*) that aimed at rendering girls obedient, humble, respectful, good Orthodox Christians and silent "ladies," is also characteristic of the importance placed on virginity. The concept of "virginity" is closely related to the traditional dominance of "masculinity" as for fear of being "dishonored" by their women kin, males kept women under strict control, limiting any kind of relationships with men outside the family (Hadjikyriacou 2009). The importance placed by Greeks on virginity for women reflects traditional constructions of "femininity," according to which women ought to be passive, be subordinate to men, and stay and work in the house. These constructions of "femininity" confine women to the private sphere and domesticity. Along with this, the different curriculum that was followed in these schools (emphasis was given to French language, piano, home economics, needlework and sewing, whereas boys studied maths, geometry, physics, and physical education) is indicative of their educational aim (i.e., to prepare good housewives). In 1929, "virgins" schools were transformed to girls-only schools where a different curriculum was also followed compared with boys' schools (i.e., no algebra, less maths, etc.). This lasted until 1985 when all state schools became co-educational and girls and boys followed the same curriculum.

Women's inferior position was underpinned by Christian Orthodox values defining women as moral, totally dedicated, nurturing, and submissive to their husbands and ready to make sacrifices for their families, resembling the holy figure of Mary, the Mother of God. In the late nineteenth and early twentieth centuries, religion was closely related to education and many schools were established and financially supported by the Church. It thus comes as no surprise that gender disparity and stereotypes had a negative effect on girls' enrolment in education, especially in the secondary sector. Moreover, economic constraints led parents to "invest" in boys' education instead of that of girls who, it was assumed, would eventually get married and leave their jobs. After all, girls, especially the older ones, were "needed" in the big families of the time for raising their siblings and helping their mothers with everyday household chores. For all these reasons, up until the 1930s the percentage of illiterate women was far higher than that of men, reaching 70 percent of all women (Gouli and Kafkoula 2004). At the same period, illiteracy among women in Belgium was 6.5 percent and in Finland 16.6 percent (UNESCO 1953). The only occupation considered "acceptable" in Greece for those women who completed their studies in secondary education successfully was that of a teacher.

Conventional views about women's inferior position in Greek society started to shift in the middle of the twentieth century due to urbanization, the development of transport, communication and technology, and the expansion of artisanship and industry that created new positions for women to work outside the home. The First and Second World Wars, the Greek civil war that followed (1945–9), the migration wave toward northern Europe after the civil war and the military regime (1967–74), necessitated women undertaking different roles in society. As in the UK (Goldin 1991), during the Second World War Greek women entered the labor market at higher rates, as the male workforce was reduced. Moreover, women kept on working after the Second World War had ended, because the Greek civil war followed (1945–9) and men were either on the mountains fighting or in exile because of their political beliefs. After the Greek civil war because of the re-construction of the economies of the northern European countries that suffered from labor shortages (Dustman and Frattini 2013) and the poverty that followed a decade of war in Greece, many Greek men migrated to northern European countries. During this period, the women who stayed in Greece had to work in order to help their families and to support the Greek economy (Drakopoulos and Theodossiou 2006). Finally, less than two decades after the civil war, a military regime was established, and women had to go out to work again, as many men were in exile.

Until the mid-1970s, women in the field of education—and possibly in other fields as well, especially in the private sector—were unequally treated (e.g., there was a pay-gap between women's salaries and men's, women lost their jobs after they announced pregnancies). What is most striking is that many women in all professional areas were forced by social pressure to leave their jobs after marriage because society could not accept a working married woman (Habidis and Taratori 2008). Then in 1975, after the reinstatement of democracy, Greece adopted a new Constitution and gender equality was established in law (Nazou 2002).

Now, the Constitution states in Article 4(2) "Greek men and women have equal rights and equal obligations." However, despite positive initiatives and the huge strides toward equalization underpinned by legislation, there is still a long way to go until gender inequalities are completely eliminated. Greek society remains largely patriarchal in its structure and customs and as a result, stereotypical perceptions and attitudes toward men's and women's roles persist and decision-making still rests mainly in the hands of men, as the majority of those who hold the leadership positions are men (Athanassoula-Reppa and Koutouzis 2002, Kyriakousis and Saiti 2006, Kaparou and Bush 2007). In other words, similarly to the UK (Coleman 2009), there appears to be a gap between the legal framework that is supposed to ensure equality and the current situation.

In addition, the Church still has a strong influence on Greek society and especially on educational matters. Religious education still forms part of the school curriculum as a required course. Also, Greece is the only European country that has a Ministry of Education, Research and Religious Affairs, showing the Church's de facto position and its extensive role in education. In November 2013 the Holy Synod of the Greek Orthodox Church decided that greater involvement is needed in the writing of school books and decided to formally request the Ministry of Education, Research and Religious Affairs to appoint a Church representative to the editorial committee of the Pedagogical Institute, which is the scientific body responsible for the scientific and technical support for the design and implementation of educational policy issues, in order to influence the content of textbooks. At the point of writing there has not yet been a formal public response on behalf of the Ministry, but this is indicative of the close involvement that the Church still has with educational affairs. The Greek Orthodox Church is a very powerful institution both politically and economically. It has an active involvement in the key contemporary political controversies and national issues, including the practice of civil weddings and the legislation related to gay partnerships (Kallinikaki 2010). The Church also promotes negative perceptions about abortion and pre-marital sex and positive perceptions about traditional families (i.e., many children, working father, and stay-at-home mother).

In a climate like this, it seems that Singleton's (1993, p. 165) assertion that "jobs whilst not legally labelled 'for men' or 'for women' are still viewed by many people as just that" remains valid in Greece. The professions of pre-primary,

primary, and secondary school teacher, nurse, or secretary, among others, are still largely traditionally perceived by both genders as "feminine" whereas manual/technical, "high profile" and "demanding" jobs are mostly seen as "masculine" domains. To this end, the majority of Greek female students in higher education in Greece and abroad tend to cluster in the departments of Education, Humanities, Law, and Fine Arts while men students dominate the departments of Economics, Business Studies, IT, Engineering, and Technology (Kethi 2008, Hellenic Statistical Authority 2014[1]) similar to their equivalents in England (Office for students 2022). Clearly, the theoretically "free choice" of study and profession in Greece is in reality largely gender-determined and socially constructed.

Social expectations in relation to gender also appear to define women's and men's hierarchical position in the country. In particular women's representation in the upper echelons of public and political life is poor, with the percentage being among the lowest amongst EU members, as I show in a following chapter (section *Quota Systems* of Chapter 5).

As of June 2023, there are fourteen women and forty-eight men in the Government, including the Prime Minister (nineteen men and four women are ministers, two men and no women are alternate ministers and twenty-six men and ten women are deputy ministers). It should be noted that the women hold the positions of minister of culture and sports, of interior, of family, and of tourism. So women who participate in the current Greek government are in more "caring" posts and not in what are considered as "real" leadership posts (e.g., minister of finance or foreign affairs), Furthermore, there are six women and sixteen men representing Greece in the European Parliament and only one woman had become president since 1821 when Greece was liberated from the Ottomans and became an independent state. Only sixty-three different women have managed to enter the Parliament compared with 237 different men over the years since liberation.

Echoing the situation in the UK (Coleman 2011), in the labor market and particularly in the private sector, men still earn more than women (Livanos and Pouliakas 2012, Christofides et al. 2013). This occurs despite legislation and even though statistics show that Greek women outnumber men in higher education and frequently outperform them academically (KETHI 2008, Hellenic Statistical Authority 2014b). Unfortunately, complaints and accusations by women in the private sector that they have been dismissed from their jobs due to pregnancy continue to be reported in the press (Eleftherotipia July 2013, edupame 2010), even though there is a law stating that a woman cannot be fired when she announces her pregnancy and that her job is secure for eighteen months after giving birth. Additionally, numerous cases of violence against women in the family and sexual harassment in the workplace are still recorded by the General Secretariat of Equality (2013).

As suggested in this subsection, it appears that in Greek society gender has impacted on the distribution of power and authority in the private, professional, economic, and political arenas over time. Put plainly, gender has historically signaled different roles for men and women in every facet of life. It is against this contextual background in combination with my gendered personal/ professional experiences as a teacher that this book is developed, seeking to provide explanations for the underrepresentation of Greek women in primary school leadership.

Women and Educational Leadership in Greece

As in many other countries (Coleman 2002, Shakeshaft 2006, Lumby 2011, Chard 2013), there appears to be a disparity between the number of women teachers and those assuming headship in Greece. According to data from the Hellenic Statistical Authority in 2019, although women constitute the majority of teaching personnel in pre-primary (four to five years old), primary (six to eleven years old), lower secondary (twelve to fourteen years old), and upper secondary (fifteen to seventeen years old) sectors, only a small percentage of leadership positions are held by women. The only exception is pre-primary education where women are not only the great majority of the teachers (99.8 percent of the teachers), but make up the great majority of the head teachers as well (99.7 percent of the head teachers). This can be easily explained as early childhood education is constructed as caring and as a "mothering" profession (Lumby and Azaola 2014). It is perceived as more appropriate for women and so it is highly feminized. Also, until 1983 in Greece men were not allowed to study pre-primary education (and work as pre-primary teachers), with the first men graduating in 1987. So, the vast majority of teachers in primary education, which is the focus of this book, were and still are women. The figures for the public schools sector that are presented in Table 2, obtained from the Hellenic Statistical Authority (2013–2020), reinforce this statement.

The number of women teachers in all areas of education in Greece is consistently higher than the number of men teachers (Papanastasiou 2009, 2010). Especially in primary education (which is the focus of this research)

Table 2 Number of teachers in Greek primary schools (2013–2020)

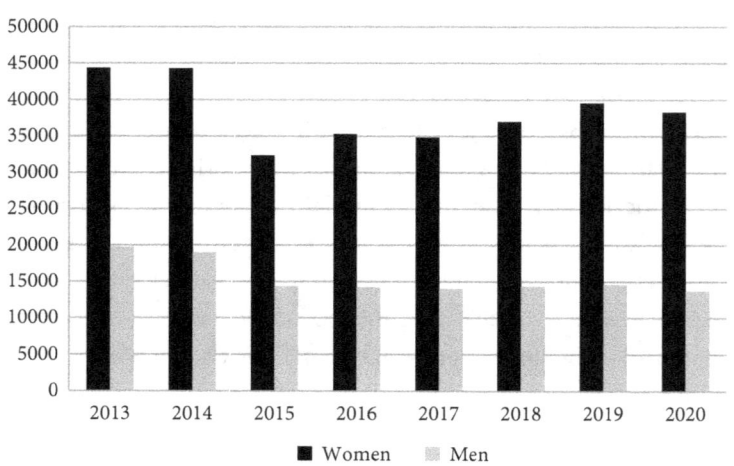

Source: Hellenic Statistical Authority (2013–2020[2]).

the number of women teachers has been more than double the number of men teachers. The statistical data in Table 2 show the interesting trend that in 2015 the number of teachers, both men and women, has dropped. In an era of recession and austerity, this can be explained by many teachers retiring and by the financial measures across all sectors and in education, which have led to reductions in pensions for those retired after 2016. In addition, because of these austerity policies very few new state employees in general and teachers in particular were appointed, as according to law, for five old employees that retire, only one new person is appointed. Instead, in order to cover the lack of teachers, the Ministry of Education, Research and Religious Affairs decided to merge or even close down schools and increase the maximum number of students in a classroom from twenty to twenty-five (plus two more when it is necessary) for all age groups. It is also interesting that in pre-primary education there are still not many men teachers despite the fact that the gender ban was lifted in 1983 leading to the first men graduates in 1987. The fact that in all areas of teacher training the studies take the same time (four years), are free of fees, and all teachers are paid the same wage irrespective of the age group they teach, may lead to the assumption that the fact that men do not study pre-primary education does not have to do with financial reasons. More likely it has to do with the assumption that the nature of the work is "feminine" and has lower status.

The trend of women teachers outnumbering men is evident in all areas of education, even in the upper secondary stage (for fifteen to seventeen years old). So, it can be assumed that education as a whole is considered a "feminine" domain. It appears that the stereotypical presumptions regarding the suitability of the teaching profession for women still persist and are partly responsible for women's preference for this traditional "female occupation." As a result, there are more women than men studying in the Departments of Education at Greek universities and more women than men graduate and finally work as teachers. To my knowledge, there have not been any attempts in Greece to attract men into teaching by emphasizing that what are considered as "masculine" attributes are part of a good pedagogy in addition to those of "femininity." Also, the contradiction that although men are underrepresented in a "feminine" profession they tend to be promoted faster than their women colleagues (i.e., the "glass escalator" phenomenon identified in the UK by Williams in 1992 and Skelton in 2002) does not seem to be incentive enough to attract more men into teaching, and even if there is no available evidence in Greece for this assumption, it may be the case here too.

With regard to headship, if men and women were proportionally represented, it would be expected that the percentage of women head teachers would be higher than that of men, with the exception of lower secondary education where it would be almost equal. This would have been a logical inference based on quantitative data from the Hellenic Statistical Authority (HAS) (2013–2020). Nonetheless, this is far from being the case. Over the years, the distribution of women in school headship has not reflected their numerical representation in the larger teaching population. It appears that Lynch's (1994) assertion that "women teach and men manage" reflects the predominant pattern in Greek education. This is true even in primary education where women teachers outnumber men teachers by more than two to one.

Data in Table 3 below illustrate the situation for the headship in primary education, which is the focus of my book. As can be seen in Table 3, although women's representation in leadership has increased in the last ten years, and especially from 2017 onwards, women are still not present in proportion to their numbers in teaching.

The decision to embark on research dealing with women's experiences of educational leadership was stimulated by this statistical picture. This is the starting point for discussing gender and educational leadership (Kaparou and Bush 2007). As the numbers indicate, women's disproportionate representation

Table 3 Percentage of women teachers and head teachers in primary education

Years	% of women teachers	% of women head teachers
2013	70.2	37.5
2014	69.5	37.8
2015	71	37.3
2016	68.6	37.4
2017	71.7	41.8
2018	72.5	42
2019	73	42.2
2020	73.6	41.8

Source: Hellenic Statistical Authority (2013–2020).

is an indicator that "things don't work properly" (Al-Khalifa 1989, p. 95) in the distribution of leadership between genders.

Being a Head Teacher in Greece

In order to understand what it means to be a head teacher in Greece it is necessary to understand the Greek educational system. As already indicated, this is characterized by a predominantly centralized structure, unified planning, and central control by the Ministry of Education, Research and Religious Affairs (Lainas 1993), like those of France and Germany (Lainas 2000). Educational matters are regulated, in their insignificant details, by a mesh of rules (laws, presidential decrees, and ministerial decisions), which are supplemented by explanatory circulars. So, educational leaders have to keep up to date to identify the most recent legislation, and interpret and apply the regulations. This practice does not offer any room for initiatives regarding the function of the school (Lainas 2000, Papanastasiou 2010).

There is an explicitly hierarchical model, at the top of which is the Minister of Education and Religious Affairs and the central service of the Ministry of Education, Research and Religious Affairs. Hierarchically graded under them are the Regional Directors of Education, the Local Directors of Education, the head teachers and deputy head teachers and, finally, the teachers. Each position has different levels of power, status, and advantages.

The leadership posts at the school level are the head, the deputy head, and the School Teachers' Assembly. According to the legislation, the head of the school unit is in charge of its smooth operation. This means in practice that the head teacher is responsible for applying educational laws and ensuring the efficient operation of school. S/he has responsibility for the implementation of the timetable and the curriculum, health and safety and protection of the school population, the cleanliness of the school, and the organization of school life. S/he also has the main responsibility for the co-ordination of school life, the observation of laws and circulars, and the application of decisions of the Teachers' Assembly. In addition, s/he participates in the evaluation of performance of the educational personnel of the school and collaborates with the school advisers and the Regional and Local Directors of Education for the more effective transaction of his/her duties.

The Teachers' Assembly (which is a governing body, comprised of all teachers in a school and has the head teacher as president) in a school is responsible for taking up some of the administrative duties. These include updating the students' records, selecting deputy heads (from the teachers who want the post) and leaders of computer laboratories, ordering and distributing the textbooks, planning the teachers' schedules, handling correspondence, and organizing fieldtrips. Some of these duties are of an administrative nature, but since in most schools there is no administrative staff, these are distributed among the teachers at the beginning of each school year, either after discussion, a draw, or some other way. Practice has also shown that the Teachers' Assembly, along with the head teacher, sometimes decides upon the school's disciplinary policy even though it is not within their legally prescribed duties. The Assembly is monitored by the head teacher who is responsible for evaluating its professionalism, collegiality, and punctuality.

It is worth noting that even though the majority of the teaching staff in all areas of education in Greece are female, the majority of the deputy heads, who are elected by the Teachers' Assembly, are men as statistical data show (Hellenic Statistical Authority 2019). So, it is likely that men put themselves forward and are elected by their colleagues, supporting the traditional construction of leadership as "masculine."

Compared with the role of the head teachers in the UK, the Greek head teacher's role is different. In Greece, there are no governing bodies in schools. Instead, the head teacher is the only one responsible for the internal organization, management, and control of the school. S/he is accountable only to the Director of the Local Educational Authorities (LEA) as far as the application of laws is concerned. Moreover, s/he is not responsible for appointing teachers, as this is done centrally by the Ministry of Education,

Research and Religious Affairs from a national candidate list. As far as the disciplinary policy in the school is concerned, the head teacher can be considered as a coordinator, as the law does not permit any freedom on ways to discipline teachers and staff. Additionally, in Greek schools there is no inspectorate even though, as indicated earlier, this is referred to a Presidential Decree but is not implemented yet, and school budgets are allocated by the Ministry of Education, Research and Religious Affairs via the local Mayor depending on the number of the students in each school.

In Greece, salaries for those working in the public sector depend on their education and years of experience, with the exception of hospital doctors, university teaching staff, military personnel, firemen, archbishops, and judges who are paid under special schemes. So, a teacher's salary in Greece is $20,643–40,720 before taxes (less than half after taxes) (depending on years of experience) and a head teacher gets paid a standard teacher's salary plus around $117 each month, so the annual head teacher's salary in Greece is $22,047–42,124 depending on years of experience (OECD 2018). At the same time in the UK a teacher's salary is $26,965–44,228 (Eurydice 2019) and a head teacher's salary can reach (or even exceed) $119,000. In other countries salaries are higher than in Greece. For example, in Luxemburg, a teacher with fifteen years of experience is getting paid $101,360, in Mexico $33,906, and in Spain $49,898 (OECD 2018). In these countries, a head teacher is being paid $116,560–161,200 in Luxemburg, $25,840–76,592 in Mexico, and $47,062–85,170 in Spain. At the same time, as it is reported in worlddata.info (2021), the cost of living in these countries is $1678 in Greece, $3789 in the UK, $6759 in Luxemburg, $782 in Mexico, and $2478 in Spain. Which indicates that purchasing power for teachers and head teachers in Greece is quite smaller than the rest of the mentioned countries.

To sum up, the head teacher's role in Greece is different from the head's role in the UK. It is characterized by hierarchical control with a top-down structure. S/he has the full responsibility for the school, but at the same time, in this bureaucratic structure, s/he has to abide by democratically made decisions of the Teachers' Assembly. But, as Kousoulos et al. (2004) note, not all head teachers abide by these decisions and some choose to approach leadership in a more autocratic way. In practice there is no way to assess and evaluate their leadership approaches as there is no formal inspection system in Greece. The teachers' union has made some formal complaints regarding head teachers' behaviors (e.g., DOE 2012) but, to my knowledge, no action was taken. So, it can be assumed that there may be tension between the teachers and the head teacher in schools where leadership approaches are considered by the teachers as autocratic. Furthermore, there is no sufficient monetary motive for someone to become a head teacher, as the head teachers' salaries in Greece is quite low compared to those in other countries.

It is important, therefore, to recognize the specific context of the Greek educational system in locating this study. The majority of research of gender and educational leadership in schools has been conducted in other countries, in particular in the UK and the United States, and whilst I draw on this research it is important to recognize the different locations in which it has been conducted.

In Greece the relevant research is limited and therefore, as I explained in Chapter 1, the major studies that exist have been conducted by Taki (2009), Brinia (2012), and Daraki (2007).

So, Taki (2009) in a book based on her PhD thesis, conducted a qualitative study of women in various leadership posts in education in the area of Thessaloniki, Greece. In her research she explores the reasons for the exclusion of women teachers from high-ranking administrative posts in primary education and also examines their underrepresentation in low-ranking posts and, finally, presents what she calls "the female perspective of educational management" (p. ii). This is the first qualitative study in Greece, based on a grounded theory approach, of twenty women who were serving or had served in administrative posts in public primary education (i.e., heads and directors of Local Educational Authorities (LEA), school advisors, and head teachers). Her results are grouped into three thematic categories: the reasons why women chose to become teachers, their career development, and the obstacles faced by women in their development. She found that most of her participants chose teaching because it was considered as "a suitable career option for women" (p. 139). However, there appears to be a differentiation between younger and older women. The younger ones appear to have planned their careers and to have worked toward achieving a leadership position, while the older ones just "drifted" into it. Finally, she found that the main problems her participants faced in their career had to do with being accepted as leaders and combining their career with having a family. As a conclusion, she proposes a new, alternative leadership model, based on the way women manage education. That is a model which is transformational, democratic, people-oriented, and based on humanist values. These characteristics of leadership approaches can be seen as informed by traditional gendered constructions of "feminine" leadership (Coleman 2002, 2005b, Van der Boon 2003), and hence are not dissimilar from the approaches and conclusions of much of the international literature discussed above.

Brinia (2012) studied the potential existence of different approaches to educational leadership between men and women in different Greek districts. She conducted a qualitative study of in-depth interviews with twenty men and twenty women head teachers using a questionnaire to examine their leadership approaches. She used Giorgi's et al. (1975) phenomenological method to analyze her data. She found several factors that may influence women to remain in teaching rather than seeking promotion (e.g., they like working with children, they have family commitments, they have limited experience, they tend to have more career breaks). She also reported that there are perceived differences between men and women in leadership approaches, with women seen by her as being more emotional, sensitive, and indecisive than men. But this conclusion seems to be problematic as Brinia draws on dominant constructions of gender which assume separate and distinct "feminine" and "masculine" characteristics. But recent research, as discussed earlier, has shown that gender constructions are more complicated than this binary model assumes. Gender identities depend on the situation, on cultural reasons, and on the individuals and their experience.

Daraki (2007) also studies the potential differences in leadership styles between women and men head teachers in Southern Greece. She conducted a quantitative study with 110 women teachers in order to see how they constructed women in educational leadership. She then interviewed fourteen head teachers (seven men and seven women) in order to see their leadership approaches and the potential differences between them. She concluded that "masculine" values that concern power, strength, superiority, rationalism, certainty, security, the penetration of knowledge, individualism, self-confidence, competition, skill, use of strategies, self-discipline, control, enforcement, and risk-taking, construct a norm which is accepted by women head teachers. But, on the other hand, she concludes that although these values are recognized in leadership, women tend to adopt a personal approach that is based on a more androgynous style. Like Brinia (2012), she concludes that leadership approach is a social construct and that it depends on the situation and on the individual.

In addition, all of them in their analysis consider gender as something static rather than fluid. They appear to consider men and women as homogeneous groups with similar characteristics because they belong to the same sex. So they adopt the idea that there are "masculine" and "feminine" ways of acting and, as a result, of leading, and they base the conclusions of their studies on this assumption. So Taki (2009) argues that:

men tend to adopt transactional leadership which is expressed with a system of penalties and punishments [....] On the contrary, women adopt the transformational leadership model, a leadership that is not static, allows collegial solutions, encourages participation, information and power distribution. (p. 345)

Brinia (2012) also argues that "personality characteristics [that are based on sex] diversify the way men and women [...] react as headmasters [sic]" (p. 179). Both of them argue that women approach leadership in a different way from men. So, they consider them as a homogeneous group different from the group of men without critically discussing their findings. But in this way they do not take into consideration the socially constructed nature of leadership and that each person, either man or woman, may draw on different identities (both "feminine" and "masculine") in their leadership approach (Reay and Ball 2000) in a way that depends on the social, cultural, and educational context and on their own histories and experiences.

Conclusion

In this chapter, gender has been used as a lens to examine literature on educational leadership. A review of the wide research in educational leadership internationally and of the limited Greek research is unpacked. The basic and pervasive stereotype that identifies leadership with men is renegotiated and I argue that the "masculine" constructions of leadership are likely to change. Also, I argue that the assumed differences of men and women in the way they approach leadership may be due to their different experiences and not innate. Interwoven is a discussion of the obstacles in women's pathway to headship. These obstacles can be perceived as arising from the "masculine" culture that seems to dominate educational leadership, the social understandings about women, and the conflict between the multiple identities that women draw on.

The Greek context is discussed later on. The different roles and expectations from men and women in the Greek society throughout history are discussed. And the disproportionate representation in the distribution of leadership between the genders follows. This created the starting point for researching gender and educational leadership and writing this research. It is important, therefore, to recognize the specific context of the Greek society, the leadership roles in the country and to present the limited, but existing, Greek bibliography on the subject of gender and educational leadership.

3

Constructions of Becoming a Head Teacher

In the previous chapter (*Women in Educational Leadership in Greece: Global and National Context*), I mentioned the underrepresentation of women in educational leadership as a fact worldwide and in Greece. I discussed some of the barriers that underpin their promotion to leadership posts, for example the internal barriers that were seen (and even today still persist in some literature) as the main reason for women's participation, the organizational culture that tends to favor men, the lack of support that women may face, the way that women are constructed as inferior to men and thus as not suitable for leadership posts and the difficulty in combining multiple identities in everyday life.

I also presented a historical overview of gender issues in Greece, the country of interest for the volume, showing how gender has impacted on the distribution of power and authority in all social arenas in Greece over time, with a special reference to educational leadership.

In this chapter, I consider the patterns of career of head teachers and teachers focusing specifically on ways in which women and men become head teachers (or not). In the first section (*Theoretical and Methodological Framework*), I introduce the methodology and theoretical framework informing my research. In contrast with the earlier chapters which compose this book, this chapter and the following two (*Constructions of Being a Head Teacher* and *Constructing Change*) adopt a more empirical focus, drawing on an original empirical study of men and women head teachers and teachers working in Greek primary schools (Papanastasiou 2009, 2010, 2011, 2013, 2014, 2015, 2016, 2020).

In the following sections, I discuss the stages through which they progress (or not) to headship, their experiences, and views of the selection procedures and the influence that family responsibilities are seen to have in decisions about their career (*Primary School Teachers and Career Choice*). Then, I explore head teachers' choice of a career beginning with those who planned to become head teachers (*Becoming a Head Teacher: Career Planning*), followed by those who did not plan for it but nevertheless became heads (*Becoming a Head Teacher: Drifting into Headship*) and moving on to those teachers who indicated that they did not want to become heads (*Unwilling to Become a Head Teacher, or Not Willing Yet*).

In the next section (*Selection Procedures*) the emphasis is put on the selection procedures of the head teachers. Networks and gender are discussed as the main determining factors to the selection that the research participants construct.

Theoretical and Methodological Framework

The theoretical approach underpinning this chapter is consistent with the broad principles presented in Chapter 1 and also draws more specifically on social constructionist and feminist theoretical framework. So, knowledge is seen as a human construction and as such it cannot be an objective process (Burr 2003). It is also co-created between the researcher and the researched and therefore knowledge is seen as local and specific to the people who participate in the research. As a social constructionist research is characterized by context (like historical and cultural influence), rich or thick explanations of events, participant inclusion, researcher reflexivity, and meaning generation (Gubrium and Holstein 2003). It rejects the assumptions of universal knowledge and certainty claims (Fontana 2003) and is viewed as focusing on "attention to context, embedded meanings, acknowledgement of the contributions of the observer and the observed, utilization of tacit knowledge and preference for interactive modes of knowledge construction" (Hoshmand 1994, p. 27). In my research I involve critical engagement with the social and historical constructions of my own knowledge production, instead of claiming objectivity. In this way, I seek to avoid "alienated knowledge" (Stanley 1990, p. 3) and an analysis that assumes what Haraway (2013) calls "the God trick" (p. 189), a gaze from nowhere which masks its own partialness by appearing to be completely neutral. By using social constructionism I address the meanings people attribute to situations by relying on human communication, shared meanings, and the contexts in which meanings take place.

The present study is grounded in a feminist research framework. This means in part, looking at the world from a woman's perspective, honoring the common experiences and histories of women in society, and at the same time respecting their different experiences. It creates a space in which the participants' talk can be analyzed and critically interpreted. It also means recognizing gender power relationships, as well. It does not mean excluding or devaluing men. Any research that uses a feminist lens is research that is informed by the current and former status of women in society. Pritchard (1994) suggests that:

> Feminist critique starts with 'women' or 'women's' issues but goes beyond to the impact of gender relations and gendered conditions of human development in all spheres of thought and action. (p. 42)

This means that feminist research is concerned not only with gender inequality but also with issues related to race, ethnicity, class, sexual orientation, and physical ability. Intersectionality is an important factor in feminist research, as Hill Collins (2004) discusses in detail, because it helps us understand the differences among women. In my research I study the perceptions of men and women in relation to gender and school leadership in Greece. My research is feminist, as its aim is not just to conduct research about women and gender in educational management, but to produce research for women. It is not research that aims to measure "masculine" and "feminine" traits, as this is "not informative" (Keener et al. 2017, p. 4). It is research that "does not merely generate new knowledge about women for the sake of knowledge, but conducts research with the purpose of empowering women" (Langellier and Hall 1989, p. 195). I focus on the accounts built by and about women in educational leadership (Ramazanoglu and Holland 2002). It is my intention that this inquiry will produce knowledge that will assist other women and policy-makers in applying policies that raise awareness about and increase the participation of women in educational management in Greece. As feminist scholar, I engage in social research in order to contribute to the welfare of women as well as to contribute to knowledge (Ramazanoglu and Holland 2002) and I aspire to make a difference to the world (Taylor 1998).

On a methodological level, this chapter and the following ones are informed by a qualitative study based on semi-structured interviews with forty men and women teachers and head teachers based in Greece (Papanastasiou 2016). Women head teachers were interviewed, as I was interested on their experiences on the job. Also, I approached women teachers who had all the necessary qualifications and requirements but who chose not to become head teachers or whose applications were unsuccessful. I also wanted to see how teachers viewed their head teacher, whether women or men. In addition, I wanted to include men head teachers and teachers as well, because I wanted to compare their views and perceptions to those of the women. Furthermore, I wanted to ensure that there were participants of diverse ages and school types (urban/rural, large/small) in order to gather a variety of experiences and views. So, four geographical areas were chosen, based on their distinct population characteristics (areas with highly mobile populations and multicultural as there are minority populations and repatriates and migrants from Eastern Europe, "poor" areas, who have lost since the 1950s almost half of their population through emigration, mostly to the Americas). These four areas have never been included to one of the researches mentioned beforehand (section *Being a Head Teacher in Greece* of Chapter 2). The practicalities of access (Burgess 1984) were also a major concern, as official research permission from the Greek Pedagogical Institute was necessary and I needed more than six months to obtain. Also, potential research participants had to be contacted. Out of the initial forty people that I approached, five teachers did not want to be interviewed (all women) and four head teachers (one woman and three men). The reasons they gave for their decision were that either they never participated in research, or that they were very busy and could not fit me into their schedules. Those who were more willing to participate were the older head teachers, the younger teachers, and those who had at some point been a member of the teachers' union. The probable reasons for this are that they were experienced in expressing views (members of the Union) or they had nothing to be afraid of (older head teachers) or they had experiences of doing research because they had graduated recently or they were doing research themselves as part of a post-graduate dissertation (the younger teachers). The ones who did not want to participate were replaced by others with similar characteristics (age, gender, years of teaching experience, role, area).

Using interviews is about getting "people to explain their answers at length" (Drever 1997, p. 6) and drawing on these statements to identify common features and differing views across the interviews. A space was created where the respondents could engage in a dialogic process and feel more at ease and less mechanical in their relationship with me as the researcher (Oakley 1981, Rubin and Rubin 1995, Bechhofer and Paterson 2000, Denzin and Lincoln 2005).

Interview schedules were piloted with a selected group of informants, which included one woman head teacher, one man head teacher, one woman teacher, and one man teacher before being finalized, although this chapter, like the other chapters (*Constructions of Being a Head Teacher* and *Constructing Change*), does not directly draw on these pilot interviews. Interviews were conducted in Greek which was the first language of the participants and then translated into English. If the respondents are able to speak in their own language, they can express themselves in a more precise way, the answers are richer and the respondents feel more relaxed (Bryman and Bell 2007). This was a challenging task, because as Birbili (2000, n.p.) argues, while translating interviews "even an apparently familiar term or expression for which there is direct lexical equivalent might carry 'emotional connotations' in one language that will not necessary occur in another." An example is the word "*fylo*" which I presented in Chapter 1 (section *Gender and Educational Leadership: A Brief History*).

The analysis of the data was initially guided by a general inductive approach (Dey 1993, Miles and Huberman 1994), which builds categories gradually from the extensive raw text data (Thomas 2006). The analytical categories emerged from the repeated reading of manuscripts and through this, following Miles and Huberman's (1994) methods for finding patterns and developing conceptual themes, initial concepts and ideas for possible themes were identified. They were refined as the fieldwork progressed, leading to the final identification of themes and sub-themes. After all the interviews were first analyzed, the list of themes that emerged constituted the thematic framework that served as the coding tree for the purpose of coding in the NVivo program. NVivo was especially useful due to the importance of what Weitzman (2000, p. 813) calls "poking around in your data" for a more inductive approach. So, this program helped summarizing the data by area, by gender group, and by role, so as to identify commonalities and differences between men and women teachers and head teachers within each area as well as between members of the same gender group based in different or the same areas.

Primary School Teachers and Career Choice

A comparison of how men and women interviewees became (or not) head teachers reveals that, men and women provide different explanations for their choice of a career. They seem to have similar views about the selection procedures even though their experiences are different and report different influences of family responsibilities on their career decisions.

Choosing a Career

The head teacher participants during the interviews had the opportunity to speak about how they became heads. In addition, the teachers who participated in the study were given the opportunity to talk about their future career plans and aspirations. It can be seen that some of my participants had plans for a career in educational leadership and worked toward this goal. Other participants seemed to have become head teachers without aiming to do so, and, finally, some of the teachers who were interviewed indicated that they were not willing to become head teachers at all. In this section, I discuss the participants' choice of a career, beginning with those who planned to become head teachers, followed by those who did not plan for it but nevertheless became heads and moving on to those teachers who indicated that they did not want to become heads.

Becoming a Head Teacher: Career Planning

There were two distinct groups amongst the head teachers in my research, those who became head teachers because they wanted to and aimed for it, and others for whom the route to headship was serendipitous. It is the former that it is discussed in this section.

Although literature from the UK (Evetts 1994, Coleman 2002, Guihen 2019) and elsewhere (i.e., from Norway (Abrahamsen 2017), from Malta (Vella 2022), and from South Africa (Bodalina and Mestry 2022)) suggests that most heads follow a career path that leads through deputy headship to headship, even though research has shown that not all deputies aspire to a headship career (Harris et al. 2003, NAHT 2016), in my research it was only a small minority of the heads that were deputies in the past. This may suggest that the career progression to headship in Greece is not a linear series of steps, from teacher to deputy and then to head, identified in previous literature from other countries. This may be the case for the whole of the country, but as the research sample is small, I do not know if the pattern is replicated nationally.

In this study, out of the twenty-five participants (fifteen women and ten men) who were head teachers at the time of the research, only five women and no men had been deputy head teachers before becoming a head teacher. Three of the women who had been deputy heads did not talk about how they got their deputy post. The other two (Gina and Danai) discussed being a deputy head. Gina, a woman head teacher, said that she got to the post of the deputy head and then to that of the head "out of personal ambition" (Gina, WHT, 40–49). And then, she adds, she became a head teacher because "it was the next step," as was suggested in the literature mentioned above.

Danai, another woman head teacher, noted that:

I was a deputy head at a very large school,[…] After being a deputy head for 3 years and because I managed it, I said why not give it a try? I decided to try it. It was the next step. I knew the job, as well. (Danai, WHT, 40–49)

She became a head teacher because she felt, as she said, contrary to the general belief, that being a deputy head teacher was much more difficult than being a head teacher, as the role can be characterized as intertwined between control, support, and having influence (Abrahamsen 2017). She explained that she had more responsibilities and a more difficult task, because she had to be the link between the teachers and the head teacher. She seems to think that as a deputy head she was a forgotten leader in the school, similarly to how Beycioglu et al. (2012), Cranston et al. (2004), and Guihen (2019) describe deputy heads in Turkey, Australia, and the UK. This was because she had similar responsibilities to the head teacher (she said "I knew the job"), but did not have the authority and the status that a head teacher may enjoy, as Hausman et al. (2002) notes about deputies in Maine, US.

But the role of the deputy head teacher in Greek schools is not the same everywhere. Their role, as it is described by Law 1566/1985, is particularly related to, and heavily influenced by, the head teacher as the head teacher is the one who defines the deputy head's duties. The same is noted in the UK by Garrett (1999) and Abrahamsen (2017) in Norway. Greenfield (1985) also notes that the deputy's duties could be defined as the head's will. As Dean (2002) argues, many deputy heads in New York find that they need to negotiate their role even where there is a clear job description, because it depends upon the management approach of the head teacher. There appears to be a similar pattern in Greece, too. Therefore, the tasks and responsibilities of deputy heads vary from one school to another and may be vague and unclear, as Harris et al. (2003) and Guihen (2019) noted in the UK. In Greece although there is a legal framework for the head teacher's duties and responsibilities, this is not the case for the deputies.

Irrespective of whether they approached headship via the route of deputy, some of the potential applicants seem to have a clear idea of what "steps" they should take in order to enhance their potential candidacy for headship and this includes gaining more academic credentials. Three of the respondents (two women and a man) talked about further developing their qualifications as a key to enhancing their advancement. For example, a woman teacher indicated:

> In the future ... [I may apply for the post] if I were more experienced or had studied further .... A kind of specialization [would have been useful]. So I could be useful in a senior post. Maybe an MBA, or a Master in administration. (Loukia, WT, 30–39)

A woman who had made it to the top and became a head teacher also explained:

> At first, university was not enough for [my husband], so he got another degree. Then it was a Masters. I followed him, as well, or maybe he followed me. We graduated together with a degree in political sciences. Then we did a Masters in teaching, I in language teaching, he in mathematics. (Lea, WHT, 50–59)

Aspiring women in this study tend to have more qualifications than men (even if they have someone to keep them company on their journey to obtain them, as in the case of Lea). According to the Hellenic Statistical Authority in the academic year 2017–18, women represented 60.1 percent of students in Master level courses rising from 43.4 percent in 2013 (Hellenic Statistical Authority 2013b, 2020b). Also, according to Hellenic Statistical Authority in 2019 women comprised 70 percent of all the primary education teachers with post graduate degrees (Hellenic Statistical Authority 2019), while ten years ago they were 65.5 percent (Hellenic Statistical Authority 2010). Coleman (2002) also noted that in the UK, during the period of advancement and planning women and men who aspire to headship are likely to obtain further qualifications. A similar trend is noted in other countries as well (i.e., in South Africa by Bodalina and Mestry (2022), in Malta by Vella (2022), in the Philippines by Rosario (2018), in Israel by Addi-Raccah (2006), in the Palestine by Khattab and Ibrahim (2006) and in the United States by Johnson and Fournillier (2022)). This problematizes the assumptions that women do not progress because they are less qualified (Coffey and Delamont 2000) and does not offer satisfactory explanations for the underrepresentation of women in educational leadership. Women tend to be better qualified than men (Koenig et al. 2011, Gipson et al. 2017), but the experiences that they may have regarding leadership and gender can often lead them to feel unprepared and unqualified to lead (Hill et al. 2016). In contrast men often overestimate their qualifications and competence about their leadership abilities and thus are far less hesitant than women to proceed for leadership posts (Wigfield et al. 1996, Pajares and Schunk 2001). Blackmore and Sachs (2007) also note that women who tend to progress are not the ones who are better qualified, but rather those who tend to follow stereotyped, "masculine" career paths, and have little or no desire to challenge the dominant leadership style. The end result of these social dynamics is that women may be less likely to perceive themselves as sufficiently qualified to enter the formal leadership procedures and hence be less likely to self-select and apply for leadership posts compared to similarly qualified men (Fuller et al. 2018).

In Greece in 2019, 61.5 percent of primary education teachers with second Bachelor degrees were women (Hellenic Statistical Authority 2019b). In my research only two men held a second bachelor degree (in Management and in Economics), while eight women held second bachelor degrees (in Mechanical Engineering, Nursery Nursing, Beauty Studies, Political Science, and Religious Education) and three held Masters (in Education). Taki (2009) interviewed Greek women in the urban area of Thessaloniki who held a variety of leadership posts in education (head teachers, Directors and Heads of Local Educational Authorities, and educational advisors). By comparing the qualifications of the women applicants for these posts to those of the men applicants, she also reached the conclusion that women appear to obtain more qualifications than men. This may be a local and a fairly recent phenomenon as earlier research from other international studies produced different results. For example, Coleman (2002) found that in the UK over 50 percent of the men head teacher participants in her study held a Master's degree, 10 percent more than the women. Also, in the United States Shakeshaft (1989) reported that 71 percent of male secondary school principals held graduate degrees compared with under half of the women. My search for more up-to-date data on the gender distribution of teachers with further qualifications in the UK did not yield any result. However in 2020–21 there were more women postgraduate students (57.7 percent) than men (42.3 percent) in the UK as Higher Education Statistics Agency (2022) reported. So, it seems likely that nowadays in the UK female teachers are also more likely to hold postgraduate degrees than male teachers, as in Greece.

Logan (1999), Peterson and Runyan (1999), and Warsal (2015) argue that the desire for more qualifications that some of the women have may be due to stereotyping women as having lower self-esteem and lacking confidence (as could be argued for Lea in my research) and so having more qualifications would perhaps make them feel more confident. Similarly, Brunner and Grogan (2007) suggest that women's low self-esteem may lead them to seek to further develop themselves in order to prove to themselves and to others that they are qualified enough to become leaders. This could suggest that low self-esteem may be directly affected by the way some women perceive the constructions and expectations that others hold for them. So, if women are constructed as inferior to men, then they may act as if they are (Wilkinson 1991, Gupton and Slick 1996), by possibly internalizing some aspects of gender stereotyping. So, women may doubt their own abilities to become head teachers and may be less likely to apply for jobs for which they are adequately qualified (Coleman 2022). Liu (2000) argued that the higher demands on the professional role of women teachers in China make the conflict between self-respect and feelings of inferiority even more acute. He explains that because of traditional cultural images, some women teachers might feel inferior and lack confidence. Therefore, when women are challenged in work, they may doubt their ability, and often stop advancing (Liu 2000). In addition, research has found that some women appear to be less aspiring toward school leadership than men (Gupton and Slick 1996, Riehl and Byrd 1997, Allred et al. 2017). Of course there may be other reasons for the fact that women stop advancing, like family responsibilities, workload etc., but low confidence may be viewed as a possible reason, too. Riehl and Byrd (1997) in the United States reported that women were not as likely as men to want to leave teaching. Women teachers had degree credentials in educational leadership at rates consistent with men's, indicating that they probably were interested in this kind of work, but they were less likely to leave the classroom, and less likely to apply for leadership positions. Similarly, Cleveland et al. (2000), drawing on international literature, argue that men are more likely to be hired for managerial positions than similarly qualified women. Similarly in the present study, although more women than men held second Bachelor Degrees and Masters, as indicated earlier, only one of them chose to pursue a leadership career. Therefore, based upon these measures, women teachers either appear to be less actively seeking school headship than men, perhaps assuming that they would not get the job or they are less likely to be appointed. Furthermore, gaining more qualifications may be an attempt to counter the assumed preference for men candidates in the selection processes (an issue that is discussed in the section below).

Becoming a Head Teacher: Drifting into Headship

Many of my interviewees (seven out of the fifteen women and three out of the ten men) saw their appointment as head teachers not as a result of a systematic career plan or strong career aspirations, but rather as an unplanned, even abrupt, event in their career. It seems to be a case of what Gold (1996) described as "drifting" into educational leadership and Sachs and Blackmore (2007) also argue, few women aspire to leadership positions and have planned career trajectories, while most women have careers they describe as accidental with few having career trajectories that were planned.

In most cases, respondents explained that their application came about as a result of others (including their colleagues or the Director of the LEA) suggesting they apply. For example, a woman head teacher said:

> [I became a head teacher] [c]oincidentally. I never dreamt of it, I never aspired to it, it never crossed my mind. Because being a head teacher is only being a clerk, not a teacher. You have to be an accountant, you have to know about computers and there is no, or limited, opportunity for direct contact with the classroom. You don't have your own class. You don't have your own children to devote yourself to. You don't feel that special relationship between the children and their teacher. Because of all that it never crossed my mind to apply. But then in 2005 the head teacher of my school retired and the post was advertized. My colleagues urged me to apply. They believed I could handle it. I have been in this

school since 1993, when it first opened, so I know all the problems, all the needs. So I decided to apply. I was thinking of taking the post just for a year. Then I said, ok one more year. Then I applied again for another 4 years this time. But to tell you the truth it was not an easy decision, because I wouldn't have my class. (Kiki, WHT, 50–59)

Kiki constructs headship as very technical not compatible with her own priorities and experiences. She sees headship as administrative in nature ("being a head teacher is only being a clerk [...] You have to be an accountant, you have to know about computers"). She identifies herself as wanting to work with children and devote herself to them, reflecting priorities traditionally constructed as "feminine" and connected to women (i.e., proximity to children, emotional expressions). Her traditional image of headship implies a "masculine" construction of the head teacher's role as someone who has to deal with money and work with technology, professions that in Greece are associated mostly with men (Alipranti-Maratou and Tsakmakis 2008). In conjunction with "masculine" constructions of management as technicist and requiring knowledge of new technologies (Al-Khalifa and Migniuolo 1990), the head's job conflicts with traditional notions of "femininity" (Reay and Ball 2000). So, from what Kiki is saying it may be suggested that the assumed "masculine" nature of headship may perpetuate women's low aspirations of attaining a management position (Evetts 1994, Blackmore 1999, Oplatka and Tamir 2009). Put differently, the belief that women tend to value caring and having relationships with others could be perceived as being at odds with "masculine" values of management and as a negative incentive for women's desire to pursue career progression (Limerick and Anderson 1999).

Furthermore, Kiki appears to lack confidence when she had to decide whether to apply for headship or not. She had to be "urged" to apply as her colleagues believed she "could handle it." So, she can be assumed to be drawing on constructions socially ascribed as traditionally "feminine," even though as I will show below, some men in my research also appeared to lack confidence in their abilities to handle leadership (e.g., Yannis). So, it can be argued that lacking confidence, although it is traditionally constructed as a "feminine" characteristic, may also associated with men, too. Though men who display a lack of confidence tend to be seen as "not manly" enough, as they do not correspond to the traditional notion of "hegemonic masculinity," that constructs men as unemotional, confident, and independent (Connell and Messerschmidt 2005).

Yannis, like Kiki, did not plan to be a head teacher. He explained:

I would say that I became a head teacher without aiming for it. […] When I was talking to other teachers and heads they were all telling me to apply. But this didn't affect me. I didn't believe I was suitable for the post, that I was the right one or that I could manage the whole school. The Director of LEA, though, who was a close friend of mine and kind of a role model, told me that I could do it and that I should apply. (Yannis, MHT, 50–59)

He is an example of a man head teacher who did not plan to become a head teacher and needed a "push." Similarly to Kiki, he seems to have low confidence, although this is traditionally assumed to be a "feminine" characteristic (Oplatka 2006). He was encouraged by a man Director of the LEA and by the Director's belief that he was capable of being a head teacher. Yannis therefore may be viewed as someone who benefited from homosocial networks (which is discussed below) to enhance his career. His talk is also indicative of the assumption held by some of the respondents (seventeen out of the forty) that becoming a head teacher has to do with networking and the people you know. Networking maybe of a political nature as eighteen of the respondents believe, or it may be of other nature (e.g., religious, knowing people who are in senior positions). Yannis falls into the second category because his appointment as a head teacher was supported by the Director of LEA, who was also a man (as it is evident in the Greek word *"proistamenos"* that he uses). In this case networking appears to be based on homophily in a way that has powerful implications for the information people receive, the attitudes they form, and the interactions they experience (McPherson et al. 2001, Coleman 2022). Yannis was supported not only by a man, but also by someone holding power (i.e., the Director of LEA). According to the literature, men tend to move onto the leadership ladder because those who make the decisions and have power usually want to maintain the status quo (i.e., to have men and/or those who draw on traditionally "masculine" identities in leadership posts) (Jakobsh 2004).

Other head teachers in this study entered their current role due to the former head teacher's retirement or career transition as they have moved to different posts (e.g., Director of LEA). The important aspect in their story is, nonetheless, that events brought about a need to recruit a person as a head teacher and they were chosen to fill this position. Notably, the women head teachers (and some men too) underscored the fact that they had not initiated the application for the vacant position. On the contrary, they indicated that they had been persuaded to apply by someone else, using phrases like "I was the most experienced teacher in this school, when the former head retired, I was offered the post and my colleagues insisted that I accept" (Christina, WHT, 30–39).[1] Perhaps they talk like this because they are not so sure they are capable of doing the job, or it may be the opposite, they wanted to stress to me that they were thought of as able and appropriate for the post by their colleagues and/or superiors.

Other head teachers talked also about becoming heads even though they had not planned for it.

> I was appointed this year, because a head teacher retired and they didn't have anybody else to appoint. I don't think I was the best person for the job. I don't even think I was prepared for it, I didn't think that then and I don't think it now. I still don't have any qualifications in management. In other schools there were better people, but the new head teacher had to be from this school and I was the only teacher with a permanent post. (Kostas, MHT, 50–59)

Here, Kostas also appears to lack confidence as he says that he was appointed as a head teacher as a last resort, because there was no other person to take up the job. He does not appear to believe that he became a head teacher because he was the right person for the job. Later on he repeats almost the same words "it was just an empty post, they didn't have anybody else and so they gave it to me." His appearance is quite "masculine." So, according to Greek understandings and constructions of "masculinity," his physical appearance and his moustache, which in modern Greece is considered a symbol of a virile man (Christianopoulos 2004, Christidou and Kouvatas 2013) even though in other countries (i.e., Iran and UK) it can be associated with homosexuality (Khosravi 2009), one would expect that his behavior would have also been "masculine." But he appears to draw on a more "feminine" construction (like Yannis above) as he appears to lack self-confidence and to devalue himself. This highlights how gender is socially constructed based on stereotypes and behaviors that do not necessarily correspond with men's and women's own identities.

Unwilling to Become a Head Teacher, or Not Willing Yet

I asked the teachers who participated in my research if they planned to apply or if they were thinking of applying for headship in the future. Out of the five men and ten women teachers that I interviewed, only three were planning to apply for headship sometime in the future (two women and one man). Out of the five men teachers that I interviewed, two had applied in the past but had not been successful and had now accepted that they would not be heads. The other eight women and two men were not willing to apply.

Five of those women who were not willing to apply indicated that the tasks of headship are not of interest to them at this point in time, because they entered education to teach. Some typical quotes from their responses are:

> No. For the time being I am not thinking about it. I am very young and I want to work with my class. I really enjoy the contact with the children and the way they behave. (Roula, WT, 30–39)

> I like teaching. This is what I want. […] I don't think I will ever apply for headship, because it will mean that I would have to abandon teaching. (Loukia, WT, 30–39)

Perhaps the most important point in these quotes is that both of them are from women teachers, and that only women made this point. No man in the study discussed the enjoyment of being a teacher and being close to children. Kiki should also be mentioned here, too, because, even though she became a head teacher, she would still prioritize being in the classroom with children over leading a school. These are claims despite the legal framework that indicates that head teachers do have teaching responsibilities, as I showed earlier. It is assumed that teaching is traditionally constructed as a feminized practice associated with care (Noddings 2005), reflecting a dominant discourse of "femininity," where women are seen as caring and nurturant, and are thus considered to be "naturally" focused on the role of a teacher. Also, as I have discussed in Chapter 1 (section *Gender Identity*), "femininity" is traditionally associated with an ethic of care, contrary to "masculinity" which is associated with professional prowess (Charlebois 2012), resulting in the assumption that "men manage and women teach" (Ozga 1993, Coleman and Fitzgerald 2008, Whitehead 2013).

One other reason that the participants put forward for their decision not to apply for headships is that of family responsibilities and work-life balance. One of perhaps the biggest challenges women and men face today is combining a career that is satisfying with the rewards of family life. Women's participation in the workforce is increasing comparing to a few years ago, with working women reaching almost 62.6 percent of all women in Greece even if it is quite lower than the rates of the EU (73.1 percent) (Eurostat 2022). Given the sort of demands that the head teacher's post holds and the fact that women are more likely to take the responsibility for children and home, it is not surprising that many women, both in my study and in other studies worldwide (Lewis 1994, Coleman 2002, Oplatka and Herzt-Lazarowitz 2006, Shah 2022), find it difficult to combine career with family.

Caring responsibilities around the world tend to be still strongly identified with women and seen as women's work (Warin and Gannerud 2014, Shah 2022);

this may cause ethical dilemmas to women who may aspire for leadership posts, as they may be caught between a conflict of professional/moral obligation to the school and the moral value of caring for their family (Moorosi 2022, Mythili 2022). This assumption produces imbalanced patterns of working practices and responsibilities across a whole range of contexts including within the teaching profession.

Additionally, while almost all of the women participants appeared to talk lovingly about raising their children, most of those who planned to apply for headship wait until their children are grown or more independent. They indicate that they do not think that they could do the work required to be a mother and a head teacher at the same time. A woman teacher aspiring to headship indicated:

My child will be older [when I plan to apply], he is 8 now, in two years time he will be 10, he will be independent … ok, I have only one child, I don't have a lot of other engagements … (Eleni, WT, 40–49)

A similar account was given by another woman teacher:

I haven't thought about it. Also, because I have connected headship with major responsibilities, it hasn't crossed my mind. Also, I have 2 children who need my attention. They are young. They can't cope without their mother! I also have my husband and my house to take care of[…] And I have to be a mum, a housekeeper and a wife on top of that! These are jobs with great demands, as well. (Mina, WT, 30–39)

She offers the view that being a head teacher is a very demanding job with great responsibilities. This, combined with the fact that she has two young children (ten and seven years old) and domestic responsibilities, feels too much to handle and so she does not think of applying for headship. McLay (2008) in her study on head teacher career paths in UK schools also found that most of her respondents did not take their first headship before their children were aged fifteen or over. Similar are the results of Mahmood's (2018) study in Pakistan. Domestic responsibility is also a very important point raised in Mina's talk. Responsibility for care and domestic work is not shared equally between women and men, regardless of women's employment status in the UK (Delamont 2001, Kodz et al. 2003, European Social Survey 2013). As I discussed in Chapter 2 (section *Barriers to Career Progression for Women*), women perform the majority of housework in European and other countries (Ferrant et al. 2014, Moreau 2019, McMunn et al. 2020, Lumby 2022). In Greece, data by Mencarini and Sironi (2009) who conducted a comparative analysis of the data collected in the European Social Survey (Round 2, 2004) found that women do more than 75 percent of the work around the house. More recent data from European Social

Survey (2013) indicate that women in Greece do even more domestic work, reaching 80 percent of the total. The explanation for this increase may rest with the recession in Greece, as women face unemployment in greater numbers. As a result, they stay at home and undertake more of the domestic work. Of course, the situation is not that different from the past, when women did not face such high numbers of unemployment. Another explanation may also be that more men than women tend to have second jobs in order to make ends meet and support their families after the pay cuts and the price increases that have taken place over the past years due to the recession in Greece and the worldwide energy crisis (Livanos and Zangelidis 2012, To vima 24/7/2011, Ognjenocik 2022). So, as men are away from the house, women have to shoulder even more responsibilities and housework. On the other hand official data show that unemployment is almost 22 percent (DYPA 2022) and even if the rates of unemployed women are much higher than those for men (almost 679,000 women and 382,000 men), a lot of men are out of work. So, one might have expected that men would have shared domestic duties, as many of them do not work anymore. But, as Kambouri (2013) also notes, this is not the case.

In today's modern nuclear family, women usually do not have practical support from other members of the extended family and this tends to place extensive pressure on women teachers as Home (1998) indicates in the United States. Household and family responsibilities can also be seen as barriers for women in leadership positions (Home 1998). Faced with both social and household responsibilities, as well as career and family, the great majority of women try to make the best of both worlds. Most working women are trying to balance a successful career and home and at the same time are attempting to establish acceptable social identities as mothers and wives (Litosseliti 2006). A study of managers aged thirty-five to sixty-four in the UK found that 88 percent of men managers were married, compared with 69 percent of their women colleagues (Charlesworth 1997). In the field of education, Coleman (2005a) found that 78 percent of the women head teachers were married and 63 percent had a child compared with 96 percent of the men who were married and 90 percent who had a child. So, she concluded that although there were difficulties in both men's and women's lives, the lives of women appeared to be more deeply affected in both studies. An important feature of leadership work is the long hours that both men and women have to spend at work in order to gain recognition and eventually promotion (DfES 2007). Even though there is no official data about the amount of time men and women in leadership positions spend at work in Greece, I can assume from personal knowledge and experience that it is longer than non-leadership work. So, women who desire both a family and a career often juggle heavy responsibilities in both domains (Reay and Ball 2000, Griffiths 2002, Woodhouse and Guihen 2022). It can be practically impossible to reconcile the long hours of leadership work with the amount of time needed to care for a home and children. In this context, time is very much a gender issue.

For women, combining a senior post with motherhood is difficult and this may lead women to prioritize their goals. It can be assumed that society's expectations are that women play the lead role at home and in childcare and this may cause conflicts between family and career. My respondents' choice to delay their entry into the headship may suggest that it might be difficult for these women to perform as both heads and mothers, given the dominant constructions of these roles, if their children were still home. While these women may need to overcome many barriers to obtain their head teacher position if they decide to apply, it is possible that their delayed entry serves to perpetuate the underrepresentation of women in educational leadership. Dana and Bourisaw (2006) in their study about women as superintendents in the United States explain:

> One of the most traditional sex-role stereotypes is the woman as family and home caregiver. Because women are the childbearers, they are also expected to be the primary family caregivers, which traditionally has meant the women stay home to rear the children, fix the meals, maintain the house and all family operations, and, since they are at home, take care of the secretarial, organizational, and social duties for the family. Men are expected to be the financial providers for their families. (p. 22)

Similarly, in the Greek family the mother is constructed as taking care of everything in the house and the father as the main breadwinner (Stratigaki n.d.).

These expectations seem to be grounded in dominant constructions of "femininity" and perhaps make it difficult for women to access a head teacher's position. The head teacher's position tends to be defined around more "masculine" constructions, as being always present in the school without any other responsibilities and spending long working hours there. Women tend to see promotion as an intensification of labor, while men view promotion as "leading to more opportunities to delegate and hence more freedom and autonomy" (Blackmore and Sachs 2007, p. 142). So, it does not seem to be a post that a woman with traditional family responsibilities can easily cope with as it may collide with the dominant constructions of "femininity."

Furthermore, a woman teacher in my research who did not want to apply for headship (Dina) seems to have images of headship that can be seen to draw on traditional constructions about "masculinity" and "femininity" and to corroborate "masculine conceptualizations of management" (Gray 1989). For example, Dina notes that:

> [A man head teacher] reacts differently in certain situations, he can enforce discipline, he can set up rules, he is fair. A woman is afraid, she is insecure, she becomes unfair, she bases her decisions on gossiping and not facts. A man can handle staff, while a woman can't. (Dina, WT, 40–49)

The assumption that an effective head teacher ought to be assertive, aggressive, determined, persuasive, strong, and charismatic makes it easier to understand why this woman teacher felt that headship does not fit with dominant constructions of "femininity." So, in some instances women like Dina may be put off applying for senior positions because leadership is often associated with "masculine" characteristics which can be unappealing to them. Dina seems to downgrade women head teachers by associating them with behaviors that have a negative connotation, like gossiping or by considering them as afraid and insecure, contrary to men. A view like that coming from a woman is very interesting and in contrast to other studies from the business world that have found that women peers tend not to downgrade other women (Ibarra and Obodaru 2009). On the other hand, in the field of educational leadership Gupton and Slick (1996) report "an unexpected wrinkle" (p. 5) in a woman high school principal's experiences in her new job when she revealed that "many teachers were […] not inclined to accept leadership from a woman. And the women teachers were less inclined [than men]" (p. 66). Bell (1995) tried to explain this phenomenon by stating that women in educational leadership are in the unusual position of having one foot in each camp, being members of a majority (women in education) as well as members of the few (women school leaders). She concludes that the experiences of women leaders "encompass both authority and influence as leaders, and isolation as women in a male dominated occupation" (p. 289).

Similar to Bell's (1995) argument is Funk's (2010) assertion that members of oppressed groups tend to lash out at their peers in response to oppression instead of attacking their oppressors. Dina appears to be doing this, as she denigrates and attacks other women who have made it and reached leadership posts.

It is not only women who find the idea of headship and the amount of work involved deterring. Vassilis, a man teacher, noted:

[I don't want to be a head teacher] [b]ecause a head teacher has so many responsibilities that I don't even want to think about the fact that I could have been in his shoes.[…] A head has so many other jobs, so many documents, has to run around, asking, or begging, for several things, like for extra teachers, or for money for the heating. A lot of work! (Vassilis, MT, 30–39)

The amount of work that headship involves appears to deter him, too. He feels that the head teacher is overloaded. The head teacher is perceived by Vassilis (as was perceived by Kiki earlier) as having so many administrative duties (e.g., dealing with bureaucracy) that do not seem to be directly linked to leadership and management. He also perceives the head teacher as the one who "begs" for things, like money or teaching personnel. It is true that in Greece the money allocated to the schools by the local authorities is usually not enough to cover schools' basic needs (i.e., utility bills and heating), let alone stationery and maintenance. Also, it is rare that all the teaching posts are covered at the beginning of each school year or during the year should a teacher leave because of health reasons. The head teacher usually has to turn to their superiors in order to have the empty posts filled. So, Vassilis believes that these responsibilities are overwhelming and, so, a headship post does not appeal to him.

Finally, one more reason for not wanting to be a head teacher seems to be the pervasive culture of heterosexism (Papanastasiou 2015, 2020). Teachers who are LGTBIQ+ have to make a personal decision about whether to "come out" or not. Grace and Benson (2000) argue that this is "a risky business" (p. 90). A man participant identified himself as gay and said:

….this will happen [the application], if it ever happens, in the future. First I have to work on being accepted as a teacher and as a person. I try not to provoke anyone. I behave as normal as I can, as "manly" as I can. I don't know … I feel it in the air that they would rather not have me around here, but I don't give up! I am here to stay! Whether you like it or not, I am a teacher, I am a good teacher I think, and my sexual orientation is nobody's business. I am not a gay teacher, but I am a teacher who happens to be gay. But it causes problems and it will cause more problems if I dare apply! (Petros, MT, 30–39)

The dilemma he might have had to face is described by Gust (2007) who wrote: "The choice of a teacher to be 'out' in the classroom is perhaps unadvisable, possible joyous, potentially disastrous, positively political, and just plain hard" (p. 43).

At the time of the interview, his colleagues at the school had figured out his sexuality and, as he was guessing, not all of them were OK with it. He suggested that the information about his sexuality has been passed on through "word of mouth," suggesting that a school can be what Foucault (1995) calls an "observation machine" (p. 173) as when something is spoken or assumed (especially if this is someone's sexuality) it becomes public property. Also his opinion that he may be criticized for his work based on his sexual identity is in line with Endo et al. (2010) who found that teachers who disclosed their identity to others were viewed differently, as sexuality became the identity that defined them, exceeding other identities.

The conflicting sentence "I am not a gay teacher, but I am a teacher who happens to be gay" may show that Petros is ambivalent about his sexual and professional identity. He seems to try to distance himself from the label he himself used before, insisting that his professional identity is separate and more important than his sexual identity. Neary (2013) argues that "LGTBQI teachers engage with processes of resistance at different levels as they negotiate their identity positions within the school" (p. 596). Petros in this research draws upon "particular positions for [himself]" (Mills 1997, p. 1) and resists by managing his identities (Ferfolja 2007) and by avoiding to come out. Maybe he is afraid that if he comes out as a gay person he will be assigned all that constitutes the label in the Greek society and his act of disclosure will be just limiting and not "both liberating and limiting at the same time" as it is suggested by Neary (2013).

From Petros words it can be assumed that in a pervasive culture of heterosexism, heterosexuality is taken for granted as normal, natural, and proper. But, individuals who resist this norm, can create new identities and ways of knowing, that is, Petros draws on being a teacher as a professional, "a good teacher," as he says. Similarly, Ferfolja (2007) in a study in Australia note that those who do not follow the "acceptable" standards of (hetero)normativity in a school, may be "punished" through overt or covert harassment, stigmatization, ostracism, and exclusion. So, as a consequence many gay teachers in Australia choose silence, because their sexuality may be considered an "illegitimate" discourse and practice as the prevailing dominant discourse normalizes heterosexuality.

Gray (2013) interviewed twenty teachers in the UK and aimed at illustrating the complexities of the coming out process. She noted that some of her participants also chose not to come out within their professional lives. The reasons for their choice were multiple and "were related to school location and participants' understandings of the communities that surrounded their workplaces as being socially conservative" (p. 5). As it is with Petros, the participants in Gray's research felt that school's pervasive heteronormative culture involved a risk, that sometimes it was too great to take.

Petros describes his behavior as trying to be "manly," reflecting the "normal," hegemonic form of (hetero)sexuality and the dominant form of gendered social relations that are constructed in an institution like a school.

When I asked him if he was thinking of applying for a headship in the future, he said:

> [My sexuality] it will cause more problems if I dare apply!

He believes that his gay identity may disrupt his career progress as Boatwright et al. (1996) explain in their study. So this highlights not only the fact that the head teacher is constructed as "masculine," but also as heterosexual, as Kanter (1977) suggested. Blount (2003) in his study in the US context suggests that there is understandable reluctance on the part of gay (or lesbian) administrators to identify themselves given societal bias. Petros is brave enough to identify himself in the interview but, as it appears from his account, not at school. He seems to believe that by breaking the code of silence through disclosure he will not perceive less heterosexist bias but would have to deal with a lot more and this could be costly. So, he is trying not to draw attention to his identity but this consumes much of his time to hide his identity and he places himself outside the regular channels for advancement. But Petros does not reject headship at all. He considers it for the future, after he has been accepted as gay.

Later on he adds:

> I don't know how they will react if I, or somebody else who is gay, apply. I guess I will have a problem, as I am not the typical man who goes around giving orders. I am more approachable and cool with everybody.

Here Petros challenges dominant constructions of "masculinity" as someone "who goes around giving orders." He presents himself as more approachable and democratic and constructs a different/alternative "masculinity." He chooses not to conform, but rather challenges the prevailing constructions of "masculinity" and "femininity" (i.e., being assertive like a "typical" man). Reay and Ball (2000, p. 149) draw on Ganderton (1991) and Gunter (1997) to suggest that those who "challenge organizational views, including orthodoxies around the 'best way to manage' are unlikely to be promoted to the position of head teacher" and this seems to apply to Petros. Although he chooses in the interview not to remain silent about his sexuality, he is silent in the school context as indicated earlier. His reaction seems to confirm what Reay and Ball (2000) note, that "the powerful in society, regardless of their sex, share more in common with each other than they share with relatively powerless members of either sex" (p. 150).

Greece is considered a conservative country where most people regard homosexuality as a taboo issue (Eurobarometer 2007) and non-heterosexual people as an invisible group (Giannelos 2000). The Greek Orthodox Church, a major and influential institution in the country, considers homosexuality to be a sin and those with homosexual orientations as sinful. Similarly, several high-profile politicians have openly expressed disdain toward homosexual people and the media often promotes an image of exaggerated and ridiculous homosexual characters or even censor homosexual scenes in prime-time series (e.g., a kiss between men shown in the British TV series "Downton Abbey"). Qualitative research findings suggest that the population in general holds a rather negative picture of homosexuals and believes that homosexuality poses a danger to society (Tzamalouka 2000). Even many social work students in a study of their perceptions appear to have negative views of homosexuality and admit that they would not treat a person who is gay/lesbian as they would treat heterosexuals (Papadaki and Papadaki 2011, Papadaki et al. 2013). Homosexual populations in Greece are stigmatized, marginalized, and often subject to homophobic behavior (Tzamalouka 2002). A few years ago, an MP from the far-right political party of the Golden Dawn denounced homosexuality as "sickness" (the Guardian 16/7/2014) and a former Minister (who is also a doctor) during an interview characterized it as "a spreading disease" (iefimerida 19/1/2017). In a cultural climate like that one can understand why Petros chooses to remain silent about his sexual orientation and why he thinks he has almost no chance of getting a head teacher's position.

Shakeshaft et al. (2010) draw on research from the United States and the UK that analyzed the history and experiences of gay and lesbian educational leaders and conclude that their reluctance to identify themselves as homosexuals is understandable. They add that gay/lesbian leaders in the United States "still risk immediate termination based on the belief that gay, lesbian, and transgender administrators post a threat to the stability of the school community" (p. 115). In Greece, although the Greek Constitution, which was established in 1975, does not allow discrimination based on gender, race, and religion, sexual orientation is not included as a nondiscriminatory category. So, maybe Petros is right and if he chooses to become a head teacher now, he will have to deal with a lot.

To sum up, from my research it seems that the ones who feel able to apply for headship are mostly men who may want it or have been urged by their colleagues or superiors to apply, even though there are some women who have applied or think about it in the future. Regarding women, it seems that those who want to be head teachers usually plan it beforehand and work toward it by obtaining more qualifications. It should be mentioned that the younger women appear to have more qualifications than the older ones (from the seven women participants with a second Bachelor and/or a Master's degree, only Loula and Lea were over forty years old, while the rest were in the age band thirty to thirty-nine). Also the women who have fewer domestic and/or childhood responsibilities are more likely to seek headship. The reasons why women and some men do not want to be head teachers seem to be because of the demands of the post and because of how they construct the role of the head teacher. This latter issue will be analyzed in the next chapter (*Constructions of Being a Head Teacher*).

Selection Procedures

In order for teachers to become head teachers they have to go through a selection procedure. In Greece, this is done in every geographical area, every two years. The assessments and selection are done by a council which is composed of three teachers (experience in leadership is preferable but not mandatory) selected by the Director of Regional Educational Authorities after a public announcement for the post, the Director of Local Educational Authorities, and an Educational Coordinator. The assessment and selection procedure involves a points system with two subcategories. The first one is where the applicant's qualifications (bachelor, postgraduate degrees, seminars, and conferences attended, papers presented at seminars or conferences, publications, knowledge of foreign languages, etc.) are judged and the second one is an interview where the applicant's personality and management knowledge and ability are assessed.

For the participants in the present research two factors were highlighted that may assist or hinder career progress for both men and women: Networks and constructions of gender.

Networks and the Selection Process

Although in Greece the selection procedure for head teachers is intended to be objective and transparent, the head teachers and teachers who participated in the present research believe that the procedures are anything but objective. All but one of the respondents felt that political beliefs played an important role.

A man teacher, who failed to be selected as head, discussed the role that political beliefs could play in the selection procedure:

> [I wasn't selected] [b]ecause, the final decision was based on criteria that were not objective, they were subjective.[...] You had to be a friend of the government or you had to be in agreement, politically, with the selection panel in order to get a high mark and to be selected. (Thodoris, MT, 50–59)

And another one commented on the selection procedure and the influence of politics:

> [I wasn't preferred because] the other [applicant] was a political ally of them. He was a member of the governing party and he had been involved with the union for many years. He was known to them. I was just a simple head teacher that wanted to keep my post. I had never expressed myself politically, I wasn't an active member of the union. So, the other guy was preferred.(Lakis, MT, 50–59)

This is similar to the findings of other studies in Greece about women in educational management (Taki 2009) and about gender and the selection procedures in educational management (Andrikogiannopoulou 2010). Both of these studies concluded that the selection of educational leaders is an unfair procedure, open to manipulation based on political networks and influence. A woman head teacher, who used to be a member of the selection panel in her area when she was involved with the teachers' union, admits that "I myself was influenced by factors outside the procedure, like the 'correct' political party" (Gina, WHT, 40–49) (she indicated the inverted commas with a gesture). The respondents agree that favoritism based on political beliefs can be applied equally to men and women and by men and women.

However, an interesting point in my data is that it is men who reported that they failed to be selected as heads because of political networks. The women in my study, although they acknowledge the existence of these networks, did not report any personal experiences related to this. This may relate to the different ways in which men and women present their political affiliations. Men tend to be more overt about their membership, something that women do not appear to do, as Kiki below indicates. She believes that her political affiliation did not play any role in her appointment as a head teacher, as her political beliefs are not known to the public. So, she assumes that the selection panel probably appointed her on other criteria and not politics:

> Because we are Greeks, I believe politics could be an influence. Personally, all these years I try to keep my political beliefs outside of the school. Politics is not my passion. So, I have never given the right to anyone to judge me for my political beliefs and I don't think that it has affected my appointment. (Kiki, WHT, 50–59)

But even so, a selection based on political beliefs may also be a gendered selection, as this woman head teacher indicates:

> The one who is closer to the panel's political beliefs [is selected]. And because men have more time to get involved in politics, they would choose the man. (Rena, WHT, 30-39)

She offers the view that women are less involved with politics because of gender roles and especially the role of women in Greek society. As discussed above, women are constructed as being the ones responsible for the house and the children. The public sphere is the male preserve and the private, or domestic, sphere is the designated sphere for women. So, in a traditional society, like the Greek society, the tendency is for the men to be involved in politics and for the women to identify with traditional constructions of "femininity" and this is suggested by Rena. A family with two breadwinners usually means a dual burden for women and unequal distribution of domestic work (OECD 2001, Kodz et al. 2003). As was noted earlier, responsibility and care in Greece is not often shared equally between women and men either. So, while women teachers have to work at school and then take care of their homes, families, and children, men teachers have time after work to deal with other things, like politics and networking.

So, some men and women participants feel that promotion in the Greek education system can be subjective and obscured by political motives. This view was also shared by the teachers who participated in several researches, like by the Greek Teachers Union (DOE) in 2002, by Bakalbasi and Fokas in 2016 and by Voulgaridis in 2018. It can be suggested that this widespread view stems from the way that educational managers are selected. In addition, the existing legislative framework (Presidential Decree 25/2002) does not establish consistent selection criteria (Saitis 2002) or requirements that interview questions should be the same for all applicants. But even if there were, this does not imply that favoritism would cease, as research in the UK, where the same questions for all candidates is standard policy, has shown that the applicants' gender affects selection (Coleman 2002). Even though Coleman's and the Greek studies were conducted several years ago, Rena clearly feels that gender is still influential.

Another hindering factor, besides political networks, that is suggested by some of the participants in my research is what has been identified in the literature as the "old boys' network" (Coleman 2002, p. 81). White men have known for a long time that networks are important for career success (Cocciara et al. 2010). Variously termed the "Old Boys Network" (Blackmore 1993) or

"Good Old Boys" network (Shakeshaft 1989, Rosario 2018), these networks have developed through school ties or social organizations, such as country clubs. Such networks serve an instrumental function in providing career-related information (Coleman 2002). In essence, the literature suggests networks provide resources, such as information, feedback, and social support, to the individual. Moore and Webb (1998) argue that for many women, who lack access to information and social support in the workplace, effective networking might be crucial for career success.

Women who seek leadership positions often find that informal networks of leaders control the recruitment and selection process, as Linehan (2001) found in her research in the area of corporate management in Ireland, Belgium, Germany, and France. Women usually do not have access to the kinds of informal contacts that usually ensure advancement in a career. Most women feel left out because the "old boys' network," a male communications network among leaders, exchanges professional and personal information that often deals with job advancement and placement opportunities as Fagenson (1994) notes for the corporate world. It can be argued that the situation is similar in education, as well. In Greece this informal networking usually takes place in coffee shops in the afternoon. Coffee shops are traditional places where men gather and where women are not welcome. As Papataxiarchis (1992) and Loizos (2003) note, the coffee shops (*kafeneia*) in Greece are places where "masculinity" is usually demonstrated by swearing, playing cards and backgammon, drinking, smoking, and engaging in discussions and are in contrast with households, which are considered as "feminine" fields. So, women are traditionally excluded from such networks and as a result they do not have information about open leadership posts. Although in my research the participants did not refer to the places where informal networking tends to take place, personal experiences show that this is in coffee shops, football grounds, and private clubs.

Years ago, Linehan (2001) indicated that, throughout Europe, the "old boys' network" was strong in most organizations. More research conducted in Ireland by Drew and Murtagh (2005) indicated that there are many established networks in the corporate world in which women are not allowed to participate. The "Old Boys' Network" is also challenging for women in South Africa (Rammund-Mansingh and Seedat-Khan 2020). Finally, Piterman (2013) argues that in Australia "the Old Boy Network is alive and well, despite all talk of diversity and corporate change" (p. 101).

Women are excluded from "old boys' networks" which have been composed of men who have power and information (Linehan 2000). The exclusion of women from male networks perpetuated the more "masculine" customs and negative attitudes toward women leaders. The detrimental effects of exclusion from male networks could be blocked promotion, discrimination, and lower salaries even if they hold similar qualifications to men.

In the international literature in relation to education, the "old boys' networks" may be viewed in relation to mentoring and sponsoring as Taylor (1995) noted in Canada and Coleman (2002, 2022) in the UK. Mentorship and networks may facilitate the progress of women (Coleman 2010, Fuller and Berry 2019). Although mentoring and/or sponsoring by experienced heads was cited as an important aspect of training and contact with others (Coleman 2002, Sherman et al. 2008, Taylor 1995), inside information and acquaintance with gatekeepers, that is, selection panels, women tend not to have full access to mentoring schemes. A reason for this may be that the majority of mentors are men, so they form patriarchal and homosocial support systems (Bagilhole and Goode 2001) from which women are usually excluded. But given that Bagilhole's and Goode's research was about women in higher education in the UK, and not in primary education, where women are the majority of head teachers in the UK, it would be interesting to see if the situation is similar in primary education in Greece where women are the minority of head teachers, as I have shown in an earlier chapter (*Women in Educational Leadership: Global and National Context*).

So, although one may have expected that women in Greece would have formatted their own networks to balance men's, the only women's networks in the country are for women who suffer from domestic or other kinds of violence, the Women of SYRIZA network that is mostly concerned with political issues (e.g., the anti-globalization movement) and the White Women Front, a network that the far-right political party Golden Dawn has formed in order to inform women. I suggest that more women's networks are necessary in order to help women to see themselves in a different way, to raise consciousness, to see new possibilities, and to gain the benefits and information deriving from networking.

In Greece, there are no formal mentoring schemes even though there is legal provision since 2018 (Law 4547/2018 has never been implemented), but many of my participants talked about support that they received from a former head teacher or from the head of the LEA.

> During my first year I just took the place of the former head who retired and really believed in me and helped me a lot with everything during the first year. He was the one who, kind of, pushed me to apply ....he believed I could do it. (Alexandra, WHT, 40–49)

> I won't call it a proposal ... information is the right word [from the LEA]. [...] they proposed to me. And then, ok, it was a whole procedure. But I knew there was a will to open this school and to appoint someone experienced, like me. (Maria, WHT, 40-49)

What is interesting is that Maria and Alexandra were both head teachers who discussed their approach to leadership in ways that could be seen as associated with traditional "masculine" constructions (i.e., making decisions on their own and not consulting the other teachers, relying a lot on the law and not being flexible, not caring about the others' emotions etc.) (as is discussed in Chapter 4 *Constructions of Being a Head Teacher*) and their "sponsors" were men. It is also interesting that the research participants (men or women) who tend to draw on what are considered as traditionally "masculine" leadership approaches were mainly supported or helped in their career progression by men. So, maybe homophilous and/or known colleagues (in the cases of Alexandra and Maria they were the former head teacher and the Director of LEA) act as attractors and they provide a familiar underlying structure for the head teacher to return to, as men tend to help other men (Coleman 2010) or those who are similar to them (McPherson et al. 2001, Chewning and Doerfel 2013). Maria, like Yannis earlier, had inside information about the post from the Director of LEA. But, contrary to Yannis who did not initially plan to be a head teacher, Maria wanted to and had already been a head teacher at another school before this post became available. So, maybe it was not a case of homophily as the case with Yannis, but a matter of acquaintance. The Director of the LEA knew Maria from her previous post and knew that she was experienced and the appropriate person to lead a new school.

But, it is not only the lack of support from those who hold an "important" position that may hinder the selection process. The fact that selection panels consist mainly of men (something that most of the respondents stressed) can also hinder women's career progression. This was something that all of my respondents (men, women, head teachers, and teachers) agreed upon.

> T: [The selection] depends on who is conducting the interview and what there is in his mind.
> E: If the panel is all men, do you think it is more likely they would select a woman or a man?
> T: A man.[..] Because he will be one of them (Anna, WT, 30-39)

> [The selection] depends on who is on the panel that is conducting the interview. Most Heads of LEAs are men and birds of a feather flock together! Of course they will select a man! (Kostas, MHT, 50-59)

It is worth noting that Anna uses the single form of the Greek masculine grammatical form (*tou*) when she is talking about the people conducting interviews. Although the panel consists of five people, Anna seems to consider it as something coherent that is also male. While she is doing this she can be viewed as drawing on traditional gender assumptions, that is, that the norm is that men occupy the upper echelons of leadership and the selection panels. Kostas draws on the same constructions as he argues that the panel consists of men and he does not refer to any women on it as though women on selection panels do not exist (even though they do exist, and Gina, a woman head teacher who participated in this research, had been a member on the selection panel of her geographical area before she became a head teacher herself). They both appear to draw on the assumption that homosociability can be reproduced in the selection process, as Surgue and Furlong (2002) also note. Other studies (Grummell et al. 2009, Holgersson 2013, White 2018, Steed et al. 2021, Fuller 2021, Coleman 2022) have also noted that there is a tendency for school leadership posts to be filled by "safe" applicants who "best fit" the school and this is influenced by homosociability (Blackmore et al. 2006, Walker and Kwan 2012) where the successful applicants often mirror their selectors.

Wood (1997) and Coleman (2002) in the UK, note the absence of women role models who manage to balance family and career. It does seem often that the demands placed on the head teacher have demoralized others (both men and women) who might aspire to such posts as Hall (1996) and Strachan (1999) report. Women head teachers have to prove that they are capable of dealing with the workload and even prove that they are equal to if not better than their men colleagues and at the same time can handle family responsibilities.

> If they select the woman, she would have to do much more than the man to prove that she was the correct choice. A woman has to prove her value after the interview as well, while the man's work ends there. (Roula, WT, 30–39)

It can be assumed from her account that women are more likely than men to feel that they have to prove themselves and believe that they have to work harder than men to earn their place. The need to work harder is fuelled by the traditional stereotypes about women that associate them with domesticity and caring, not with leadership. There has been a lot of research which shows that women need to work much harder to prove their value (i.e., Reay and Ball 2000, Gupton 2009, Brezinski 2011, Coleman 2022) and to "break away from their stereotypes" (Coleman 2002, p. 82).

So, the contact between people who appear to share similar identification, that is, are men or those who are more "masculine," seems to create a tie between them (McPherson et al. 2001) and seems to disadvantage those who are different (i.e., the men and women with more "feminine" behavior) or the ones who do not correspond with the dominant construction of head teacher (i.e., "masculine" and heterosexual) like Petros who was discussed earlier and is not planning to apply for headship in the near future because of concerns about the likely reactions to his sexuality.

Constructions of Gender and the Selection Process

As discussed above, Coleman (2010), in her research about networking in education in the UK, argues that the selection panels are influenced by gender stereotypes which associate women with the home and the family. She also argues that this link is difficult to break. Nevertheless, in earlier research of men and women head teachers in England and Wales she found evidence that traditional gender constructions had not proved a factor hindering promotion. In fact, she found that caring roles associated with "femininity" were "almost equally common in the life history of the male and female heads in the survey" (p. 19). She argued that this may indicate a reduction in the stereotyping of women in such "softer" roles. Equally it may also mean a reduction in the stereotyping of men as suitable for headship, suggesting that the link mentioned earlier is starting to break. But, according to Grummell et al. (2009) in Ireland assessors of educational leaders tended to outline a range of personal criteria and qualities that they associated with leadership positions. These, as Grummell et al. (2009, p. 336) argue, "evoke the concept of hegemonic masculinity (Connell 1995)" and excluded many people, mostly women, who were judged subjectively based on their perceived suitability for the post. So, women tend to be considered as suitable for "softer" roles and low status tasks, not for headship (McLay 2008).

The head teachers who participated in my study were asked whether they had encountered any discrimination because of their gender when they applied. Also, all the participants (teachers and head teachers) were asked whether they believed that gender could be a hindrance in the selection of head teachers. The responses of my participants illustrate that women seem to be systematically overlooked because of traditional constructions that do not associate women with leadership.

When a woman head teacher was asked whether she believed that there was an inequality issue she noted:

> There is! There is! There is the pattern that has been inherited by us, the pattern that younger people adopt because this is what they have learned. (Maria, WHT, 40–49)

My data suggest that there are two reasons why women may not be considered suitable for the role of head teacher. The first is that women may not be seen as capable of being heads. So women are not seen as suitable choices, even if they are more qualified than men, because headship is seen as being too hard for women. The second reason is that being a head teacher requires a heavy time commitment and women do not have time. One respondent indicates this by arguing that perhaps a woman is not preferred for headship because she usually has care responsibilities while a man does not.

> But if there is an issue of selecting between a man and a woman, I think they will prefer the man, because he wouldn't have the responsibilities that a woman has, not because he would be more capable. (Yannis, MHT, 50–59)

In relation to this, one woman head teacher had to deal with a question during her interview about her ability to combine headship with her family.

> [They asked me] [h]ow will you do it and what will happen with your family? (Alexandra, WHT, 40–49)

The question that Alexandra was asked can be linked to the perceptions discussed earlier about the difficulty for women in juggling career and family responsibilities. The selection panel seems to draw on traditional constructions about women that appear from earlier discussion to be widespread and common including among some of the research participants.

Both of these quotes illustrate that women may be constructed as the "other," the one who is different from the dominant construction of the head teacher (i.e., being always available with no other responsibilities). The panel members may feel the need to "protect" women from this heavy duty by not adding another responsibility on them and they may assume that a woman will have trouble managing work and family. Martin (2006) calls this: "paternalistic masculinity." "Paternalistic masculinity" keeps women in their traditional unquestioned social identities, thus devaluing their identities as professionals and leaders. Women are constructed as weak people who need to be taken care of. The "father" figure is central and guides and protects his family members. It perpetuates gender stereotypes and constructions: women have responsibility for taking care of the children, while men are responsible for other things. Men tend not to have to justify the arrangements they will have to make even if they themselves have families and children.

In addition, my data indicate that women applicants are seen as different from men when judged against the ideal stereotype of the strong, authoritarian, masculine leader. As one woman said: "A man who is believed to be a good leader is treated differently [during the selection procedure] from a woman, who can be seen as more emotional and caring" (Jenny, WHT, 50–59). So, as leadership is often associated with "masculine" characteristics, women applicants may have to appear as more "masculine" in order to be appointed. Reay and Ball (2000) observe that "female managers are operating in a context of male hegemony" (p. 145) and as a result they will have either to conform with it and become more "masculine" or fail to be selected (Lekule 2018).

As another participant indicated:

> I have heard "why does a woman want it?" and I have also heard "A man can use a Black and Decker, what will a woman do?". (Danai, WHT, 40–49)

I suggest, therefore, that the role of head teacher is constructed through the distinctions that are made in society between men and women and that these distinctions may hinder women who are seeking to occupy roles as leaders. The gender dualism that underpins the selection panel's thinking about women and men influences their perceptions of the worth of both. Paechter (2001) refers to:

> dualisms deeply implicated in gendered/power relations, aligning themselves with and underpinning the distinction between masculinity and femininity. They include participation in civil society versus rootedness in hearth and home, hardness versus softness, activity versus passivity, reason versus emotions. (p. 48)

Within these dichotomies more value is placed on civil society than on the domestic arena, on hardness, activity, and reason rather than on softness, passivity, and emotion. Moreover, "femininity" is constructed as a homogeneous concept, that is, all women are assumed to be caring and emotional. But, in contrast to such constructions, "femininity" is dynamic, various, and changing, hence allowing for multiple "femininities" (Paechter 2006). The above dichotomies are the foundation for how the roles that men and women play in society are viewed and how gender is constructed. The construction of women as caring, domestic, and, implicitly, of lesser importance and status than men impacts on the experience of women in positions of leadership which are identified with stereotypical "masculinity." This stereotypical, or "hegemonic masculinity" as Collinson and Hearn (2000) and Connell (1995) term it, also has implications for men who choose not to operate in traditional ways. On the other hand, claiming that being "feminine" is of lesser value and importance than being "masculine" is not so simple. Hence, Lumby and Azaola (2014) argue that women by being "feminine" attempt to change "the rules of the game" (p. 11) and import the values and norms of their personal lives into their professional lives and use them in order to gain power and deploy their agency (Bradley 1999, Barlow and Chapin 2010). So, it can be assumed that it is too simplistic to view all women as drawing on specific constructions that are considered as negative for leadership, like being caring and emotional. Similarly, it is also simplistic to view all men as drawing on a different set of distinct constructions that help them in becoming and being leaders.

Judgments may be made about the leadership capacities of men and women on the basis of personal characteristics that are being assessed during the interview part of the selection process. Men tend to be seen as the "reference point" and women as the other that may differ from this reference (Oppenheim Mason 1986). In some instances even men who are different from the dominant "masculinity" may be treated as "other" by the selection panel, as Petros, the gay teacher discussed earlier, indicated:

> I have heard people saying that women head teachers don't cope with things as easily as men do. That men can be more assertive and are heard, while women aren't so much, there is more order in schools that are managed by typical men. I don't know how they will react if I, or somebody else who is gay, apply. I guess I will have a problem, as I am not the typical man who goes around giving orders. I am more approachable and cool with everybody. (Petros, MT, 30–39)

Here Petros challenges dominant constructions of "masculinity" as someone "who goes around giving orders." He presents himself as more approachable and democratic and constructs a different/alternative "masculinity." He chooses not to conform, but rather challenges the prevailing constructions of "masculinity" and "femininity" (i.e., being assertive like a "typical" man). Reay and Ball (2000, p. 149) draw on Ganderton (1991) and Gunter (1997), as mentioned earlier, to suggest that those who do not conform to organizational views, including around the "best way to manage" are unlikely to be promoted to the position of head teacher, and this seems to apply to Petros. Although he chooses in the interview not to remain silent about his sexuality, he is silent in the school context as indicated earlier. His reaction seems to confirm what Reay and Ball (2000) note, that "the powerful in society, regardless of their sex, share more in common with each other than they share with relatively powerless members of either sex" (p. 150).

Conclusion

The chapter starts with a brief presentation of the theoretical and methodological framework that underpins the research in this book. And continues with the way the research participants construct the aspiring teacher's way to headship.

The route to headship is difficult for both men and women in this study. Both sexes have experiences of rejection, albeit very few (two men and one woman), and may lack confidence about taking on this difficult job. For a surprisingly large proportion (seven out of the fifteen women and three out of the ten men head teachers) there is a lack of planning and even an element of surprise in finding themselves in a head teacher's job. What seems to be significant is the perception of both men and women that the female gender can be an "obstacle" to becoming head teachers. Women are also likely to encounter stereotyping that is unhelpful in making career progress. Although women appear to be dealing with the difficulties stereotyping might cause them, the data confirm that culturally women tend to be assumed to be less capable than men of holding head teacher positions.

As far as the selection procedure is concerned, almost all of my respondents suggest that networking, either political or other, can influence the final appointment. Almost all also offer the view that the selectors, who tend to be men, have difficulty in overcoming the stereotype of women as linked to the family and home. So, my research shows that at the beginning of the twenty-first century the majority of women and a proportion of men judge that gender stereotypes and dominant constructions of "femininity" and "masculinity," still play an important part in the selection of the head teachers.

Finally, family life can be considered as a factor delaying or even hindering career progress for women, as balancing life and career is bound to be a difficult issue, when the responsibility of childcare and domestic work is largely placed on women. The women in my research seem to believe that they are the ones in the family that often have to sacrifice their own career aspirations for the benefit of their family.

4

Constructions of Being a Head Teacher

This chapter follows from Chapter 3 (*Becoming a Head Teacher*) and draws on a similar theoretical and methodological approach. Although Chapter 3 focuses on head teachers' "choice" of a career, including in its gendered dimension, Chapter 4 is concerned with head teachers while in the midst of their career, with consideration of their professional and "personal" lives and of how gender intersect with these.

Much of the research worldwide on gender and educational leadership is about assumed differences in leadership approaches between women and men head teachers (Adler et al. 1993, Oplatka 2006, Fuller 2009, Brinia 2012). This may reinforce the binary between men and women as it draws on the assumption of inherent characteristics for each gender. On the other hand, Francis (2010) argued that gender characteristics are not tied to biological sex. Rather, she notes, men can draw on "feminine" and women on "masculine" approaches, depending on the situation and their socialization. In the same vein, Reay and Ball (2000) offer the view that "gendered identities are in context more fluid and shifting […] as a result female leadership […][is] both multi-faceted and more contradictory" (p. 145).

A critique of the notion that head teachers' behavior and interaction with students and teachers may be predicted on the basis of their gender is reinforced through my research about gender and leadership approaches. Kessler and McKenna (1978) and later Speer (2005) pointed out that once a gender attribution has been made (a person identified as male or female), their behaviors tend to be understood with reference to that attribution. So, a similar behavior may be read as "aggressive" in a man or as "bitchy" or "manipulative" in a woman (Francis 2000, 2002).

Head teachers' performances of gender and their leadership approaches are explored in this chapter. In the first section of this chapter (*Theoretical and Methodological Framework*) after recalling some of the theoretical and methodological principles underpinning the original study that are presented earlier (section *Theoretical and Methodological Framework* of Chapter 3), in Section 2 (*Constructions of Authority*) I draw on data from the participants (men and women head teachers and teachers) to analyze the extent to which they may draw on authoritative approaches to lead their schools. The findings highlight the diversity in women and men head teachers' practices and in their constructions of gendered subjectivities and leadership, hence providing evidence to question assumptions that head teachers lead in particular ways due to their identification as belonging to the male or female gender. The analysis emphasizes the fluidity and complexity of gender in head teachers' performances, and is supportive of the argument that gendered behavior is not necessarily tied to biological sex.

In the following section (*Construction of Caring and Nurturing*) the emphasis is on the way men and women head teachers have extended their potential caring roles as fathers, mothers, wives, parents, and carers into the workspace, into their leadership approaches and the impact of this on their lives. Contrary to this assumption that leadership approaches stem from gender identity, the analysis of data from my research suggests that there are many different approaches to leadership, not necessarily tied to gender or biological sex.

In the next section (*Constructions of the Ideal Head Teacher*) I will discuss the way the ideal head teacher is constructed by the teachers who draw on a nuanced construction that combines both "feminine" and "masculine" characteristics.

In the section that follows (*Combining Career with Family*) I discuss how men and women head teachers combine their career with their family and the responsibilities they assume in both their roles. As women have the major responsibility for the house and the family, it is primarily women who are "juggling" these different roles. On the other hand, men tend to have a more hands-off approach to domestic responsibilities.

Theoretical and Methodological Framework

As noted previously, the broad theoretical and methodological framework underpinning this chapter is similar to the approach spelled out in Chapter 3 (*Becoming a Head Teacher*). That is, it draws on data from semi-structured interviews that were analyzed using a social constructionist and feminist theoretical framework. This chapter is also more specifically informed by a sociological discussion of gender issues in being a head teaching, including in relation to issues of "masculinity" and "femininity," to the division of work according to gender constructions and combining career with family (Acker 1989, Coleman 2002, Skelton 2002, Moreau et al. 2008). This approach to head teachers' lives also acknowledges that individuals' identities are multiple and complex and are affected by several power relationships which simultaneously open possibilities and constrains to what head teachers can do.

Constructions of Authority

In this section, I aim to illustrate and analyze diverse performances of gender and authority on the part of the head teachers, both women and men. In doing so, I seek to unpick some of the discourses on gender and headship underpinning their performance of gendered subjectivity in the school and to apply this analysis to draw conclusions regarding the relations of power.

When I asked the participants how they deal with everyday issues at the school and what they do if they have a problem, six out of the ten male head teachers in my research said that they usually give orders to the teachers, or carry everything out by themselves.

> Normally, I should let the teacher solve the problem [that may occur with a child], but I always intervene, because I don't think that teachers and especially the women, can enforce discipline (Takis, MHT, 50–59).

> The head's word is one and only. The head should be clear about what is in his mind. No tensions are allowed in the school and nobody is allowed to do whatever comes into his mind. They should ask me first. Discipline among the teachers is a must. I know best what to do and I can advise them (Stefanos, MHT, 50–59).

Knowledge and ability to enforce discipline are constructed as being held exclusively by the (man) head teacher, and the other teachers (and especially women) are positioned as devoid of authority. So they are positioned as "lacking" something. Both of the head teachers construct themselves as the possessors of knowledge. Harding (1991) has noted that this construction as "authentic leader" and "keeper of knowledge" is a profoundly "masculinized" one. So, these head teachers draw on a model of the head teacher as an authority, as possessing knowledge and power, with teachers lacking both. This deliberate concentration and "ownership" of power and the distancing approach they seem to be taking to their colleagues may be considered as typically "masculinized" constructions.

It is interesting that a head teacher, Dimitris, refers to the teachers in his school as "kids." He says: "I feel very lucky that the kids who are working here in my school are a team" (Dimitris, MHT, 50–59). He positions himself as the adult, the father, who is in control of the school and the "possessor of knowledge," and the teachers are being constructed as "kids," who teach other kids. Thus the teachers are positioned in non-egalitarian relationships with their superiors (i.e., the head teacher). So, in a way he seems to infantilize the teachers and imply that they do not understand and cannot be trusted.

Another man head teacher, Nikos, adopts physical violence to discipline children in his school:

> … what I am doing is grabbing their arm and shaking them. They have to understand that someone else is in charge. That is what I do. I always walk between the children, because if you want to be effective, you have to know and see everything. Now, once I had to hit a student. He climbed up to a window, which had metal bars, managed to pass through the bars and was sitting outside the window. The other students told me what he did, I called him into my office and I had to slap him in the face because he could have been hurt or even killed, had he fallen over. It was a mistake, I know it, but that was my decision at that moment. (Nikos, MHT, 50–59)

Corporal punishment is explicitly prohibited in schools in article 13 (8c) of Presidential Decree No. 201/1998 on the Organization and Functioning of Primary Schools and those who enforce discipline in that way face legal disciplinary procedures and even dismissal. Despite this and despite the extensive campaign that has been running in Greece for several years against corporal punishment, Nikos acts that way and shows his power over the young boy. His last words indicate that he understands his fault, but does not appear to regret his actions. Sometimes as a direct, forceful, and painful assertion of power, corporal punishment stimulates repressed feelings of guilt and frustration (Rydstrom 2006). His decision at that moment was perhaps indicative of his assumption about authority and traditional "masculinity." Connell (1995, p. 84) notes that corporal punishment is "part of a system of domination, [it] is at the same time a measure of its imperfection." It can be argued that the imperfection lies in the inability to maintain power which triggers the identity "and violence is a means of resolving the crisis because it acts to reconfirm the nature of a masculinity otherwise denied" (Moore 1994, p. 69). Also he can be assumed to be drawing on positional power (Bradley 1999) that stems from his higher position in the school compared with the students.

There is also another head who, although he uses dialogue in order to deal with disciplinary problems, believes that it is not the appropriate method. He said:

This is a general problem, especially today when there is a general drop in the values in our society, there are many immigrants that don't know about the value of the family, so things are difficult. On the other hand, there are the laws that forbid us some things just like that, there has never been an organized study. There has never been research that proves that punishing the children corporally is bad. But the law forbids it. But I see that in America and England things are turning to more traditional disciplinary actions. Here we still have to deal with the problems through dialogue. Dialogue with the child, dialogue with the family ... How much dialogue? Anyway, I follow the law, even if I don't like it, even if it is very difficult to communicate with the parents who are immigrants or whose first language is Turkish, because they don't want to learn Greek. (Giorgos, MHT, 50–59)

He appears to hold racialized assumptions about the non-Greek students and their families. This is an issue that has been present and studied in other countries as well. Studies in England indicate the prevalence of racism in schools, mainly in terms of teachers' (un)intended attitudes, behaviors, and practices (Gillborn and Mirza 2000, Gillborn 2008). In particular, it has been found that some teachers may treat Black, Muslim, and Asian students in stereotypic or hostile ways and may assume that these students have behavior problems (e.g., Connolly 1998, Archer 2003); some teachers' constructions are found to be grounded on racialized, gendered, and classed assumptions (e.g., Archer and Francis 2005). Similarly, research in other European countries (e.g., Belgium and the Netherlands) shows how some Belgian teachers discriminated against Turkish children (e.g., Stevens 2008), or some Dutch teachers disregarded Moroccan children (e.g., de Haan and Elbers 2004). In addition, research in the United States shows that some teachers' negative stereotypes and low expectations of children from minority groups partly explain the overrepresentation of culturally and linguistically diverse students in special education programs, which, in turn, affects the eventual educational outcomes of these children (e.g., Harry and Klinger 2006). These representations of children from minority groups may be grounded in homogeneous perceptions of identity and color-blind perspectives and place the burden for adaptation to the norms of the majority on minority children (Phoenix 2002, Stevens 2007). Most of these studies argue that teachers draw on racist constructions in their classrooms either without realizing it, or meaning to, or while they deny it to researchers (i.e., speech and practice are different). Giorgos does not deny his assumption about non-Greeks, and his belief in the need to use corporal punishment, rather he appears to be quite proud of it and tries to support his view by referring to studies from other countries.

Giorgos makes clear, however, that he believes that he is fair and democratic. He says "I discuss everything with everyone. I hear all sides, sometimes there are more than two, and I make the fairer decision." He articulated his impatience when he explained how he deals with students from various social groups (as mentioned earlier). He projects a deficit onto "foreigners" who may be seen as demonized and as the ones responsible for their assumed behavior issues ("they don't know about the value of family," "it is difficult to communicate with the parents [...]because they don't want to learn Greek"). So, he presents himself as politically informed and at the same time as a democratic, firm, demanding head teacher, with high expectations, in contrast to those students he finds "challenging" because of their "Otherness" (i.e., their nationality or language). Generally, his approach might be read as a highly "masculine" construction of self, that is, assertive, self-assured, intellectually invested (as he wants me to know that he is informed about studies on pedagogical matters), rule-bound, and maybe even aggressive, similarly to what Francis (2008) argues in her study.

Both of these head teachers set strict rules. The first one, Nikos, even hits a child to discipline him and the second one, Giorgos, believes that dialogue is not an appropriate problem-solving technique contrary to "more traditional disciplinary actions," hence we see a "masculinized" performance of authority. Corporal punishment is partly based on authoritarian education practices and male teachers are considered to be more authoritative and therefore they seem to prefer corporal punishment more that female teachers (Bogacki, Armstrong, and Weiss 2005). But, as Nikos notes later on in his interview and is discussed below, he seems to adopt more mediating approaches, which could be read as a more "feminine" approach, as he claims that he encourages children and teachers and listens to them ("But I am trying to discuss it with all the involved parties").

It is interesting that when asked to describe their leadership approaches with the teachers, all the men head teachers interviewed described their approach as a democratic one based on dialogue.

But when they were asked to give actual examples of how they lead their schools (i.e., my question was "what would you do in a difficult or problematic situation?") almost all referred to issues or problems with the children's behavior and they appeared to construct their approaches in a more autocratic and "masculine" way, showing a contradiction between their account of how they treat teachers and the accounts they give about their actions with children. Maybe this contradiction appears because they have learnt the "correct way" to answer theoretical questions, but when they have to talk about actual practice, a rather different account emerges. For example, Dimitris said that he uses deprivation in order to discipline children.

> [T]here were very few occasions ... very few, that we had, not to punish, but to deprive the kid of something. And that was it. (Dimitris, MHT, 50–59)

Nikos, who also claims that he follows a democratic leadership approach, as mentioned above, does not hesitate to grab the children or even hit them. And Takis, although wanting to lead his school in a diplomatic way, appears to be autocratic, as he says he always intervenes and even threatens the parents "with expelling their child or with going to social service [...] [This way] a problem is always solved" (Takis, MHT, 50–59). Here it can be argued that they appear to change their approaches when they have to deal with someone with less power than them (i.e., the children). In the Greek educational system, the head teacher does not have any disciplinary power over the teachers, so they have to count on their good will to accomplish tasks, hence perhaps the emphasis on dialogue. On the other hand, the head teacher has disciplinary power over the children, for example, by calling their parents, by keeping them in their office, by depriving them of excursions etc. Therefore, it can be assumed that the contradiction between how they should say they deal with issues and how they say they actually deal with them, in part affects the power dynamics. Their actions are assumed to be based on their power over the children and they gain their power from what Bradley (1999) calls "positional power" which is their authority and position within the hierarchical system of the school.

These cases illuminate the way in which particular gendered leadership approaches and practices can be considered as constructing a powerful "masculine" position for the head teacher compared with the powerless other (teachers and students). In the present cases and in the case of the head teacher that I will present next, power seems to be located in the head teacher's hands. They exercise power in specific instances by calling on the disciplinary practice of the school and by concentrating everything in their hands and not giving any responsibilities to the teachers. So, power is constructed as something that is initiated by the individual (i.e., the head teacher) based on his/her place in the hierarchy.

In my research there were a number of participants (seventeen out of forty, eight women and nine men) who argued that women have to modify some of what might be considered as their "feminine qualities," in order to conform to the expectations of the head teacher that are centered around masculine discourses. Vasso below indicates this:

I don't want to be liked, I don't care. Of course these behaviors are in the school. When I leave here, I become a different person. Inside the school, I like to have everybody else as, please forgive my wording, slaves, I want everything in my own terms [...]If she is tough by nature, then she can be herself. Otherwise, she should become tough and autocratic. There is no room for good people here. (Vasso, WHT, 40–49)

From her account it becomes apparent that she draws on a leadership approach in which she is less inclined to build personal relationships with her colleagues and adopts an identity more strongly associated with "masculinity" than with "femininity" in order to be successful. Acquiring power in school may lead a woman to play out her gender in many ways that are "different to those realized in normative, socially subordinate femininities" (Reay and Ball 2000, p. 146) and adopt a more androcentric style (Oplatka 2006). As Reay and Ball (2000) comment, "it is arguable whether many of the women or men who succeed in becoming head teachers are able to challenge and stand out against expectations that they manage according to contemporary orthodoxies" (p. 150).

Similarly, Vassilis, a man teacher, argued that a woman head teacher "When she is at school she should leave her real, kind and emotional self at home and take up another role. A meaner role" (Vassilis, MT, 30–39).

Vasso and Vassilis do not seem to draw on the gender constructions that are ascribed to "femininity" (being caring, kind, passive, emotional, co-operative). Their constructions about women head teachers appear to be quite different from this dominant construction and they believe that every woman who aspires to leadership should also follow a similar approach (i.e., refrain from being emotional, be strict etc.). This may be viewed as demonstrating that women like Vasso are active agents in the production of women's various subjectivities as they consciously draw on different identities and, as a result, leadership approaches.

A man teacher said about his former woman head teacher:

She was making some decisions that we, the rest of the teachers, were listening to, but when the time came and the school was being inspected by the head of the LEA about these decisions that were her personal decisions, then suddenly she tried to put all the teachers forward in order to defend her. [...] She wasn't listening, she was the ultimate ruler of the world! She wanted to enforce her opinions. (Andreas, MT, 40–49)

The conventional or "expected" approach for a woman head would have been to listen to the other teachers, consider their views, and make a collegial decision. On the contrary, according to Andreas, the head decided to be more autocratic and so can be seen to draw on "masculine" approaches. So, being in a powerful position of authority, she can be assumed, from Andreas's talk, to be drawing on aspects of a more autocratic identity. Yet, when she was inspected by the director of Local Educational Authorities, who was a man, she appeared to draw on aspects of a more "feminine" identity, which perhaps reflects the hierarchical relationship between the director of the Local Educational Authorities and her. Hence, this woman head teacher seems to be constructing her identity through constant negotiations of power and hierarchy, showing that power can be seen as a resource that can operate differently in different sites and under different conditions (Bradley 1999). Her identity also can be seen as fluid and dependent on context.

Constructions of Caring and Nurturing

School leadership is regularly expressed through metaphors (Earl and Katz 2006). One of the most common metaphors is that of the school as a family, meaning that there is the expectation that the school is lively and has a warm atmosphere like a family (Akbaba-Altun 2007, Taylor 2021, Ozdogru 2022). It also recognizes the adult-child relationship of power and authority (Stobo-Gaskell 1995). Baker (1991) and Mahlioson and Maxson (1998) stated that the school is usually perceived as a family when the protective and training characteristics of the family for their child are noted. When the family metaphor is projected onto the school, then the women in it are usually seen to be drawing on aspects of the role of the mother and the men that of the father (Saban et al. 2007).

So, in this section, the emphasis is on the way men and women head teachers' potential caring roles seemingly spread from their personal to their professional lives incorporating characteristics of care into their leadership approach. In addition, the way their leadership approach impacts on their personal lives is discussed.

Contrary to the "masculine" and authoritative approach that I discussed in the previous section, Thanos, a man head teacher, can be seen to articulate a different approach. Power differences between the head teacher and the teachers are less overt. He evokes an "equal" relationship between the teachers and himself, although this could be hiding unequal power differentials that come from the different hierarchical positions between the head teacher and the teachers.

> [If there is a problem] I would try to find the golden medium. We come to the school in order to be calm and do our job properly. Quibbling and fighting is not good. I will never enforce my opinion. We discuss here, we don't enforce. (Thanos, MHT, 50–59)

This head teacher seems to construct himself as respectful and as wanting to solve problems and issues through dialogue. However this may also be considered as a "masculine" discourse (Walkerdine 1990, Harding 1991), because it is associated with reason and mind, while discourses associated with emotion are considered as "feminine." Similarly, his emphasis on being calm is associated with "masculinity" as he can be assumed to reject any emotionality. But, it may also be argued that practices based on respect for the others' point of view and are more collaborative, represent more "feminine," "soft" leadership approaches (Alvesson and Billing 2009). So, gender constructions are more nuanced than just simple constructions of "feminine" or "masculine," and "such nuances need recognition" (Fuller 2014, p. 334).

An approach that does not comply with traditional notions of "masculinity," but rather seems to be more complex, is also suggested by Yiannis:

> I am always trying to come close to [the children and the teachers], to hear them, to discuss with them. I don't know if I achieve it. At least I want to believe that I do. (Yiannis, MHT, 50–59)

Yiannis says he performs in a more nurturant, "feminine" way in his relationship with the children and his teachers/colleagues. But there are suggestions that his authority might have been questioned, as he said:

> This year we had a small problem with 2–3 parents. You know, rumors and stuff against me [...] Most parents mean well, but there are also others who are wrong, who may be vicious ... (Yiannis, MHT, 50–59)

He told me when the interview was finished, that there was a rumor at the school that he was incompetent in his leading of the school. His account suggests that the parents (at least some of them) are seen by Yannis as positioning him as slightly incompetent. Perhaps there are issues of power differentials, where Yannis is seen as less powerful than some of the parents, despite him being a head teacher, a post usually associated with power and status. So, this is indicative of the shifting status of power as a resource that can operate differently in different sites and under different conditions (Bradley 1999).

This interpretation is supported by Yiannis's somewhat self-depreciating construction. For example he said "I am not perfect" and "I don't know if I achieve it. At least I want to believe that I do." This slightly anxious and unconfident subjectivity produces characteristics socially ascribed as "feminine" rather than "masculine," although his unexpected "feminine" approach does not appear consonant with his "masculine" appearance (very tall, dark, with moustache[1] and deep voice). This realization may be showing how constructions of gender are usually based on gender stereotypes and gender expected behavior that may not correspond with what happens in practice (Papanastasiou 2013).

Another man head teacher also indicates the complexities of gender constructions when he offers an approach that differs from the traditional construction of "hegemonic masculinity."

> The head teacher should inspire everybody, be an example, and be the first to do what he is asking. If the head teacher is avoiding things, he can't expect the teacher to do the work. The head teacher should give responsibilities to everyone and everyone should know what has to be done. (Stefanos, MHT, 50–59)

He did not talk about the inadequacies of the others and he stressed that in a school responsibilities should be shared. He also noted that an important aspect of the head teacher's role is encouraging the others and setting an example of good practice. Here this man head teacher constructs his professional role not as a disciplinarian and authoritative person, but rather as a colleague to the teachers and a father (his wording) to the children, contrary to Kiki discussed earlier (section *Becoming a Head Teacher: Drifting into Headship* of Chapter 3), who constructs the head teacher as an administrator. Drawing on Francis (2010) it can be argued that he draws on constructions of "masculine femininity," indicating that leadership approaches are not based on the binary dichotomy between "feminine"/"masculine," but are more complex.

As discussed in Chapter 2 (*Women in Educational Leadership: Global and National Context*), men tend to be seen as more capable of leadership positions (Cox 1996, Wajcman 1998), as they are believed to be better at enforcing discipline. The notion that men are more suited to leadership is embedded in the public discourse of gender and leadership (Cammack and Philips 2002) and is based on the stereotype of a "'natural' male violence" (Burn 2005, p. 5) which is constructed in opposition to female "caring." Kaufman (1994) argues that men are required to "suppress" nurturing and caring in order to prove their "manhood" and hence they may appear as more "violent." Also, with regard to care, dominant forms of "masculinity" are characterized by the need to avoid closeness in relationships and to fear emotions (Kimmel 1994, Connell 1995).

But, in my research, some men head teachers may be viewed as "caring" figures. In particular one of them said:

> [The children see me] [l]ike the father of all! I mean, that all of the children, whether the youngest or the oldest ones, whatever they need, they will go to their teacher [uses the female form for the word 'teacher' in Greek] and then they will come to me. They would ask for my advice, or my help, or for something to be done immediately. (Pavlos, MHT, 40–49)

Here, he can be seen as taking up the role of the caring father, the one who is wise enough to advise the youngsters, who can take action immediately, who is available, and willing to help. At the same time, by using the female gender when he talks about the teacher, he may be viewed as constructing an image of teaching as a women's profession (and as a consequence leadership as a men's one) and an image of men as being more capable than women (the woman teacher cannot deal with issues, so the children turn to the man head teacher).

The "masculine" and "feminine" differentiation of the jobs and the construction of the "appropriate" professions for each gender can be also assumed by the way respondents talk about the head teacher's role. They tend to use the masculine personal pronoun and masculine suffixes to nouns and adjectives. For example Stefanos who was quoted earlier, uses the Greek word "*diefthindis*" which means the "man head teacher," when he talks about the "head teacher," contrary to "*diefthindria*" which means the "woman head teacher." Then, he uses "**his** colleagues," "**he** is asking," "**he** can't expect." The words and the pronouns that he uses are very important, as they can be considered as a social resource for constructing different accounts of being a head teacher, as either a man or a woman. Similarly, in Porter and Fahrenwald's (2022) research some of the participants used masculine pronouns to refer to leaders, especially coercive ones. Contrary to Stefanos, the rest of the participants used both the masculine and feminine words and pronouns (i.e., *diefthindis/diefthindria, o/i* etc.). As Burr (2003) notes, "To the extent that our constructions of the world are founded upon language [...] then language underpins the forms of action that it is possible for us to take" (p. 61). So, this head's culturally shared expectations that head teachers are (inevitably) men can be considered as the source of his using the male grammatical gender in his speech.

Dominant constructions of motherhood in society reflect notions of love, responsibility, selflessness, and sacrifice, as is reported in Sikes's (1997) study. Also it is expected that what are often assumed to be "maternal instincts" are available for teachers to use with all children, and particularly primary stage children. Women have been seen to be particularly suited to teaching young children through a symbolical representation of the teacher as the loving mother (Burman 1994, Peeters 2008). At the same time, men are able to assume a "privileged responsibility" toward caring duties because it is not seen to be their "natural work" (Tronto 2002, Zembylas et al. 2014). Consequently, care, when performed by men, perhaps is not recognized as such (King 1998, Hjalmarsson and Lofdahl 2014). Along these lines, thirty-eight out of the forty women and men participants shared the view that women are the most appropriate teachers for young children, as they are assumed to be more caring and nurturing.

The participants, with their dominant constructions of "motherhood," also reproduce dominant constructions of "femininity." So, according to them the woman is constructed as caring, emotional, approachable, nurturant, and sensitive to children. These traditional constructions then lead to the assumption that women are suitable mainly for a role that includes the abovementioned constructions, that of the teacher of younger children. Therefore, as it is argued by Lumby and Azaola (2014), women may be perceived as less of a match to the traditional stereotype of the leader. Hence, women who wish to achieve headship should probably step outside of the acceptable construction of their "female" identity in order to match the leadership stereotype. This means that women who take up headships may face persistent stereotypes. Swann et al. (1999) argue that many women struggle against the negative assessment of themselves as having limited value and struggle in order to change this stereotype.

Women are expected to take care of their families (children, husbands/partners, or extended families) willingly (Wajcman 1998, Charlebois 2011) and as an extension of that, they are expected to take care of their schools. It would not be a surprise to find a woman in a school perceived as taking up the role of the mother, as a supportive, caring figure. Sometimes their colleagues even expect them to behave like that, as described by Reay and Ball (2000) and found in my own study.

A woman head teacher said that when she first entered the staff room as the new head teacher, some of the men teachers greeted her saying:

> "Go to your kitchen and leave us alone"! Somebody else told me to make him his coffee every day, because if I wanted to learn how to manage, making coffee was the first step! I thought they were just stupid! (Vasso, WHT, 40–49)

Her men colleagues construct her according to the typical traditional woman, i.e., staying at home, caring for and serving the man, creating particular configurations of "masculinity." Their expression defines "masculinity" in ways that lead to social constraints and power inequalities. So, these men appear to assume that they hold the power and that "women's place is in the kitchen" or "she should be making coffee." It can be argued that the men teachers deliberately put Vasso down and treat her as a woman rather than as a head teacher. Telling her to make coffee can be seen as overt hostility against being managed by a woman. This brings to mind Walkerdine's (1990) study in a nursery school, where she found the roots of patriarchal violence against women in the sexual banter of two four-year-olds who verbally assaulted a girl classmate and a woman teacher:

> Terry: You are a stupid cunt, Annie.
> Sean: Get out of it, Miss Baxter paxter.
> Terry: Get out of it, knickers, Miss Baxter.
> Sean: Get out of it, Miss Baxter paxter.
> Terry: Get out of it, Miss Baxter the knockers paxter, knickers bum.
> Sean: Knickers, shit, bum.
> Miss Baxter: Sean, that's enough, you are being silly. (pp. 4–5)

Walkerdine argues that the boys' talk, though resistant and transgressive, is far from progressive or emancipatory. These boys succeed in resisting the authority of the teachers and the school, but only by reproducing the patriarchal power available to them by being male.

As in the case of Vasso, the power shifts between oppressors and oppressed here is clear. The men/boys resist the authority of the head teacher/teacher by exploiting a sexist discourse in which they, as the males, have power. In both cases there is a blatant sexist challenge and both women respond weakly and ineffectively (Miss Baxter says "I think you are being very silly" and Vasso says "I thought they were just stupid"). Their responses do not seem to help them resist the subject position they are being offered (i.e., the traditional, subordinate, powerless woman).

Hence, Vasso is constructed by the men in the school as only suitable for more subordinate roles rather than leading a school, maybe because they do not believe that she is capable of achieving her role, or maybe because they do not want anything that changes or challenges the patriarchal norms of the Greek society (Gassouka 2004).

A woman head teacher who claimed she took up a "mothering" role in her school explained:

> I care about children and cherish them. I am their mum. Instead of having 2 children, my own children, I have also the 27 children from the school, a total of 29! So many!!!! (Marianthi, WHT, 40–49)

"Masculinity" and "femininity" are not simply properties of bodies, but they are discourses, contextual, cultural, and situational. As such, they are not stable but they may shift and adjust. So, they are intertwined into everyday practice and into the management of schools. Perhaps this is why it "feels" acceptable for women and mothers to be primary teachers, because there is the expectation that only women share these assumed "maternal instincts," and they may gain pleasure and power from this.

Also, as some women head teachers (four out of fifteen) in my study place an emphasis on the "image" of the school (what others say about the school, what festivals they organize, what extra-curricular activities they have, etc.), it suggests the head teacher may feel vulnerable and exposed. Perhaps if they "fail" to present a good image, the effect may be to expose the head teacher to public scrutiny and blame (from the parents). Since women are often seen as "outsiders," as they are perceived as less of a match to the ideal construction of a leader, they may therefore experience this effect to a greater degree than their men colleagues (Moreau et al. 2007).

One illustration of the way in which identity is constructed in the context of dominant discourses of "femininity," "masculinity," and school leadership is provided by Katerina, when she described how she dealt with an issue at school.

> ... there is a child at the first grade who is very naughty. His teacher has warned him many times, so I called his father to come here. So, the father came and started telling him off before the morning assembly and before the prayers. Here in the hall. I told him to come into my office because the other children were watching. He continued shouting at his child there, in front of everybody. Later, when the school was over and the mother came to pick up the child, I told her that I and her son's teacher had to speak with her husband, because he behaved really badly in front of all the children. And that we wanted to tell him some things. So, the father called me and told me that I was not a good teacher, I couldn't do my job properly, I couldn't handle young kids and that he was going to talk to the TV channels about the way I behaved. In five minutes he came here and continued shouting. I told him, I want to help you. I want to help your child. What you did, shouting at your son in front of all the students, was wrong. You can't threaten your child by saying that you are going to kill him. You can't tell him that he is a constant problem. This is going to be a boomerang for you, because your son will never forget it. And I also told him, that we have studied these subjects, we know something more. He is your child, but we are responsible when he is in the school. He said that he was going to stop schooling for the child. So I told him, do what you want, but I will do what I have to do, and that is call the police to protect my child. And

then he started saying that he was sorry, that he had overdone it. (Katerina, WHT, 40–49)

She can be seen to draw on a discipline-oriented identity, when she calls a student's father because he was obstructing class. Yet, despite being in a powerful, authority position, she is drawing on aspects of a more caring identity, as well, when she protects the child from the (potentially) abusive father and when she shows interest in the child continuing school. In studying her words and the way she negotiated and constructed multiple, shifting identities, we find that she draws on another aspect of her identity, at odds with the subordinate woman, when she stands up to the father (the man) and threatens him. So, her behavior can be understood as multiple, fluid, and dynamic. Her role as a "mother" who tries to protect her "child" in this quotation is being put forward as a source of power, as it allows her to face and even threaten the father in order to "protect" her child. She can therefore be seen to challenge traditional constructions of female identity (powerlessness, non-assertiveness etc.) (Reay and Ball 2000, p. 153) and to draw power from one of the most powerful women's roles, that of the mother.

Katerina may be drawing power from her identity as a mother who cares about her child and at the same time (finally) enforces discipline on the father. But when she deals with the initial problem (the naughty child), she does not seem to consider the mother of the child as powerful and as able to discipline him. She called for the father to come to the school and not the mother, or a parent in general, in order to deal with the disciplinary problem. Yet she met the mother every day, as the mother was the one who regularly took the child to the school and picked him up at the end of the day. "Fatherhood" and "motherhood" in this quote are constructed in accordance with dominant gender assumptions about "masculinity" and "femininity." So, the "father" is constructed as the one who is able (and has responsibility) to discipline his child. He is portrayed as a dynamic, powerful, authoritative, and disciplinarian figure. At the same time, she appears to construct the "mother" as passive, powerless and "unsuited" to discipline (Bjornberg 1991). This construction of gender and parent roles does not take into consideration the fact that identities are being constantly negotiated and are not stable.

Katerina's account indicates that the father, himself, rejects the head teacher's power in school and constructs himself as the authority and Katerina is constructed as the weak woman who, he assumes, will be afraid of him. According to Katerina, he presents himself as tough and masculine (threatens, shouts, etc.). This suggests that he undervalues women who, he appears to believe, are not able to do the job, particularly the disciplinarian part of it. But, in this case, the head teacher produces change in the father's behavior by being strict and authoritative and by drawing on what tends to be seen as more "masculine" gender constructions.

Katerina, the head teacher, experiences the crisis as emotionally demanding, but also rewarding to deal with, because, as it can be concluded from her words, it was important and meaningful in the context of her key responsibility (i.e., safe-guarding of the children in her care). So, she successfully negotiated what was potentially a difficult situation. Similarly to a head teacher in Reay and Ball's (2000) study, Katerina, as in the case of the woman head teacher described by Andreas in the section before (section *Constructions of Authority*), draws on a range of subjectivities that are assumed depending on the situation (Papanastasiou 2013), and therefore gender binaries should be re-examined.

Power has often been an uncomfortable issue for women as it is usually linked with control and "masculinity," while women are believed to be understanding, caring, and more emotionally motivated (Meyers 2002). For one of my women head teacher participants the context where she was working was difficult and she spoke about the conflicts that she experienced in an attempt to reconcile her managerial identity with that of the understanding woman.

> There are teachers who say, OK we have a woman head teacher, she will be more tolerant. Especially the women teachers. Do you know how many times they have asked to be excused and leave earlier from the school for various stupid reasons? […] They think that I will sympathize with them or cover for them. But no! Lady, do you have to be at school and be inside the classroom? So, you will be at the school. You won't be out for coffee or at the super-market because duvets are on sale and they will be over when the school finishes![…] She thought that because I am a woman, I would have understood the importance of good duvets and that I would have let her leave the school and cover for her!!! (Jenny, WHT, 50–59)

The women teachers referred to in this quotation constructed the head teacher's identity on assumptions around "femininity" and "being one of them," as belonging to their group (Krishnan et al. 2006, Warning and Buchanan 2009). They seem to have assumed that there was going to be an affinity because of their common gender and so thought that they would get privileges as a result of that. So, Jenny, the head teacher, struggles with being a supportive woman head teacher who is available and understanding on the one hand, with being an authoritative, strict but fair figure who demands things, follows the laws, and does not cover for other women. Hence, Jenny may be viewed as struggling with her identities, as a head teacher and a woman. On the one hand she shares a feminine identification with the teachers, but on the other hand she appears unwilling to set aside the expectation people have of her as a head teacher. She finds it very difficult, especially, when it comes to dealing with other women and distancing herself. As Reay and Ball (2000) say, women head teachers "are expected to lead and still remain equal, to be tough and simultaneously kind and nurturant" (p. 152). This influences the ways in which colleagues relate to them (as she is expected to be understanding and caring and nurturant).

Perhaps headship is felt to be less acceptable for a woman by society because in the combined role of being a woman and a head teacher, the ambitions and identity of the head teacher are beyond what is acceptable or outside the identity created for women (and so often, accepted by women) in society. And when women decide to become head teachers they "are drawing on a range of subjectivities, at times as a maternal figure, at times as stereotypically woman, but at other times constructing an identity as a powerful person which cuts across and conflicts with the other historically derived aspects of feminine subjectivity" (Reay and Ball 2000, p. 153). Dominant discourses related to the presumably caring role of women in our society may place powerful expectations and pressures on women who are mothers (Lynch 2008). The interplay of identities was examined in a study of head teachers who are mothers, too (Bradbury and Gunter 2006). The researchers found that rather than having one coherent identity, identity differs according to context, so at the same time their participants could identify as mothers and head teachers, drawing on different aspects of these identities. This does not imply that women head teachers have fractured identities, rather that as individuals they are multiple and complex. As Burr (2003) indicates, they actively create multiple, dynamic, and sometimes contradictory identities. Each of these aspects of identity defines women and yet women could not be fully understood unless each of the aspects of their identities was considered.

So, in my research, a woman teacher talked about her former head teacher, whom she considered as a very successful one, explaining:

> She had a very strong personality and she managed the school by herself. She would drive to the children's homes everyday to pick them up for school. She was like the mother in the house. (Anna, WT, 30–39)

Here, she describes her head teacher as a motherly figure, showing the traditional "feminine" behavior of care and interest and because of this she gains respect and is accepted by both the children and the parents. This behavior is similar to the feminine behavior that is being put forward in Greece by television advertisements, popular women's magazines, and school books. That is the woman who, although she is working, manages to take care of everyone and everything without help. At the same time, the head teacher in this quotation is pictured as powerful and dynamic; characteristics that tend not to be constructed as "feminine" but rather as "masculine." It can be argued that she constructs these shifting identities in order to be seen as an authentic leader. She made a very difficult decision (even if it was unconsciously), to construct and assume a different role from what was accepted for her female gender, because she felt that it was necessary. So, she takes on a caring but at the same time authoritative identity by being interested in the children attending school and almost coerces them to attend.

Anna later adds about this head teacher:

But they couldn't not love her! She was a mother for all! Even for the mothers! She was there for everyone! (Anna, WT, 30–39)

She was perceived as a "mother for all," someone who is available and present and sacrifices her own needs (i.e., free time as she drives around and picks up the children) for those of her children (i.e., the students) (Hays 1996, Peters 1997). As Sikes (1997) commented "traditional notions of nurturance demand absolute commitment to the needs of others [...] If you are being an 'ideal' mother there is no space for you to do anything else" (p. 139). Being caring and being selflessly always available for others, helped build strong relationships and acceptance by the parents. Legitimizing "motherhood" in order to explain why the women head teacher is being seen as accepted and powerful may help women have fewer difficulties in gaining a leadership position (Reay and Ball 2000, Tangonyire et al. 2022). There seems to be an interplay of the constructed "motherhood" identity and the head teacher identity, and a blurring of the identities boundaries.

However, there are scholars who consider the idea of professionals who lead by drawing on a "mothering" identity from a different angle. For example, Mudau and Ncube (2017) argue that women who try to combine "mothering" and professionalism may be seen as inadequate and weak leaders. Similarly, Adler (2005) concludes that women who lead in a more nurturant/"mothering" way in a patriarchal system, may be considered weak and inadequate. Blackmore and Sachs (2007) also report that "femininity" in the field of educational leadership can be a negative discourse. Khelan (2010) also argues that adopting a mothering role in the school may embed further the belief that women's approach to leadership is limited as they tend to adopt a nurturing rather that a more aggressive or strategic approach to leadership and therefore an approach that is less effective. Despite this the head teacher in this instance drew on the construction of a "mothering" identity and assumed a more powerful position among the parents and the teachers and in line with a participant in Wilkinson and MacDonald (2022) who argued that being a students' mother is a necessity in leading a school, even after the troubling questions that this raises when it is viewed from an intersectional lens (Wilkinson and MacDonald 2022).

Grummell et al. (2009) see senior leadership posts as "care-less" positions which advantage those who are "care-free." But far from being carefree, in Anna's talk the woman head teacher's care extends over her professional life, being reflected into her headship role and leadership approach. As Anna sees it her head teacher established rapport easily with the parents and the students, because she was always available and drew on aspects of a caring identity. She is also perceived as a dynamic woman who takes initiatives in order to succeed in her aim. So, in order to educate the children, she drives to their homes and picks them up. She draws on aspects of a caring subjectivity and at the same time of a responsible head teacher. She is juggling with different aspects of her identity according to context, so at the same time she can be identified as "motherly figure" and as head teacher following the laws, drawing on different aspects of these identities. It is most likely that these different aspects of identity rather make her stronger that weaker as a leader (Tangonyire et al. 2022).

Constructions of the Ideal Head Teacher

In the interview I asked the fifteen teacher participants (ten women and five men) what the ideal head teacher would be like. Most of their responses were about constructions of the head teacher as the one who controls the school and enforces discipline. These views draw on more "masculine" approaches to leadership (Coleman 2002).

Even if headship is considered as a post suitable for men because of its assumed "masculine" nature (see earlier discussion in Chapter 3 *Constructions of Becoming a Head Teacher*), in my research there were teachers who expressed negative opinions about their men head teachers, showing that there seem to be differences between the idealized notions of what a "good" head teacher should be and how they were reported as doing it in practice.

So, a woman teacher said about her man head teacher:

He discriminates against people. He likes some people and he dislikes others … [He discriminates] based on beauty! […] He behaves differently to women that he likes, and usually they are young women, and differently to people that he doesn't like, and they are men and older women teachers. […] To us, because we are quite young, he is milder. He doesn't give us extra work, we don't have many gaps in our daily programme, and that is not fair for the others. He hasn't tried anything more, but I guess that if we were more open, he would raise his hand. (Roula, WT, 30–39)

This can be perceived as discriminatory and perhaps sexual harassment. The "Gender Equality Duty" (2007), which is a guide for authorities in England, qualifies comments about someone's appearance and actions that stem from appearance as sexual harassment. McDonald (2012) and Dorwart (2020) argue that sexual harassment in the workplace is identified as an issue that women experience all around the world. In Greece, Manesi et al. (2022) drawing on a series of studies, report that 85 percent of women have experienced sexual harassment in the workplace.

Although sexual harassment is a common practice in Greek workplaces and is carried out both by employers and fellow employees (Magliveras 2005), the State has not adopted any relevant civil and/or criminal legislative measures specifically to deal with it. However, there exists a general legal framework consisting of provisions in the Constitution, dealing with equality between men and women and the protection of human personality, provisions in the Civil Code and in the Criminal Code which could be applied by analogy, and in various collective employment contracts, as well as general principles of Labour Law and in the Penal Code. Arguably, this framework does not afford victims of sexual harassment a satisfactory regime for seeking redress and it depends on the court and on their own willingness to formally complain. In this case, the head teacher can be seen in Roula's account, to draw on aspects of "hegemonic masculinity" and is assumed to be using his power to give privileges to young and beautiful teachers by means of disempowering or giving extra work to the others. At the same time, as Roula argues, he does not seem to be afraid of doing it, perhaps because of the lack of legal framework or perhaps because this behavior is normalized. He may be viewed as drawing on forms of hierarchical relationship of dominance and subordination (Connell 1987) between himself and other men and women.

When teachers' expectations from, and perceptions about, the "ideal" head teachers were the focus of studies in the UK and the United States, it was found that they constructed "feminine" desired relationships according to which the head teacher demonstrates that s/he trusts the teacher, listens to their opinions and feelings, increases their autonomy, develops coaching relationships, and promotes professional growth (Blase and Anderson 1995, Blase and Blase 1998). Also, the ideal head teacher is usually perceived as honest, considerate, optimistic, firm, knowledgeable, moral, and flexible (Blase and Anderson 1995, Hsieh and Shen 1998, Law and Glover 2000, Thylefors et al. 2007), qualities that may be considered as a mix of "masculine" and "feminine."

The teachers who participated in this research organized their conceptualizations of educational leadership around qualities attributed to the idealized head teacher, his/her leadership approach, and the desired relationships between the head teachers and the teachers in a school: the head teacher as a flexible and tolerant person, a moral leader, an emotional—friendly person, a coach, and a strong person.

Most of the teachers who participated in the research shared the view that the head teacher needs to be attentive and open to the needs of the teachers. Some said that a flexible head teacher is important because sometimes they do not feel competent enough on some issues, leading them to expect a tolerant person as a head teacher. Like Anna:

> I would like a head teacher who wouldn't just give an order to do something. I would like **him** to explain to me what I am supposed to do. I don't know everything! (Anna, WT, 30–39, my emphasis)

This ideal construction is consistent with a "feminine" approach to leadership, which is assumed to be more accepting of differences among people, more tolerant of deviance and more considerate of others' needs (Gray 1989, Shakeshaft 1989, Hurty 1995, Oplatka 2001). It has to be stressed, that Anna uses the masculine grammatical form in Greek when she talks about the ideal head teacher. So, it can be assumed that she may be implying that the ideal head is a man or that usually the head teacher is a man, although she appears to want the head not to be typically "masculine" and autocratic.

Likewise, the ideal head teacher—teacher relationships have also been constructed by the teachers as including positive attitudes toward the teachers' opinions, even if they are different from the head teacher's. The head teacher is expected to "like new ideas, new teaching ideas I mean" (Loukia, WT, 30–39) and "[a] good head teacher should be open and flexible and should accept the novice" (Roula, WT, 30–39).

Another teacher expressed the view that the ideal head teacher is "a person who is open to advice and opinions, one whose decision is not necessarily the final one" (Mina, WT, 30–39). Another teacher expected "to be supported, encouraged, and feel that someone is listening to me, to my ideas" (Andreas, MT, 40–49). The words of Anna, Roula, and Mina are similar to reports on head teachers who are depicted as listening to different viewpoints (Hurty 1995), encouraging collaboration (Regan and Brooks 1995) and advocating a consultative approach (Coleman 2002). These approaches to leadership (listening, consulting, and collaborating) have traditionally been constructed as "feminine."

Notably, and congruent with the "feminine" ideal (Gray 1989) and with observations on women head teachers (Fennell 1999, Oplatka 2003), as the ideal head teacher is constructed as open-minded, s/he is also constructed as an open-to-change person. So, the teachers would have the opportunity to work within a dynamic, creative, and innovative environment.

Some of the teachers (five out of the fifteen) hold beliefs that the head teacher should be moral. Consistent with Sergiovanni (1991) they claim that the head teacher should lead with integrity and honesty. This kind of belief is also shared among teachers in other studies (Blasé and Blasé 1998, Blase and Anderson 1995) and can be seen to draw mainly on "feminine" leadership approaches (Coleman 1996, 2002).

All of the teachers in my research, however, also highlighted the instructional and more "masculine" aspect of leadership. The ideal head teacher was constructed as knowledgeable in pedagogic issues and theories (not so much in practice), a source of organizational information, and a mentor. For example, the ideal head teacher was constructed as "up-to-date in classroom issues, so that I [if I were a head teacher] could teach the other teachers. Inform them about new techniques and staff" (Rea, WT, 30–39).

The emphasis on pedagogical knowledge as a core element in the educational leadership approach of the head teacher was stressed by many participants (twelve out of fifteen) despite the fact that they all had at least ten years of teaching experience. One respondent in particular said:

> The head teacher should be a teacher first. Obviously **he** should know how to deal with the bureaucracy, but **he** should never forget that **he** was and still is a teacher. (Andreas, MT, 40–49, my emphasis)

Furthermore, the "ideal" head teacher was also constructed as a source of providing systematic information about the school. It is anticipated that s/he guides, directs, and makes the teachers' acquaintance with the formal and informal structure of the school organization. This view was clearly expressed by a male teacher who noted that the head teachers should help the teachers, especially the younger and inexperienced ones, with school practice, show them their obligations and rights, and inform them about the educational legal framework.

To sum up, the ideal head teacher as constructed by the teachers who participated in my research, is not consonant with stereotypes of traditional "masculine" leaders. Rather, the construction of the ideal head teacher is more nuanced and draws on a mix of both "masculine" and "feminine" characteristics.

Combining Career with Family

It is assumed that one of the major factors affecting the difference between women's and men's experiences as head teachers in the UK is family responsibilities (Coleman 2002, 2022). American women high school principals in Lad's (2000) study identified the expectations of family responsibilities as a strong influence in their professional lives. Marital status also impacted their ability to carry out the responsibilities inherent to their post. Among the Australian women head teachers in Limerick and Anderson's (1999) study about their perceptions regarding how their lives changed when they reached headship, only a childless head teacher did not report having problems in achieving a balance between the conflicting work-family demands. More recently, Reilley (2022) also reported balancing professional responsibilities with family responsibilities as a challenge for women.

As noted in the literature (i.e., Hall 1996, Limerick and Anderson 1999, Lad 2000, Coleman 2002, 2005b, 2022) women tend to see more "obstacles" in their career pathways, such as dual responsibilities at home and at work, the need to have a supportive partner who could lighten the load of domestic responsibilities and perhaps even a partner prepared to put the other's career ahead in importance of their own.

As discussed in Chapter 3 (*Constructions of Becoming a Head Teacher*), there is compelling evidence that the family responsibilities of women head teachers correlate strongly with a relative lack of career progression in both the UK and elsewhere (Coleman 2002, 2022, Oplatka 2006). In a study in Greece, Brinia (2012) interviewed twenty women and twenty men head teachers in various rural areas. She found that family commitments make it difficult for women to be head teachers. Career breaks for child rearing interrupt career development and make it likely that women will be older than their men counterparts if and when they seek promotion to headship (Powney et al. 2003, You and Ko 2004, Reilly 2022). Contrary to this, in my research in Greece the men head teacher participants tended to have more years of leadership experience than the women who belonged to the same age group, even though women head teachers as a whole tended to be younger than the men. So, it appears that the women became heads at a younger age than their men peers but men probably keep their posts for a longer time. Only one woman head teacher out of the fifteen I interviewed had twenty-one years of headship experience. The experience of the rest of the women varied from one year to eight years. At the same time, the men head teachers participants had experience as head teachers that varied from one year (one participant only) to fifteen years.

Powney et al. (2003) found that almost 33 percent of the disproportionately low number of women head teachers in their research about English teachers actually lived alone, without partners or children, whereas only 2 percent of the men head teachers were without partners at home. For women in education, they conclude, as for women in other occupations, career and promotion may be more frequently sacrificed (by choice or under duress) in order to cope with family responsibilities. This seems to be far less frequent in the case of men. In the present research, all but three women head teachers were married (two had never been married and one was a widow) and two men heads had never been married. Even so, taking into consideration that women head teachers appear to have fewer years of experience as head teachers, it may be assumed that perhaps career and promotion for women probably are sacrificed or postponed in order to cope with family responsibilities. So, this may indicate that career progression is taking place, but, only when major child responsibilities are over, as the majority of the women head teachers had children who were over eighteen years old when they became heads. This may indicate that women tend to have children earlier in their lives or that they tend to plan their careers and have their children before assuming headships.

Powney et al. (2003) also found that women head teachers tended to have more "personal circumstances" (p. 40) that they believed were hindering their attempts to combine work and family. These "personal circumstances" are compounded by the heavy workload that head teachers had. Similarly in Greece, as one of my participants believes: "there isn't anybody else with such a workload as a school head teacher." She goes on by saying that at the school the head teachers should:

... be secretaries, cashiers, accountants, referees, psychologists, nurses especially now with the flu, lawyers ... everything. (Katerina, WHT, 40-49)

Also, the note that women appear to have to work harder than men to achieve the same result (as indicated in the previous chapter) and that along with the large amount of work that headship entails, impacts on women's family life. Given these difficulties in reconciling work and family life it is not surprising that women leaders are less likely to have children than their men colleagues (Coleman 2002, 2005a, Duxbury and Higgins 2013). In my study in Greece the head teachers who participated were in a different situation as only five (three women and two men head teachers) did not have any children. Out of the rest, only two of the women heads had a child under the age of ten when they were appointed as heads, while three of the men heads had young children. If we take into consideration that in Greece the average age of all mothers was 31.6 years in 2020 (Hellenic Statistical Authority 2020) (while in the UK it was 30.7 years (Office for National Statistics 2020c)) and that in my research, the women head teachers who were interviewed tend to have fewer years of head teaching experience than the men, it may be assumed that many women tend to postpone their careers.

Being a head teacher leaves little time for the additional family responsibilities that women continue to bear unequally alongside their men peers. As one of the respondents in Thornton's and Bricheno's (2006) study about men and women in education in the UK commented, it is easier for men as they do not have restrictions from their families and they can "drift" into things.

Unlike women head teachers, men with families are more likely to be promoted earlier than their women peers, and they are far less likely to feel they are held back by their families (Coleman 2002, 2005a, Khanam et al. 2022). And maybe even in Greece the higher percentage of men heads with young children indicates that men do not have to take care of them, as this is a woman's work, as a man teacher who used to be a head said:

I can say that I didn't face these problems [taking care of the children and family]. But, to be honest, my wife played a huge part. She took care of all the family while I was devoted to my duties as a head teacher. (Thodoris, MT, 50-59)

Perhaps the most important point in his words is that it seems that "motherhood is mandated and fatherhood discretionary" (Clarke and Popay 1998, p. 226). Women, although they participate in paid work, appear to have to accommodate their work in their caregiver role. Responsibility and domestic work are not equally distributed between women and men regardless of women's employment status (Fagan and Burchell 2002) and men seem that they have the opportunity to choose over spending more time with their children than women can (Hanna et al. 2018). Also, along with their family and children, they have to deal with everything that is (or is assumed to be) included in the head's role.

The conflict between gender and headship was also constructed in this study as some of the women appear to have deeply embedded "feminine" identities that emerged throughout our conversations. Almost all (twenty out of twenty-five) of the women participants in the research mentioned the assumption that a woman will get married and have a family, do the domestic work, take care of her children, husband, and parents and always be available for them and be considerate. One example of this is Marianthi who talked at length about the importance that her husband put on the fact that she had a job with higher status than his.

> Also, I think that the fact that I was going to have a higher status job than him, he was just a bank employee, played a part in this [i.e. his bad reaction when I was appointed]. Of course, I never saw it like that, but this is how men are! (Marianthi, WHT, 40–49)

Similarly, as she has young children, she commented:

> The truth is that I was a little scared [when I applied], because I had 2 young children, each morning was very difficult, I had to prepare them for school, make my husband's breakfast, prepare his clothes and get myself ready for work. As a head teacher I had to be at school very early, every day, before everyone else, I had to open the school, ventilate the classrooms, turn the heating on, make coffee for everyone else … that's usual practice in our school. Also, I had to leave later than the others. The school day was over, everyone was leaving and I was staying because I had other administrative work, I had to check if all the windows were closed, if the classrooms were in order … do you know how many times I had to carry desks and chairs because classrooms were a mess? (Marianthi, WHT, 40–49)

Marianthi describes some of the duties of a head teacher in Greece. These duties appear quite domestic (e.g., opening and closing windows, making sure that the classrooms are tidy) and in a context different to the Greek one, they might be a care-taker's responsibility. Also, they are quite feminine and not connected with those of an authoritative figure. This may raise the question as to why a man would want to be a head teacher. An explanation might be the assumption that being a head teacher is usually associated with having higher status and prestige (Paustian-Underdahl et al. 2014), but neither Marianthi nor any other participant in this research connected headship with status. Nevertheless, as I said earlier, men head teachers are the majority of the head teachers in Greece.

In discussing women in educational leadership, Brunner and Grogan (2007) explain: "Societal norms do not work in her favour, so she must address this particular aspect of her life in some way in order to move forward in her career" (p. 43).

Some of the women in this study have overcome this hindrance by seeking help from their husbands for these responsibilities. These women were convinced that they would not be able to be head teachers without this help, because they were still their responsibilities/jobs. Loula indicated:

> He [my husband] helps me a lot. He does a lot of things at home, cooking, cleaning, taking care of children although they are old now. If he had refused to help ... then we would have had a problem! (Loula, WHT, 40–49)

Lukia commented on the same issue:

> A woman who has a husband who doesn't do anything at home or with the children, she doesn't have time for this.[...] If her husband believes it and helps her, then yes she can do it. Otherwise, definitely no! (Loukia, WT, 30–39)

However, another head's experience with this barrier has been quite different. Marianthi decided to become a head teacher without having any support from her husband. She still takes care of all the house duties and the children. However, she appears to have changed her mind about going into headship and she is thinking of resigning, as her home and head teacher's responsibilities seem to be in conflict with each other.

> No. I don't like it [headship]! I think that it was my mistake. I am not suitable for these things. I am very tired. There is more work at school and there is the work at home, the children, my husband ... I have thought of quitting. (Marianthi, WHT, 40–49)

Similarly, Rena said:

> No! [I don't have any help] Who will help me? My husband? He has his own work. He is a good man, but he is a man. The woman is the one taking care of the home. (Rena, WHT, 30–39)

In both of these quotes, and in the one that follows, gender binary is reified through the reinforcement of "masculine" and "feminine" expectations. Additionally, these women themselves are seen to utilize this form of essentialism, by conceptualizing their experiences around the binary expectations for men and women. So they seem to believe that there are specific tasks for women (i.e., taking care of the home) and for men.

Another head teacher, also does not have any help at home, because, as she indicates:

> My husband is a farmer. He doesn't help at all. He is a traditional man. He wants everything in his hands. (Katerina, WHT, 40–49)

Her husband appears to conform to traditional constructions of masculinity and does not renegotiate his identity even though his wife is working, too. He can be seen to exert masculine power in a patriarchal family system, where the roles of each gender are clearly stated. So, the woman's role is to have the responsibility of the household and of the children, even if she has a quite demanding job, and the man's role is to be the main breadwinner. Gender differences are profound in the domestic realm and the woman seems to be subordinate to man. The constructions of "masculinity" and "femininity" continue to be embedded in the work-family discourse, modified only to allow for greater movement between the domains, so that women are "allowed" to work (Runte and Mills 2006).

Conclusion

Being a head teacher is a complex situation for both women and men. Different identities are constructed for them, by them, and by the teachers. Many of the difficulties women encounter are related to the perceptions of teaching as a "woman's work" and management as a "male field." As noted, explanations of "care" (Noddings 2005) have depicted women as better carers, because they may experience motherhood, and thereby are suited to teach young children. But this essentializing perception of nurturance and care has been seen to devalue women's skills within institutions and may be considered as contributing to their low status.

Further, it appears that men head teachers, although they are expected to be drawing on dominant constructions of "masculinity," seem to be drawing on a range of available "masculinities" (Haywood and Mac an Ghaill 2003) in order to construct their approaches to school leadership. They revealed constructions of "hegemonic masculinity" along with "masculinities" that were more sensitive, caring, and nurturing.

Similarly, the women head teachers do not simply either adopted "feminine" or more "masculine" approaches to leadership. Rather, they appeared to draw on "gender heteroglossia" (Francis 2010) and sometimes their behavior tended to be different from traditional "feminine" behavior.

The teachers also construct the "ideal" head teacher in terms of "masculine" and "feminine" leadership approaches (Lord and Maher 1993). So, in conjunction with the "feminine" leader, the ideal head teacher is conceptualized as open-minded, attentive, responsive, emotional, and supportive. The ideal relationships between the teachers and the head teacher are conceptualized as caring, considerate, equal, and as a source of knowledge and growth (Blackmore 1999, Fennell 1999, Hall 1996, Oplatka 2002). But when it comes to discipline and order, the constructions seem to be more "masculine," in that they are assumed to include the ability to use power and authority in order to discipline people. The head teacher is expected to be a strong person who has control over staff and children and also combine qualities that have been assumed to be both "masculine" and "feminine."

Finally, the question of life and career balance for people as busy as head teachers is bound to be a difficult one. The research responses show that the solutions to the problem include examples of negotiation and compromise between partners, and of probably hard decisions made by women. The implications of the responses are that the men's lives are dominated by the demands of work and that, in the majority of cases, this can happen because they have the support of their wives who provide continuity to the family as the main home-making partner and the one who often sacrifices their own career aspirations. Despite some changes in the Greek context, as it can be concluded from my participants' responses, it does not appear that the "male" model of career is being challenged, or that an alternative model that would offer a better life and work balance for women and men is becoming widely established.

5

Constructing Change

This chapter comes after Chapter 3 (*Becoming a Head Teacher*) and Chapter 4 (*Being a Head Teacher*) and draws on a similar theoretical and methodological approach. Although Chapter 3 focuses on teachers' "choice" of a career, including in its gendered dimension and Chapter 4 is concerned with teachers while in the midst of their career, with consideration of their professional and "personal" lives and of how gender percolates these, this Chapter discusses what they suggest the future holds for women in educational leadership in Greece and how they believe women's participation in educational leadership could be increased.

I asked the participants in my research to propose ways for improving women's participation in headship. Their suggestions for change will be examined under three sections: individual change, social change, and state/policy change. In the fourth section I will discuss the suggestions that no change is needed or that change is not possible.

It is worth noting, that some participants (five, one women head teacher, one woman teacher, and three men head teachers) answered that they did not know how to improve women's participation in headship. Taking into consideration the context of their interviews, this may imply that they did not consider it much of a problem, or that it is not possible to change.

Individual Change: Change the Woman

According to several scholars (i.e., Shakeshaft 1989, Coleman 2002, 2022, Cambell and Cambell-Whatley 2020) women are constructed as lacking confidence, aspiration, and motivation. A narrow majority of the participants (twenty-two out of forty, fifteen women and seven men) suggested that in attempting to change the current situation in educational leadership in Greece and increase women's participation, the responsibility rests on the individual.

So, they suggested ways in which the women could help themselves toward headship by changing themselves and their presumed self-belief, as not being adequate enough for the position of a head teacher.

One participant said:

I believe it's just an issue that women themselves have to deal with. If they decide that they can meet the demands of the post, they will apply. (Marios, MHT, 40–49)

And another said:

Women have to be willing to apply, because they have the same qualifications and abilities as men. They can do the same job. We, men, do not have more brains; we are not more intelligent than them.[…] Usually, men are more accepted because they are considered as better and because they can be at the school at any time, so they have one more advantage, but a woman can be accepted, if she fights and proves that she deserves it. (Kostas, MHT, 50–59)

Although these men head teachers do not assume that men are superior to women and recognize that women do have leadership skills and knowledge, they do attempt to "blame the victim," in this case the women themselves. It is assumed that it is because of their personal choice that they do not apply and as a result there are few women head teachers.

Kostas recognizes that men tend to be seen as the norm ("men are more accepted, so they have one more advantage"). According to him, men are generally assumed to be better than women, indicating the common perception, which was also discussed earlier, that "management is male" (Schein 1994). In the suggestion above made by Kostas, that it rests on the women themselves to apply and fight to prove their worth, Kostas indicates that even if a woman wants to apply and even if she is successful, she will then have to fight and prove that "she deserves it." It is assumed that for a man being a head teacher is something "natural" and a "rational advancement in his career." But for a woman, headship is not natural. It is something strange, and she will have to fight to establish her right to be in that place. As Shakeshaft et al. (2010) and MacKinnon (2019) noted, a woman has to work harder to prove her value to teachers, children, parents, and others and to be considered as successful. The situation in Greece is similar to what Wahl (2010) indicates about general management in Sweden: "[managers] describe a masculine culture where women are excluded or expected to adapt. It is clear how a manager should be, and consequently women have to perform more" (p. 11). Wahl suggests that some of the Swedish managers she interviewed believed that there are differences in the way men and women managers are treated because of the organizational cultures that privilege men and "masculinity" over women and "femininity."

It was not only men in my study who held these views, but also women (nine out of the fifteen women head teachers and six out of the ten women teachers) who suggested that it is women's personal responsibility to bring about change and increase women's participation in educational leadership. It is also important to note that the women who held these views were from all age groups.

"Women should stand on their feet" said Jenny, a woman head teacher in her fifties whilst Anna, a woman teacher in her thirties, noted that "women tend not to want it."

A woman head teacher in her forties, married with two children aged twelve and sixteen, told me:

> Women should find the courage and apply! Only that! We are not weaker or subordinate to men. We can do the same things. We shouldn't be afraid of anything. (Loula, WHT, 40–49)

She suggests that future change rests on women who should be more courageous. The implications of Loula's words are that she considers women as a whole "different" from men as they lack the courage to apply. She implies that women seem to be lacking some of what are considered as the main characteristics for the post. But she believes that women can do it as she herself has done, by sharing the family responsibilities with her husband and by dealing with other activities, like home finance. Also, she has relied on her husband for help and she appears to believe that this is the exception ("I am a different case!", she says). "My husband is very supportive" she indicated, which seems to have helped her in being a head teacher, as he is the one taking care of the home and the children. The relationship between motherhood and leadership is frequently treated with skepticism (Sachs and Blackmore 1998, Eveline 2004, Sinclair 2004), because motherhood is considered as a social expectation with characteristics and behaviors usually associated with or attributed to women while leadership is associated with dominant "masculine" constructions, although as I discussed earlier, Reay and Ball (2000) argue that motherhood can be a source of power for women. Despite the assumption regarding motherhood and domesticity, Loula has managed to reverse the popular domestic situation, where the "female" role is the caring one, and the "male" is the breadwinner. Loula's words can also mean that women actually need more courage to apply, because they may be faced with rude, sexist, and aggressive male staff, as I described earlier in the case of

Vasso who had to deal with colleagues telling her to make them coffee (section *Constructions of Caring and Nurturing* of Chapter 4).

Other women also suggested that women should change their attitudes toward educational leadership:

> Maybe women themselves believe that they won't be able to do it. They put up the barriers to themselves. [...] Women should believe in themselves and take the huge step! (Roula, WT, 30-39)

Roula suggests that women lack confidence and self-esteem and she also suggests that if women are more confident and believe more in themselves, then there will be an increase in their participation. Similarly, Lea said:

> But most importantly, they should want it. They should be ambitious and most women aren't, they should be more confident, stable, methodical and strict. This way they will become head teachers and they will become successful head teachers. (Lea, WHT, 50-59)

The stereotype of women as "passive" and "not confident" is indicated in both of their responses. They seem to hold essentialized notions of gender in which the female identity is conceptualized as stable and homogeneous, with generalized characteristics and attributes. So, women are depicted as lacking ambition, confidence and stability, and as being less methodical in their work. They are assumed to be passive recipients of the dominant constructions of "femininity" in a patriarchal society, in which women and their experiences have often been silenced. So, these notions of "femininity" expressed by Roula and Lea may be socially imposed constructions and products of the patriarchal society that enforces "public patriarchy" (Walby 1990) through segregation and subordination of women within the public sphere. Roula uses an essentialized and homogeneous construction of women, drawing on what Reay and Ball (2000) call "the universal feminine" (p. 146) and she does not consider the existence of any differences between women because of personality, experiences, and time. However, Lea seems to ignore the fact that men and women may draw on many different aspects of identity that could influence their relationship with others (Moi 1988). Women may also draw on constructions of "femininities" that position women as powerful, as "femininity" is dynamic, various, and changing (Pyke 1996, Shah 2022). Hence, even if it remains a paradox for women to occupy a leadership position because it contradicts the notion of traditional "femininity" (Reay and Ball 2000), female identities, as I have shown in previous chapters (Chapter 3 *Constructions of Becoming a Head Teacher* and Chapter 4

Constructions of Being a Head Teacher), are inextricably interwoven and fluid, shifting across time and context, ranging from subordinate to powerful in different contexts, while structures of inequality may be durably reproduced. As a result it can be argued that it is inappropriate to blame women for their low representation in educational leadership.

Sam et al. (2013) also noted that many of the respondents in their research about the constructions of the female leadership stereotypes of heads in the Ashanti Region, Ghana, held the view that women lack self-confidence and courage to apply for headship. This notion of women being less courageous is reiterated in Cubillo and Brown (2003) and Gupton (2009) who also found that in the United States women's so-called lack of courage was more to do with lack of familiarity with the headship territory than with a lack of courage in their abilities. So, maybe women indeed lack courage as in headship they often have to work within and around institutional, cultural, and societal contexts that may be authoritarian, oppressive, gendered, and a possibly unknown territory. As indicated earlier, in Greece the traditionally male-dominated field of educational leadership is a field of networking and power and, as Sinclair (2013) and Lee (2023) observe, women are usually positioned as "outsiders." This outsider status frequently requires courage, a familiarity with "not belonging" and a willingness to be nonconforming (Sinclair and Wilson 2002). But as Jenny and Loula argue, this presumed lack of courage should not constrain women from applying for head teachers posts.

These "blame the woman" accounts are compatible with Schmuck's (1980) "individual perspective," Shakeshaft's (1989) account of the "internal barriers" that hinder women's position and Ortiz and Marshall's (1988) "person-centred explanation." Despite these multiple labels, all seek to explain the persistent and continuing underrepresentation of women in educational management from a psychological orientation and not from a social one. That is, they look to the women themselves for the "cause," exploring such things as personal traits, characteristics, abilities, or qualities. However, as Schmuck (1980) recognizes, when the focus is on person-centered causation, individuals are "held responsible for their own problems, with the solutions to those problems found in terms of changing the defect or weakness in the individual" (p. 9). A similar perspective was expressed by other participants in my research as well. They said: "There should be no excuse! They have all they need. All the help with the children. The state is there for them" (Takis, MHT, 50–59), "Women do not have goals" (Stefanos, MHT, 50–59).

So, as Shakeshaft acknowledges, such emphasis on women's so-called internal barriers lends itself to what she describes as a "blame the victim" perspective (p. 82). Although Shakeshaft insists that from a psychological perspective these "internal barriers" do exist, she feels they take the focus away from societal barriers that deny women's advancement. Shakeshaft (1989) cautions, "If we accept that inequity is due to some inadequacy on the woman's part, then there is a tendency to not look at any other external causes" (p. 84). However, from a sociological perspective, "internal barriers" are created by the culture and social context in which women develop (Sadker and Sadker 1994). As has been seen earlier, the way society perceives traditional constructions of "femininity" and "masculinity" has led to views of women as weak and as lacking self-esteem, unable to achieve certain tasks, like leadership, although my research has shown that some men may also lack self-esteem and may also be considered as unable to lead. Also, Shakeshaft (1989) suggests from this perspective that "[The] remedy is for women to be resocialized so that they will fit into the male world" (p. 82) and as a result, women are the ones who have to change. Such a perception also reads as suggesting that there is a binary distinction between men and women and the way they approach leadership, but I have argued in a previous chapter (Chapter 4 *Constructions of Being a Head Teacher*) that leadership is fluid and shifting, as I have shown that there is no single "feminine" or "masculine" approach. Rather it is more nuanced and, drawing on Francis (2010) that gender is "complex, contradictory and fluctuating" (p. 485), I argue that both men and women may draw on both of what are considered as traditionally "feminine" and/or "masculine" leadership approaches. This pluralism may mean that it is fruitless to believe that change means the adoption of a "masculine" leadership approach as it appears that there is not one clear "masculine" or "feminine" approach. So, as Collinson and Hearn (2003) suggest there is a need to move away from viewing women as having distinctively different ways of managing and leading. A more critical approach toward gender and leadership seems to be needed, given that the differences between men and women are socially constructed and dependent on the situation (Burr 2003) rather than imposed by nature and/or biology. With leadership traditionally defined in "male" terms and with women being blamed for their underrepresentation, the option of taking up leadership roles may be less appealing for some women. And as Shakeshaft (1989) concludes, contrary to popular assumptions:

> Molding ourselves to be imitations of men or becoming successful while the doors are closed to other women will do nothing to restructure society so that the barriers will cease to exist. (p. 144)

In order for a reconceptualization to take place, societal beliefs about women need to change instead of women having to continue to learn how to navigate and adapt into a system that is men-centered. And as I have shown previously (Chapter 3 *Constructions of Becoming a Head Teacher*), women do face a number of hindrances, when they think about or decide to apply for headship and not only so called "internal barriers." These hindrances are based on traditional "masculine" constructions of leadership and gendered assumptions about women's place in society. As Shakeshaft (1989) notes, it is not only women who should change, but also the structure of the society.

Furthermore, although several of the participants in the research (nine women and five men) indicated that women should aspire to leadership in order to increase women's participation, my research has shown that many women do have these aspirations. As I indicated in an earlier chapter (Chapter 3 *Constructions of Becoming a Head Teacher*) nine out of the fifteen participating women head teachers had clearly planned to apply for headship before obtaining it, and they worked toward it. As early as the mid-1980s Shakeshaft (1985) argued that women's lack of success in obtaining administrative positions was not due to lowered aspirations or lack of motivation on the part of the women. In the mid-2000s, Grogan and Brunner (2005) found that 40 percent of the women they studied in the United States planned to pursue a leadership position in education. So, a change in women's way of thinking is not enough, as women may plan their careers, but they take a more labyrinth way (Eagly and Carli 2007, Moorosi 2022).

In a previous chapter (Chapter 3 *Constructions of Becoming a Head Teacher*) I discussed the "barriers" that women face when they decide to apply for headship. Among them were the selection procedures, where most of the respondents indicated that men were preferred, and the difficulty of combining career with family. Despite this, Takis, the head teacher who was mentioned above, seems to believe that women find excuses not to participate in headship. He says that it is their responsibility because the state offers help with the children (day-care centers and whole-day schools). His view is contrary to the everyday life experiences of many women who cannot find a place for their child in a day-care facility or a whole-day school. Popular Greek newspapers and sites, like "aftodioikisi.gr" (September 7, 2022) and "Efimerida Syntakton" (September 1, 2022) gathered data from publicly available datasets in the Ministry of Education, Research and Religious Affairs and the Ministry of Labor, Social Security and Welfare and reported that last September (2022) 84,000 children aged five to twelve could not get a voucher to enroll at public after-school centers (Creative Employment

Centers-KDAP)[1] because of lack of available places. Moreover, even though the great majority of schools offer whole-day programs that last until 4 o'clock, most parents do not finish their work until 5 or 6 o'clock, or even later. So, despite the fact that there are existing "barriers," Takis considers them as just "excuses" and believes that if women stop making these "excuses" then in the future there will be more women head teachers.

In addition, in the interviews, many of the women who participated did not draw on the traditional construction of women as lacking confidence (e.g., teachers like Helen and Loukia, and head teachers like Gina and Danai). Instead, they appeared to be sure about themselves and about their abilities, even if they had not decided at this point in time to apply for headship.

To sum up, the responses from the participants discussed in this section stress the individual's responsibility where women's participation in educational leadership is concerned and tend to rest on fixed/essentialized constructions of women/"femininity." Hence, they seem to remove responsibility from the state, from men and "masculine" constructed leadership or from other factors that may be considered as "barriers" and which were discussed in earlier chapters (Chapter 3 *Constructions of Becoming a Head Teacher* and Chapter 4 *Constructions of Being a Head Teacher*).

State/Policy Change

There were seven participants (four women and three men, out of forty) who suggested that in order to have a higher participation of women in educational leadership, changes in policies should occur. They defined these changes as the possible implementation of a quota system for women, the implementation of changes to make the head teacher's job easier and more attractive to both men and women and an increase in the number of childcare facilities.

Quota Systems

Over the last half century women have made significant advances in education and in educational leadership but they are still underrepresented across the globe and in Greece, as I have shown. The limited women's presence in educational leadership leads to a consideration of whether and how this could be changed. To answer these questions, only one participant (a man head teacher) proposed direct policy interventions such as gender quotas in order to increase the participation of women in educational leadership.

> There could be a quota system, for example that 50 percent of all headships should be occupied by women. (Marios, MHT, 40–49)

Quota systems have been implemented in several countries as an attempt to increase women's participation in management. Norway, in an attempt to eliminate discrimination and inequality between men and women, passed a Law in parliament in 2003 that stipulates a minimum of 40 percent representative of each gender on publicly listed boards (Lewis and Rake 2008). Similarly, France and Spain passed quota legislation in the early 2000s (Fagan and Gonzalez Menendez 2012). In their systematic review of empirical articles on the topic of network and career advancement van Helden et al. (2021) argue that imposing a gender quota system may lead to more women in managing positions, but it will not automatically make it easier for other women to advance their careers because of (un)conscious stereotypes and biases (van Veelen et al. 2019).

The use of radical strategies such as quotas are important tools for promoting equality and are fundamental approaches in some countries, such as the Scandinavian countries. But even though they achieved gender equality there, it is also likely that the equality is a combination of social, cultural, and economic factors in addition to the use of quotas, as the Global Gender Gap Report (World Economic Forum 2022) indicates. The same report shows that Greece in 2022 has dropped almost twenty places in the global gender rating since 2013 and almost thirty places since 2006, just before the economic crisis. It is also recognized by British scholars (i.e., Malleson 2003) that the use of a quota system in certain areas such as the judiciary was likely to emerge as a political issue in the UK. A more recent study from Germany (Stark and Hyll 2014) argues that if there is no quota system, women consider their chances of getting top positions to be lower than men's and so women do not engage in applying. At the same time, less "able" men are more likely to get such positions. Gender quotas may discourage those men who are less qualified and encourage those women who are more qualified.

In Greece the first time that quotas were implemented was in 2000 and 2001 with two pieces of legislation. The first, Law 2839/2000, stipulates that both genders shall participate at a quota of 1/3 each, in departmental boards of public administration services, collective managing bodies of public organizations, local administration organizations, and related institutions and enterprises.

This was done in an attempt to ensure a balanced participation of fully qualified men and women in the decision-making processes of public administration, as well as in the entities of the private sector and the local administration agencies of 1st and 2nd degree (Mayors and Prefects). A year later, Law 2910/2001 was implemented. It requires that the number of candidates of each sex in the local and national elections must be equal to at least 1/3 of the total number of candidates in each party list.

With the first Law an attempt was made to tackle the underrepresentation of women in public administration. But the phrase "fully qualified," that was included in it, left room for individual interpretation. The qualifications can be proven by degrees, certificates etc., as well as by being assessed through interviews, where the general knowledge and the personality of the applicant are evaluated. Employing somebody is not just a process of skills sorting. It appears to be also a process of cultural matching between the potential employer and employee (Rivera 2012). Research in the UK and the United States regarding employment has shown that similarities in employer-employee gender may be a potent source of interpersonal attraction and may affect the potential hiring (Lareau and Weininger 2003, Wimmer and Lewis 2010). So, men tend to appoint other men or those who match traditional "masculine" constructions. Other research in the UK has shown that the same interview questions are not asked to men and women candidates. Instead, gender-based questions may be asked, concerning family, mobility, and leadership approach (Coleman 2002), which is illegal, but still happens, as Alexandra (a woman head teacher) commented in section *Constructions of Gender and the Selection Process*, p. 68 of Chapter 3. Alexandra said that she was asked questions about how she would manage to combine a headship post with having a family. Similarly, data from my research presented in earlier chapters show that the majority of the participants in my research believe that the applicant's gender plays an important role in the outcome of the interview. Finally, research shows that many men (who are the majority in the selection panels) have a vested interest in holding onto power and authority rather than sharing it with women (Brown and Ralph 1996). Research has found that men have a tendency to employ people who look, potentially think, and act like them, that is, they are men or more "masculine" (Oplatka 2006, Coleman 2011, 2022). As argued by D' Agostino et al. (2022) "think manager, think male" is along established phenomenon that has a major impact on women's progression in leadership. My research also indicates that several factors can interfere in the interview procedure (like political beliefs, networks, and gender). As discussed in Chapter 3 (*Constructions of Becoming a Head Teacher*), experiences of the research participants (i.e., Anna and Kostas) indicate that a man candidate would be preferred over a woman candidate with the same qualifications. So, women may lawfully remain underrepresented insofar as it could be argued after the interviews that there are no "fully qualified" women employees (or teachers in the present case) to promote. In spite of the legal framework, women's representation in the top positions in local administration and public organizations remains low. In 2018, only 9.1 percent of board seats of the largest publicly listed companies were women, while the same figure in EU was 26.7 percent (European Commission 2019).

As far as the second Law is concerned, women applicants in the elections have increased but the participation of women in political leadership has not. Maybe this is because Greek society is highly patriarchal and the leadership arena is believed to be "masculine." So women tend not to be voted for and as a result there are not many women in the political field. Publicly available data from the Ministry of Internal Affairs show that in the elections of 2012 only fifty-three out of the 300 members of the parliament were women, while in the last elections (June 2023) there were only sixty-seven women. Also, in the local elections of 2019, out of the 332 Mayors, only eighteen were women.

So, evidence from Greece shows that women's progress has been disappointing, as women's employment outcomes have not improved enough despite the existence of relevant legislation. Similarly in Australia, despite the existence of quotas, research has shown that little progress has been made with the implementation of such policies (Ainsworth et al. 2010). Ainsworth et al. (2010) in their research have confirmed Bacchi's (1996) findings, that there had been a lack of success in instituting "real" equal opportunities for women as the social and/or structural disadvantage experienced by women remained largely constant. Instead, they all found that there was an engagement in a series of debates regarding legislation and policy about the possible interpretation of quotas and the reforms it should encompass. More recently Svensson and Gunnarsson (2012) discuss how Sweden attempted to adopt a "gender neutral" equal treatment process, by considering men and women as equals, side by side. However, they note that even though Sweden recognizes the need for equality, the policy focuses more on social institutions and structures rather on the individual. But Svensson and Gunnarsson (2012) conclude that by this it appears that the main interest was the outcome (i.e., having more women in higher ranks) rather than equality of opportunities to access higher ranks. Overall, women and their lives and situations as a targeted group might be viewed as not being the priority in any of the countries studied, rather increasing their numbers in higher ranks has been a priority. As a result, issues such as the domestic division of labor may be considered as largely unaddressed (Bacchi 1996, Vincovic 2023). Other recent studies regarding the employment of women have also concluded that quota systems may increase the numbers of women but do not provide real equal opportunities as they do not promote any structural changes in the lives of women (i.e., Loutfi 2001, Reskin 2003, Bertrand 2018).

Some scholars argue that a gender quota system denies equal opportunities for men and women to compete for available posts and they advocate selection based on merit and not gender (Phillips 1995). They argue that quota systems lead to appointing or promoting less-qualified people who may perform poorly (Holzer and Neumark 2006). Quota systems may also perpetuate negative stigmas regarding the abilities of minorities, as Sowell (2005) has argued in his study of quota systems around the world. Another study in a US university regarding quota systems and faculty and student recruitment showed that a considerable percentage of faculty participants expressed concerns that quotas' recipients who are underqualified are favored over qualified non-recipients (Flores and Rodriguez 2006). Similarly, in a study of students Zehnter and Kirchler (2020) found that students perceived women quotas as counterproductive, derogatory, and unfair. So, a quota system may be seen as undermining women's efforts for equality.

Maria, a woman head teacher, who is the most experienced head teacher amongst my participants with twenty-one years of headship experience, on the one hand indicated that there should be an increase in the number of women heads, but on the other hand, that there should not be any quota system for them. Although in the past she was one of very few women head teachers and, as she noted, she had to deal with behaviors that ranged from patronizing (from the students' parents) to—what is considered today as—sexual harassment (from her superiors) and despite the fact that she appears to believe in women's abilities and the need for more women's participation in educational leadership, she is opposed to any form of quota system. She suggests that this policy may lead to reverse discrimination, as Crosby et al. (2006), Beaurain and Masclet (2015) and Du et al. (2022) also suggest.

> I am against all these quotas for women participation, e.g. in politics. [...] isn't there a danger that worthless women will be promoted instead of valuable men? (Maria, WHT, 40–49)

Similarly to common assumptions, she argues that quotas may lead to a reduction in quality as it may lead to having head teachers who are not qualified enough. She does not seem to believe that leadership is associated with "masculinity" or "femininity," rather than with abilities and value regardless of gender. But, she seems to disregard the fact that with the current hiring system many unsuitable men could be hired because of their gender and many suitable women not. Her assumption is that the reason why women do not rise to senior positions has something to do with their suitability.

But Maria seems to disregard the fact that women in Greece, as well as elsewhere, are in a disadvantaged position compared with men. As Bradley (1999) argues, the continued dominance of the power men hold over women and the way these power relations are produced and reproduced may lead women to such position.

Also, Phillips (1995) argues:

> selection by merit [...] or gender are not such poles apart for there is no process of admission or appointment that operates by a single quantifiable scale, and the numbers are always moderated by additional criteria. These more qualitative criteria [...] often favour those who are most like the people conducting the interview: more starkly, they often favour the men'. (p. 61)

Furthermore, it is argued that the larger the numbers of women represented in educational leadership, the more possibilities exist to make a difference (Karl 1995, Morgenroth et al. 2015). Karl argues that it usually takes a critical mass of women to affect change and I believe that such change may alter the stereotype of men's domination in leadership positions in Greek primary schools, reduce gender discrimination, and further the opportunities for women head teachers through the formulation of gender friendly policies. So, quota systems may help to achieve this and still remain essential as far as many women are concerned.

But the application of such policies without questioning why they are applied is criticized by many scholars, such as Harding (1991), Nater et al. (2023), Loumbourdi (2023), and others. Tamale (1997) notes that a quota system is "a single policy [...] a lonely policy, a voice in the wilderness which can achieve little without the support of the policies directed at reducing disparities" (p. 73). A quota system is geared toward increasing participation but the latter cannot be viewed in isolation from the social-economic context. Women's social and economic identities may overlap and interact resulting in interconnected patterns which often reinforce each other and this may place an unreasonable burden on both women and men. However, it seems that it hurts women more than men since it appears to be incongruent with the caregiving responsibilities that women, as the primary caregivers, are perceived or expected to have (D' Agostino et al. 2022).

In contemporary Greece, where there is a major recession and social welfare policies are being reduced since the 2007/8 crisis (Matsagianis 2013, Papanastasiou 2022, Kapitsinis 2023), women may find it difficult to participate in leadership even if a quota system for head teachers is implemented.

In conclusion, quota systems, where implemented, have not solved all the issues of society-wide discrimination. Instead, in order to achieve a better balance between men and women in senior posts I argue other forms of change might be necessary along with quota systems. Some of my participants also noted other forms of change in order to enhance women's participation in educational leadership.

Change in Head Teacher's Workload

When asked how women's representation in educational leadership could be increased, two of the respondents, one man head teacher with three years of headship experience and one woman teacher who has never thought of being a head but who has not ruled it out, argued that the Greek state should adopt policies in relation to schools that will contribute toward raising women's participation.

> The situation could be changed if we see the foundations of the system. If we break larger schools into smaller ones with 6 classes each, if we appoint secretaries to deal with paperwork and if the extra money is increased. This could encourage women to apply. (Pavlos, MHT, 40–49)

Pavlos argues that the changes he suggests should be implemented by the state, into changes to the structures of the educational system. Pavlos's proposals include reducing the size of schools, as he considers schools with more than six classes very big and difficult to manage. He also proposes the appointment of administrative staff, in order to reduce the amount of administrative work that the head teachers are responsible for. His last words ("This could encourage women to apply") may indicate that women are discouraged from applying because they find the job difficult, while men do not or maybe because the demands and the volume of the work are too much, given women's domestic and childcare responsibilities. His assumption is based on traditional constructions about women as being less able than men in certain tasks, like managing and he might be viewed as drawing on traditional constructions of "masculinity" and "femininity."

So, the changes he suggests for all head teachers include giving financial incentives and reducing the amount of work. The small amount of extra money that the head teacher in Greece receives may have led to teachers being unwilling to apply for headships. As one of my respondents told me, after the digital recorder was turned off, "During the last selection, we were 12 applicants for 12 headships. The responsibility and the amount of work to be done cannot be paid for, especially with 115 euros before taxes!"

The Greek head teacher has a variety of duties, pedagogical, and managerial. The cost-benefit analysis may appear to lead many teachers to believe that the amount of work is too great and they suggest that the responsibilities should be reduced maybe by either employing assisting personnel (e.g., secretaries) or by increasing the additional payments they are getting. So, headship then might become more attractive for both men and women.

But if the suggested changes occur, maybe more men will be persuaded to apply for headship, too. Given the construction of the job as "masculine" and that men tend to be preferred in the appointment process (as I have indicated in section *Selection Procedures* of Chapter 3), this may lead to even fewer women being appointed. Also within the current economic situation in Greece it is highly unlikely either that administrative staff will be appointed or that more financial incentives will be offered to head teachers.

Childcare

The number of women filling dual roles of mother and worker has increased significantly in the last fifty years both in Greece and in the other European Union countries (KETHI 2001). Wolf-Wendel and Wark (2006) indicate that in the United States 64 percent of mothers of young children (aged up to six years old) worked outside the home in 1999 and almost 70 percent in 2015 (US Bureau of Labor Statistics 2021), compared with 19 percent in 1960. In Greece almost 20 percent of women were working in 1960 (KETHI 2001) and this rose to almost 70 percent in 2005 (before the crisis) (Kikilias 2007). Also, Coleman (2002) draws on Ruijs (1993) who suggests that, for most women the choice of a management position means choosing not to have a family. In the early 1990s Ruijs (1993) argued that there is a clear and established relationship in most European countries between women's employment and childcare provision. In the present research, almost all women were responsible for the management of their households, despite the fact that they had a partner. Even some men head teachers (five out of ten) who participated in the interviews admitted that they could not have done it without their wives, who were responsible for the children, reflecting the findings of Coleman (2002 and 2009) in England.

Women who shoulder the major responsibility for their homes seem to be able to lead well when their responsibilities at home and at school are in some kind of balance. Achieving such a balance allows women leaders to channel their energies effectively in both spheres (Grogan and Shakeshaft 2011). So, there is a need for childcare provisions for working parents, for changes in the domestic division of labor in Greece (as I indicated in an earlier chapter women do more than 80 percent of housework) and in expectations of women and men.

There were four participants (three women and one man) who suggested that childcare facilities are necessary in order to have a higher participation of women in educational leadership. Alexandra, a woman head teacher with two older children (twenty-six and twenty-four years old) who became a head teacher when her children were twenty-two and twenty years old, argued that more childcare provision should be introduced in order to change women's participation in educational leadership.

> What I reckon is holding them back are family commitments. This is the most important issue and if she can deal with it, I don't know how, maybe by having more kindergartens and more child-provision settings so that she won't worry about her children, then the number will change. (Alexandra, WHT, 40–49)

Similarly, Takis, a man head teacher, who although he said, as noted earlier (section *Individual Change: Change the Woman*) that women find excuses for not becoming head teachers, also commented about the lack of adequate childcare provision:

> The state should give incentives to women and help with the kids should be provided. Day-care centres, whole-day schools should exist for all. (Takis, MHT, 50–59)

In Greece, a number of socio-economic changes have progressively taken place over the last forty years, such as the loosening of family ties, an increasing distance between young parents and their family of origin, an increase in divorce rates, growing numbers of single-parent families, diminished family size, a change in values, intense urban migration, a migration wave from other nearby countries since the early 1990s as well as a progressive change in educational policy (Bagavos 2001, 2005, Salvati 2018). These conditions created new demands for early childcare and education provision with such services not considered sufficient to fulfill the demand.

Greece has two types of institutions for young children: childcare centers and pre-primary school (*nipiagogeio*). Childcare centers accept children from six months to four years of age. More specifically, daycare centers/nurseries or crèche provide services for children from six months to four years. Until 2001, public childcare centers were under the auspices of the Ministry of Health and Welfare. Since then, they are funded and supervised by the municipalities with support of the Ministry of Interior. It should be mentioned that there is no universal right to access as the available positions are fewer than the children who need them. So, parents are forwarded to private centers where they have to pay nannies or grandparents. Children aged four and five attend pre-primary school (*nipiagogeio*), which falls under the responsibility of the Ministry of Education, Research and Religious Affairs. Since 2018/19, the start of compulsory education (pre-primary school/*nipiagogeio*) has been lowered from age five to four.

According to estimations, 110,000 children aged between five months and five years—representing more than the 20 percent of the population of this particular age group—attended one of the 3,000 nurseries (KEDKE-EETAA 2005, Tsoulea and Kaitanidi 2005). This figure rose to 314,153 by 2020 (Eurostat 2022) even though since 2018 the age for compulsory education was lowered to four years old.

If we add to this figure the additional numbers of preschool children, aged four and five, who attended public preschool services instead of private ones during school year 2019–20 (146,302 in public schools and 18,414 in private schools) due to the recent economic crisis then the whole picture is even more disappointing, as this makes the demand even greater and the available places even scarcer. Enrolment is influenced by an insufficient supply of childcare (Daouli et al. 2004) and more than half of the children in Greece are cared for informally, by childminders or family members (Janta 2014).

The above data, along with the note that Greece is a country with traditional patriarchal structures (Gassouka 2004) where the major responsibility for the children falls on women (Samman et al. 2016), can lead to the assumption that women cannot become head teachers or maybe even work full time. As many participants noted and as discussed in Chapter 4 (*Constructions of Being a Head Teacher*), the post demands many hours, with Jenny noting "It is exhausting! I am the first to arrive at the school in the morning and the last to leave. Sometimes I return in the afternoon [after the school is closed] because I have work to do"(Jenny, WHT, 50–59), it is easy to see why a change in the availability of childcare provisions might be necessary.

But since 2010, cuts in public expenditure in Greece have been the main reaction to the crisis. Strict consolidation plans have been introduced with IMF and EU programs. A great number of these plans involve cuts in services such as childcare (European Women's Lobby 2012). In a climate like this, it seems difficult to expect an increase in childcare provision. On the other hand, there are European funds that remain unused. In 2020, data from the Ministry of Finance that were published in the press (businessdaily.gr, June 25, 2020) show that only 35 percent of European funds were used. Maybe this money could be used, in addition to the money already being used, to increase childcare provisions.

Wider Social Change

Some of the participants in my study argued that wider changes are needed in order to increase the participation of women in educational leadership. In Greece, in times of crisis women struggle. In a country where large demonstrations have been taking place during the last years, where new forms of social movements develop, where the far right is still growing significantly, the position of women is affected. Golden Dawn, the political party that represented the far right in the Greek political scene and in 2020 the court ruled that it is a criminal organization and its leadership has been convicted to imprisonment, had formed a women's network called the "White Women Front" (WWF) and had a rather paradoxical relationship with women. Although there were women elected in the Greek Parliament representing Golden Dawn (the wife of its president was a member of the parliament) and even though one would think that WWF would have a solid position on women, gender equality, or women's rights, this is not the case (Papanastasiou 2019). Their only solid position was in their emphasis on the women's traditional roles as mothers, sisters, daughters, and the nation's breeding machines without a right to abortion (Ideological library of White Women Front, n.d.). Despite the fact that there have been almost three years since the ban of Golden Dawn, a lot of people in Greece seem to adopt its ideology about women and gender in general. During the last national elections (June 2023) a new political party has emerged (*Spartiates*/Spartans) in the far-right political scene and gained twelve seats in the Parliament, stemming from Golden Dawn and representing its ideas.

The crisis raised the rates of unemployment, especially for women (in the fourth trimester of 2022 the rates were 11.9 percent in the general population, 8.8 percent among men and 15.7 percent among women (Hellenic Statistical Authority 2022)).

But it is not only a question of unemployment. It is also a question of working conditions mainly for women, as women lead predominantly in precarious jobs and there are many forced redundancies along with a collapse of wages and labor rights (Karamessini 2011a, 2011b, Livanos and Tzika 2022).

Men, on the other hand, do not seem to face so many difficulties. Also, everyday experience shows that unequal pay in comparison with men's is the rule, pregnant women are fired or other women are obliged to commit to not having children (!) and are paid less because of this "danger," the insurance rights of women are brutally violated, and rights are abolished, including changes to the retirement age, maternity leave, and childcare. All the above, along with the simultaneous decline of the trade union movement (Avdela 2009), seems to affect predominantly the social groups which are less protected and more vulnerable to pressures of every kind (Gaitanou 2009).

Even the left political formations, that wish to be considered as fighting inequality, seem to remain quite traditional and androcentric with men comrades often prioritizing the class struggle against neoliberal globalization over other structural inequalities (such as gender (in)equality) (Kyriakidou 2010). This has led left-wing feminist women in Greece to emphasize their potential different experiences as women, reinforcing gender difference, and to create groups within existing political formations (i.e., Women of SYRIZA Network, that exists within SYRIZA, the Coalition of the Radical Left) or original political initiatives (e.g., the coalition group called "Women for Another Europe," that participated in the European Elections of 2004).

When I conducted my research, the crisis had just begun and its first consequences were evident. In a climate like this, where "masculine" constructions seem to be the dominant ones, my participants argue that a change in the way wider society constructs gender is needed. Two particular issues were highlighted: gender and domestic labor and media representation of gender.

The Gendered Division of Work

A number of the respondents (fourteen out of forty, ten women and four men) indicated that in order to increase the number of women head teachers, a change in the way people think is necessary. This includes changes in the gender roles in the household, in society, and in the way children are being raised.

Dimitris, a man head teacher married with two children indicated:

> But if women's position within society and within the house does not change, it will be very difficult for them. (Dimitris, MHT, 50–59)

His response reveals a view of Greek society as patriarchal. As was noted in Greece "the male dominated structures and the neglect of persistent gender hierarchies still prevail" (Women of SYRIZA Network declaration 2008). In Greece there is limited research about families, society, gender roles, and power with the most recent study being published about twenty years ago (Maragoudaki 2005), although in the 1980s there were some studies about domestic responsibilities and roles (i.e., Nikolaidou 1981, Moussourou 1985a and 1985b). In these studies it was noted that the fact that most women were working at that time (as they are today) can be said to have contributed to men starting to deal with domestic work. At that time there was also more help from other members of the family (grandmother, unmarried aunt etc.), so the male contribution tended to be confined to shopping, washing the dishes, and walking the children. The major household responsibilities, however, rested with women. Similarly, a study in the United States has shown that "women's work" is typically thought to include preparing meals, doing the dishes, cleaning the house, and doing laundry, whereas "men's work" includes taking out the trash, fixing things with tools, and taking care of the vehicles (Parkman 2009). As I mentioned in Chapter 2 (*Women in Educational Leadership: Global and National Context*, p. 23) in Greece the everyday situation is similar to that in the United States and the lack of literature may imply that this is the "normal" thing for women to do.

Another Greek study in the mid-1990s (Maratou-Aliprandi 1995) found that the level of men's participation in domestic work depended on their education. Men who have higher education tend to do more around the house. It also depends on the work status of women. In 1995, Maratou-Aliprandi reported that the higher the status of a women's job, the greater the participation of the husband. As women have continued to enter professional fields it may have been expected that men would become more involved in domestic work. However, data from my study suggest otherwise. Katerina, a woman head teacher participant in my study, contrasts with Maratou-Aliprandi's (1995) findings as in her family the opposite is noted, as she is the one with higher education in her family (her husband is a farmer who has not studied beyond junior high school) and yet he does not participate in the domestic chores, because as she said "he is a traditional man."

The dominant construction of "femininity" in Greek society is one that positions women as the ones responsible for the house and as subordinate to men, who sometimes, may offer their "help" with what are considered to be women's responsibilities. So, the participants suggest that this construction should change in order to change women's representation in educational management. But neither Dimitris nor Katerina offers any suggestions on how this could be achieved.

The suggestion comes from other respondents. For example, Marianthi said:

> If the roles within the family do not change, if the husband does not take up some responsibilities, then nothing can be done. (Marianthi, WHT, 40-49)

She expresses this view, because as she said earlier (laughing sarcastically):

> My husband's responsibility is the bills as he holds our money and some external tasks. Sometimes he picks up the children from their lessons, but not always! (Marianthi, WHT, 40-49)

In Turkel's (1988) view dealing with money "is [...] a symbol of worth, competence, freedom, prestige, masculinity, control and security" (p. 525). Paying the bills therefore may be seen as reassuring Marianthi's husband of his "masculinity," as research has shown that holding money and paying the bills is considered as a "male" thing (Kornrich et al. 2012).

According to Marianthi, her husband may have constructed his wife as responsible for all that needs attention around the house and for the children. Marianthi on the other hand, seems to construct the "masculine" role as the one responsible for financial issues (he pays the bills). So, she proposes that all of these should change. But again, she does not offer a view about how this could be achieved.

A woman teacher suggested that changes in child rearing are necessary. She said:

> If we continue to raise boys differently from girls then nothing will change. And everything that starts from education inside or outside of the family needs many years to have outcomes. So there is a long way ahead of us! (Loukia, WT, 30-39)

Loukia suggests that traditional constructions about "masculinity" and "femininity" in Greece can change through education. Greek education has moved forward and now all public schools are co-educational and there are no different curricula for boys and girls contrary to what was happening in the past (see section *An Historical Perspective on Gender Issues in Greece* of Chapter 2). But the school books that are used in primary schools in Greece include images of gender stereotypical behavior by men and women (e.g., women are presented as nurses, librarians, ballet teachers, secretaries and paediatricians, while men are presented as soldiers, sailors, artists, engineers, doctors, teachers, and astronauts. Also, men are presented as being involved in activities outside of the house and women as being involved in traditional "female activities" like cooking, baking, and knitting) (Hardalia and Ioannidou 2008). Even in the writing and publishing teams for the school books men are the majority and women are responsible mostly for editing (Kadartzi and Pliogou 2007).

A man teacher talked also about the need for change:

> This calls for a change of mentality in the Greek society. Roles change, slowly, but they do change. (Andreas, MT, 40–49)

Similarly, Sullivan (2006), after analyzing datasets from the National Survey of Families and Households (NSFH) conducted in forty-eight states in the United States between 1987 and 2003, proposes an approach to better explain changing gender relations. Based on both others' and his own research findings, Sullivan's approach emphasizes that the analysis of gender relations in the family should be linked with an account based on the analysis of daily interaction, negotiation, and struggle. He suggests a concept of gender awareness, the development of which, he explains, involves a process which includes a growing recognition of change in gender relations. In other words, change in gender relations can happen not only as a result of individual interactions between men and women, but also as a result of exposure to changing attitudes and norms in broader societies. By incorporating the broader concept of gender consciousness, Sullivan's approach puts even more emphasis on the "transformative potential of everyday interaction" (Sullivan 2006, p. 13), and underscores the non-static, ever-changing nature of gender relations. This transformative potential, according to Sullivan, includes two analytic components: cultural meanings, norms, and expectations on one hand, and interactive processes on the other. That is to say, change in gender relations can come from both macro-level cultural changes in the larger society and micro-scale changes in interactions between individuals, in an attempt to challenge patriarchy and raise consciousness (Hughes n.d.). So, Loukia seems to believe that traditional understandings and constructions of gender could be changed through education. According to Loukia, the potential change could come from a combination of change in cultural norms, which includes changes to a different way of raising boys and girls in the family (micro-scale), and a change in the way the wider society contributes to gender education (macro-level). Also research has shown that change in gender relations has not been as rapid as early advocates originally hoped (Sullivan 2006, Mahoney and Knudson-Martin 2009) but it is a slower ongoing process as research in the Anglo-Saxon world suggests (Lang and Risman 2006, Hook 2006). However, there has been change as one of my participants indicated:

> There has been a huge change during the last 50 years! Woman has exited from the house, she went to school, she started working, you see men that do several

things that 20 years ago they couldn't even imagine doing! This is how they will accept women in higher posts! My children maybe will see it; my grand children will definitely see it! (Jenny, WHT, 50–59)

Jenny can be seen as implying that change is inevitable in a process of linear progression. Women's situation has changed and continues to change, so equality is simply a matter of time. But equality for women is not a linear story of progress from women being restricted into their houses to equality in professional and social life. As I have shown elsewhere (see section *An Historical Perspective on Gender Issues in Greece* of Chapter 2) women's participation in the labor market has declined as well as advanced in Greece throughout history. Women have made progress in their participation in social and professional arenas, but it is not simply a matter of time until there are enough women in leadership. I have shown elsewhere (Chapter 3 *Constructions of Becoming a Head Teacher*) that women face a number of challenges when they decide to apply for leadership posts and they are less likely than men to be promoted. Her assumption is that as more women enter the teaching profession it is simply a matter of time until they work their way up and become head teachers. Her view is similar to that of Forbes et al. (1988) who argued that in the corporate world: "Although progress has been slow, women currently entering the work force already are viewing the sky through the broken remnants of the glass ceiling" (p. 9). On the other hand, Leathwood and Read (2009) and Singh et al. (2008) challenge the idea of the "pipeline" theory, that is, the argument that it is simply a matter of time until the women that are now entering the professions achieve equality with men in senior positions, as there are currently many qualified women but few in leadership positions. It appears that certain professional areas are very resistant to gender changing. As a result, the path to leadership can be described as a "leaky pipeline" as women seem to drop out on the way to higher posts (Allen and Castleman 2001, White 2001, Blinkenstaff 2005). So it is suggested that there may be a more nuanced and complex set of factors relating to career choice for women.

Moreover, the Greek educational system and the school curriculum have been described as conservative (Dimitrakopoulos 2004), as research has shown that girl-students are usually taught to maintain distinct roles in the family, with the woman constructed as a wife, a mother, and a housewife (Panagiotidou 2013). Hence, girls taught such traditional constructions probably cannot easily overcome the gendered division of work and maybe they cannot challenge them and work their way up to leadership posts. A few years ago, the left-wing party that was governing then (SYRIZA) has brought criticisms of the existing gender equality policies and reform proposals to the forefront of public debates. But, in the current recession climate in Greece, where the unemployment of women has reached 30 percent in April 2015 (Hellenic Statistical Authority 2015b) and currently is officially 15–18 percent (Hellenic Statistical Authority 2023), it is difficult to achieve gender equality.

Media Representation

Only one of my participants said that the mass media should bear some of the responsibility for the construction of change for women in Greece, as the media could play a role in raising consciousness and changing attitudes:

> The influence of cinema and TV is great on this. We see what is happening elsewhere and we want to become like them. For example, there are many films that show working women and staying-at-home dads. Why not have them as an example? (Jenny, WHT, 50–59)

As Greek society still preserves its patriarchal and traditional concepts (Eurostat 2020) and is constructed around a conservative model of behavior which attempts to suppress women's issues, by not promoting women to decision-making positions and by assimilating them into the traditional "feminine" role of wife, mother, and homemaker (Panagiotopoulou 2007), it does not came as a surprise that these ideas are reproduced in the content of the majority of the Greek media and particularly in television. The media have the power not to merely represent but also construct notions of dominant, hegemonic, subordinate, and oppositional "masculinities" and "femininities" (Litosseliti 2006). The few research studies that have been conducted in Greece on this issue show very similar results (Kakavoulia et al. 2001, Kafiri 2002, Karantonaki 2021). They reveal the stereotypes which constitute the representation of women on television and in various sorts of women's magazines. Also, during the last years there has been an increase in the number of new magazines with contents of cookery, arts and crafts, knitting, etc., which are considered as "feminine" subjects, with titles like "Sweet alchemies," "Sweet secrets," "Home and decoration," and "Burda." According to McCracken (1993), women's magazines are assumed to provide pleasure, while at the same time "naturali[se] social relations of power" (p. 3). Her argument cannot be dismissed given that their sales flourish in an era when women's unemployment rises, as these reproduce deeply conservative and patriarchal ideologies. For instance in TV series or TV and magazine advertisements, women are portrayed either as the expression of original sin, as the medium of evil, of forbidden pleasure and of sin, or as a mother who—through childbearing—accepts the superiority of man and whose primary concern is to care for the family. In particular, the woman teacher is usually presented as an unmarried woman, with clothes that are out of fashion, thick glasses, and hair worn in a bun (e.g., in the popular TV series "*Savvatogennimenes*" (Born on a Saturday) and "*Chara's Café*"). Also, she usually has suffered some kind of nervous breakdown, and is in love with someone who does not love her back. She is constructed as excessive and sometimes even as monstrous. So, as Leathwood (2003) comments in relation to the representation of women in two UK government videos that were designed to encourage applications to universities in Britain and in magazine images:

> The visual representations [of women], whilst open to multiple and alternative readings, are anchored through reference to culturally specific symbolic systems of meaning which, I suggest, re/inscribe dominant constructions of femininity and masculinity. (p. 9)

So, I argue that the influence of the media can have the opposite result to what is suggested by Jenny as traditional dominant constructions of "femininity" and "masculinity" are being presented instead of being challenged. Rarely are the issues concerning intellectual relations between men and women, career development and possibilities for young women that contradict traditional gender norms and so on, ever presented (with the exception of the TV series "Chara's Café" which is described below). Within this ideological framework, viewers are encouraged to identify with the models provided. So, the Greek woman, as presented in much of the media, should be a sweet, preferably blond "doll," who attributes her popularity to the social position of her husband or partner and her heterosexuality.

So the media tends to present a homogenized construction of women as relatively powerless, as being subordinate to men and as having to perform their femininity in order to succeed or even to be accepted. So, there is still some way to go to raise children in a way that challenges traditional "masculine" and "feminine" identities.

Jenny, the woman head teacher mentioned above, believes that this could be done through programs on television that depict situations in women's lives in other countries. But as I argued above, the way gender is constructed in several key media programs that are very popular on Greek television, does not often contest the dominant constructions of "femininity." Sometimes they confirm, or reformulate dominant constructions, although there are examples where they contest them.

Children are exposed to gender stereotypes through TV programs, too. They frequently watch soap operas, where women are often constructed as subordinate, passive, and indecisive (Bassow 1992, Witt 2000). Also, in commercials for children's programs, boys are shown more frequently in active roles, while girls are constructed as more passive and as drawing on caring roles (e.g., they are mothers) (Witt 2000, Zimianitis 2007, Botaiti 2010). So, children are getting used to these traditional constructions, may consider them as natural, and may draw upon them in their adult life.

At the same time, it should be noted that in both Greek and international television programs, viewers are not merely passive recipients of the images. I believe that they possess agency to critically examine and contest the legitimacy of such representations. Whereas some women may attempt to emulate these images, others will reject and resist them. In either case, media images may serve as cultural templates (as Jenny and Lakis indicated) for idealized notions of "masculinity" and "femininity." As a result, I suggest, media programs should not be dismissed as mere entertainment, but viewed as possible disseminators of culturally idealized gendered images which need critical scrutiny and analysis.

No Change

Out of the forty head teachers and teachers who participated in my research, two (one woman head teacher and one man teacher) indicated that they did not want any change in the representation of women in educational leadership and one man head teacher indicated that change was not possible.

Rena, one of the respondents who did not want change, was a head teacher at the time of the interview and, as I was informed, resigned from the post a little bit later. Drawing on traditional gender constructions, she said that she did not have any help from her husband because as she indicated "he is a man." So, she was responsible for all the domestic work and family care was her responsibilities. Rena said:

> Does it have to be changed? Why should it change? Why should percentages increase? Families will fall apart. It's better to have good families and small female representation, than many women head teachers and broken families. The truth is that a family is kept by the wife. The husband is just a decorative element and sometimes a burden. (Rena, WHT, 30–39)

Another participant opposed to change was Vassilis, a man teacher who was very pleased because he had a man head teacher at his school (he said "Thank God, a man [is my head teacher]"). He argued against the need for change:

> Why should the situation change? If it changes, this would mean that the woman will have to abandon another role of hers, so something will go wrong. It's better not to have so many women head teachers and more happy families! (Vassilis, MT, 30–39)

They both argue that increasing the participation of women in educational leadership will lead to families breaking down. Perhaps the most important point here is that women are seen as responsible for holding a family together ("The truth is a family is being kept by the wife. The husband is a decorative element and sometimes a burden," said Rena). So, Rena offers a traditional construction of "femininity" and women as being in charge of caring for their family and home, but as not being able to draw on the identity of a school leader because of these other responsibilities, despite the fact that at the time of the interview she was a head teacher herself, who said she was thinking of resigning from the post because of the amount of work (and subsequently did so). Vassilis, similarly, claims that women have to juggle with a number of identities and roles with that of the mother as the most important one. In addition, Rena appears as diminishing the man and dismissing him as a "decorative element." She can be seen as gaining power from her role as a mother, as Reay and Ball (2000) have argued. Also, in her talk the shifting nature of power (Bradley 1999) is indicated, as she appears as powerful in the family. Both Rena and Vassilis appear to draw on more fixed constructions of gender, where women are constructed in a traditional way that should remain stable.

Another man head teacher said that:

> The situation will never change. Women will never be equal to men. They can't reach men. (Giorgos, MHT, 50–59)

His response in conjunction with earlier responses where he indicated that men are the ones who are most appropriate for the post of the head teacher ("[They will select] the man [applicant]! He can be successful in the post not the woman," "A man always knows how to manage things, a woman will never learn") can be seen as drawing on a construction of "femininity" as necessarily and inevitably subordinate to "masculinity" and on fixed and essentialized constructions of gender (Papanastasiou 2014). He assumes that "men are made to manage" (Reay and Ball 2000) and women are not management material. So, women may be viewed as being trapped in gender constructions that have been ascribed as "feminine" and do not include leadership, and men in "masculine" superior roles. He may be assumed as drawing on hegemonic masculinity (Connell 1995) that operates through the subordination of "femininity" guaranteeing the dominant position of men ("Women will never be equal to men").

The number of the participants opposed to change may be small, as there are only three who hold such views. But these responses raise the question of what is happening more widely in the Greek society and the extent to which Greeks are resistant to change.

Conclusion

Women face a number of barriers on their way to educational leadership, as has been discussed in a previous chapter (Chapter 3 *Constructions of Becoming a Head Teacher*). Both men and women, however, suggest that change can happen. The majority of the participants in this study, both women and men, indicate that it is women's responsibility to implement change. They tend to believe that women themselves are the reason for their low numbers in headship.

As far as the state is concerned, some respondents in my research suggested that a number of changes should be implemented in order to encourage women to apply for headship. These changes include quota systems for women, provision for more childcare, and changes to the head teacher's workload. They do not seem to challenge the notion that childcare is women's responsibility and that balancing a family with a career is a difficult issue for women.

Also, some other respondents indicated that wider social change is probably necessary. They argue that the stereotype of women as linked to family and home should be overcome. Some offer the view that the media can play a part in this, because they show programs with various constructions of "femininity" and "masculinity." But I suggest that care should be taken not to passively accept these constructions, but to critically view these images of "femininity" and "masculinity."

Finally, there were participants who claimed that there should be no change or that change could not be achieved. They draw on traditional constructions of "femininity" and "masculinity," where women are holding a family together, and they assumed that women are subordinate to men.

Overall, it could be argued that most of the participants seemed optimistic about change even though in the current economic climate change is difficult to happen.

6

Conclusions

In this volume, I set out to critically engage with contemporary discourses of gender and educational leadership in Greece and to explore the way men and women teachers and head teachers construct these discourses. Despite the corpus of international research and literature on women's unequal participation in educational leadership this has been a relatively unexplored area in the Greek setting. So, this critical engagement attempted to illuminate women's and men's experiences of progressing to and holding primary school headship posts in Greece, examining whether and to what extent these experiences are gendered, understanding the reasons behind women's disproportionate representation in leadership and exploring the participants' constructions about the future and the changes potentially needed in order to improve the situation in Greece.

Chapter 1 (*Introduction*) sets the theoretical framework which is feminist social constructionism. I particularly drew on the work of Burr (2003) on the theory of social constructionism and Francis (2000 and 2010) on gender and social constructionism. In this chapter, I argue that gender identities and relations are constantly reaffirmed, challenged, and negotiated in relation to power.

My research is based on the assumption that there are multifaceted interconnected factors that may hinder women's advancement in educational leadership in Greek primary schools. It is also based on the view that there are no uniform "glass ceilings" between and within societies and cultures (Cubillo and Brown 2003). Within the sociologies of education, the figure of the seemingly universal leader is identified by Kanter (1977) as "male, heterosexual, white, glamorous and well-built" (p. 42). This means that those who deviate from this masculine norm are constructed through deficit discourses. Rather I argue in Chapter 2 (*Women in Educational Leadership: Global and National Context*) that educational leadership is a "situated concept" (Shah 2009, p. 128), which means that it is underpinned by beliefs, values, cultures, in a particular time and place. So, this research set out to identify the reasons for women's uneven participation in leadership in Greek primary education. In addition, it aims to illuminate the participants' gendered constructions of leadership and their gendered identities. Through comparing women and men leaders' experiences, the ultimate goal is not only to inform theory, policy, and practice about the "obstacles" women teachers may encounter when ascending the hierarchy in Greek primary education but also to provide recommendations for potential reforms in order to increase Greek women teachers' take up of primary school leadership.

The methodological strategy employed in this thesis is briefly discussed in Chapter 3 (*Constructions of Becoming a Head Teacher*), where I refer to the theoretical and methodological choices, and explain the philosophy and rationale underpinning them. With regard to the research paradigm and approach in particular, it was clear that in order to answer "why" and "how" research questions, a qualitative, in-depth, feminist, social constructionist approach was required. In alignment with the choice of approach and knowing that there are no "right" or "wrong" (Silverman 2009), "best" or "worst" (Bogdan and Biklen 2007), "perfect" or "useless" (Denscombe 2007) methods, only suitable and fitting ones, purposeful sampling, semi-structured in-depth interviewing and a general inductive approach to the analysis emerged as the most appropriate means for generating and analyzing the data.

The rest of Chapter 3 and the subsequent chapters composing this volume (Chapter 4 *Constructions of Being a Head Teacher* and Chapter 5 *Constructing Change*) are informed by a corpus of interviews I have conducted with men and women head teachers and teachers on gender and educational leadership in Greece.

The study generated rich data that presented the complexity of factors underpinning women's and men's access to and experiences of Greek primary school headship. The findings are briefly summarized below.

One of the key elements that emerges from the experiences of the research participants is that despite some accounts of positive constructions regarding women in leadership positions within (a) the school context (teacher colleagues, deputy heads, other principals, students), (b) the community context (parents and other professionals), and (c) the family context (family and relatives), the findings of this project appear to resonate with research elsewhere, that is, that, once in post, women frequently receive more intense criticism regarding their leading capabilities than their men counterparts (Hall 1996, Reay and Ball 2000, Coleman 2002, Reynolds 2008, Celikten 2009). Having to prove their worth before they can be accepted as effective leaders in combination with excessive identity conflict while in headship has led some women heads and some women teachers to have second thoughts about being head teachers.

My data show that the majority of the participants believe that educational leadership opportunities are highly gendered, as it appears that leadership positions are usually occupied by men, in the selection procedures men are preferred over women and old boys' networks still exist. These findings are consistent with previous research (Coleman 2002, 2007, Eagly and Carli 2003, Shakeshaft et al. 2010) that has shown that traditional gender identities are still constructed. Also, my research shows that even though universalizing "masculine" and "feminine" leadership approaches based on Western gendered identities excludes the experiences of other groups who may not be "womanly" or "manly" enough, according to traditional stereotypes, educational leadership approaches are more nuanced, ambiguous, and fluid.

As I have shown in Chapter 3 (*Constructions of Becoming a Head Teacher*) planning and being positive about the headship career and ensuring that you have a mentor are some of the strategies that were proposed as necessary for obtaining a head teacher's post. However, without planning their career, some of the head teachers (men and women) have "drifted" into their roles often seeming unaware of their own abilities. Certain people appear to have qualities that are recognized by others and so they are encouraged to apply for a leadership post. However, others, both men and women, who have achieved headship seem to lack confidence. What is interesting is that men in particular often have the confidence to apply for a job, even if they do not have all the necessary qualifications.

Covert discrimination during the interview for promotion was a theme related to career progression. The findings suggest that traditional assumptions underpinning the decisions of the interview panel along with informal discrimination favoring men for headship in primary education have been partly responsible for women's unequal representation in this sector. Even though this is illegal, research from the UK (i.e., Coleman 2002, 2010, 2011) indicates that this is a practice not limited to Greece.

Also, in the same chapter (*Constructions of Becoming a Head Teacher*) it is argued that despite the generally positive and supportive stance of colleagues, head teachers and family to participants' advancement, some incidences of anachronistic attitudes toward them, which were related to gender, are reported. It appears that the traditional construction of women's incongruity with leadership and men's suitability for it often still exists—particularly among men—and frequently underlies their prejudiced attitude toward women aspirants. Although some of the participating women had managed to become heads, a proportion of the participants said that these influences were important in their decision to reject leadership.

Although a woman may be determined and aspire for leadership posts, reconciling career and family is another matter. Many women heads choose not to have children or proceed with their career advancement after their children are older and more independent. The lack of adequate child support systems from the state is evident along with the constructions that childcare is a woman's job. As I show in Chapter 4 (*Constructions of Being a Head Teacher*) the family and personal lives of women head teachers appear to necessitate career negotiations and compromises. In order to obtain a balance in their career and life, women often say that they appear to have to make some hard decisions, while men head teachers do not seem to have to deal with the same problem, as their wives tend to take responsibility for undertaking most of the domestic and caring tasks. As Reay and Ball (2000) argue, women have to juggle heavy responsibilities and it is the women who have to sacrifice their career aspirations.

The analysis in this chapter also shows that it appears that being a head teacher is not simple for either men or women. The way head teachers who participated in my research approach leadership does not seem to be stable nor dependent on traditional gender constructions. Rather, both men and women heads seemed to draw on a range of available approaches to leadership that weren't traditionally gendered. Leadership is seen to involve negotiations of identities, as Francis (2010) and Reay and Ball (2000) also argue.

Chapter 5 (*Constructing Change*) explores provides very interesting points. The participants construct several levels of changes as necessary to improve women's participation in educational leadership. A first level of change is individual change (i.e., that women are the ones who need to change) that is supported by twenty-two out of the forty participants (fifteen women and seven men). On a second level, change is constructed as state/policy change by seven participants (four women and three men) who suggest a number of changes that could be implemented in order to help raise the participation of women in educational leadership. On the next level of change, several participants (fourteen, ten women and four men) claim that a wider social change is necessary in the form of challenging the stereotype of women as linked to family, care, and home. In conjunction with this, a woman participant offers the view that the way the media constructs and reflects "femininity" and "masculinity" can play a part in what the future holds for women. Finally, some participants drawing on dominant constructions of "femininity" and "masculinity" argue that women hold a family together and men are breadwinners and claim that no change is needed. Another participant is also against change and asserts that it is not going to happen, by drawing on constructions of women as weak, incapable of leading and as subordinate to men. As a whole, the research participants seem to be quite optimistic about change, even though currently in Greece change is difficult to happen because of the recession.

Even if limited in scope (forty participants), I argue that this research can offer a valuable substantial, practical, methodological, and theoretical contribution. It has generated and recorded the accounts of women's and men's experiences of ascending the hierarchy and working as leaders and teachers in the Greek primary sector. Moreover, I seek to understand and conceptualize women's unequal participation in Greek primary school headship. As Reay and Ball (2000) have argued, this research demonstrates that there are no particularly distinct ways in which women and men approach educational leadership. Finally, I have given an account of the things that could be done in order to increase women's participation in leadership.

Extending the contribution of this book to the international setting, I argue that, since this is one of the few pieces of local research on the topic, it provides the almost unheard Greek perspective on the issue, with all the commonalities and differences that this brings to the existing corpus of literature in the field. This research, therefore, makes a valuable contribution to research and knowledge on women's participation in educational leadership, representing the case of Greece. By taking place in the Greek context, the study aims at responding to Oplatka's (2006) plea for more research investigating women leaders' experiences. Moreover, on the basis that there is limited qualitative research about Greek women in educational leadership, this research adds to the neglected area of women's uneven participating in primary school headship.

In an era of recession, change and the questioning of the old reality is needed. I believe it is time for change in Greece in many areas, including gender equality, because as Dougherty (2009) argues "the fact that women are underrepresented, whatever its cause, is unjust" (p. xi).

Notes

Chapter 1

1 The ancient Greek "races" or "tribes" were the Pelasgians, the Acheans, the Aeolians, the Ionians, the Dorians, the Macedonians, and the Tracians. There were more Greek races or tribes in ancient Greece, but these are the major ones that affected Greek history.
2 In Greek there is also the word "*fyllo*," as in pastry, which sounds the same but the spelling is different.

Chapter 2

1 The last available data at the time of writing were for 2014.
2 At the time of writing, the last available data were for 2020.

Chapter 3

1 In Greece, when the head teacher in a school retires or resigns from the post then the next one in the list of the potential candidates takes his/her post. But if the list is finished (i.e., all the candidates have become heads) then the most experienced teacher in the school can take up the post, but only until the end of the two-year incumbency of the former head teacher.

Chapter 4

1 As I indicated earlier (see Chapter 3 *Constructions of Becoming a Head Teacher*) having a moustache in Greece is considered as an indication of masculinity.

Chapter 5

1 These are private or public centers that offer creative activities for children aged five to twelve years old. Their services are provided on a daily basis from 2:00 p.m. to 10:00 p.m.

References

Abrahamsen, H. (2017), "Redesigning the Role of Deputy Heads in Norwegian Schools—Tensions between Control and Autonomy?," *International Journal of Leadership in Education*, 21 (3): 324–43.

Acker, S. (ed) (1989), *Teachers, Gender and Careers*, New York and London: The Falmer Press.

Addi-Raccah, A. (2006), "Women in the Israeli Educational System." In I. Oplatka and R. Herz-Razarowitz (eds), *Women Principals in a Multicultural Society: New Insights into Feminist Educational Leadership*, 49–69, Rotterdam: Sense Publishers.

Adler, N. (2005), "One World: Women Leading and Managing Worldwide." In D. Bilimoria and S. K. Piderit (eds), *Handbook on Women in Business and Management*, 330–55, Cheltenham: Edward Elgar Publishing.

Adler, S., J. Laney and M. Packer (1993), *Managing Women. Feminism and Power in Educational Management*, Buckingham: Open University Press.

Aftodioikisi.Gr (September 7, 2022), "Day Care Workers: More than 84,000 Children Are out of Day Care—26,000 Vouchers Are Indisposed," 23/3/2023, Available Online: Https://Www.Aftodioikisi.Gr/Paideia/Ergazomenoi-Kdap-84-000-Paidia-Ektos-Vrefonipiakon-Stathmon-26-000-Voucher-Den-Vrikan-Domi/. [In Greek]

Ainsworth, S., A. Knox and J. O' Flynn (2010), "'A Blind Lack of Progress': Management Rhetoric and Affirmative Action," *Gender, Work and Organization*, 17 (6): 658–78.

Akbaba-Altun, S. (2007), "Harmonious Texture of Cultural Values and Democracy: Patterns of Success." In S. Donahoo and R. C. Hunter (eds), *Teaching Leaders to Lead Teachers. Educational Administration in the Era of Constant Crisis. Advances in Educational Administration, Vol. 10*, 77–97, Oxford: Elsevier.

Alipranti-Maratou, L. and D. Tsakmakis (2008), *Old and New Professions: A Gender Aspect*, Athens: Kethi. [In Greek]

Al-Khalifa, E. (1989), "Management by Halves: Women Teachers and School Management." In H. De Lyon and F. Widdowson-Migniuolo (eds), *Women Teachers: Issues and Experience*, 83–96, Milton Keynes: Open University Press.

Al-Khalifa, E. and F. Migniuolo (1990), "Messages for Management: The Experiences of Women's Training," *Paper Presented at the Conference on Equal Advances in Education Management*, December 3–6, 1990, Vienna.

Allen, M. and T. Castleman (2001), "Fighting the Pipeline Fallacy." In A. Brooks and A. Mackinnon (eds), *Gender and the Restricted University: Changing Management and Culture in Higher Education*, 151–65, Buckingham: Open University Press.

Allred, P., G. M. Maxwell and L. Skrla (2017), "What Women Know: Perceptions of Seven Female Superintendents," *Advancing Women in Leadership*, 37: 1–11.

Alvesson, M. and Y. D. Billing (2009), *Understanding Gender and Organization*, London: Sage.
Andrikogiannopoulou, A. (2010), "Research on Teachers' Perceptions about the Presence of Both Sexes in Organization and Management in Primary Education: The Case of Achaia," MA Dissertation, University of Patra, Patra.
Arar, K. (2012), "Book Review: Women and Educational Leadership," *Educational Management Administration and Leadership*, 40 (5): 641–6.
Arar, K., T. Shapira, F. Azaisa and R. Herts-Lazarowitz (2013), *Arab Women in Management and Leadership: Stories from Israel*, New York: Palgrave Macmillan.
Archer, L. (2003), *Race, Masculinity and Schooling: Muslim Boys and Education*, Buckingham: Open University Press.
Archer, L. and B. Francis (2005), "'They Never Go off the Rails Like Other Ethnic Groups': Teachers' Constructions of British Chinese Pupils' Gender Identities and Approaches to Learning," *British Journal of Sociology of Education*, 26 (2): 165–82.
Athanassoula-Reppa, A. and M. Koutouzis (2002), "Women in Managerial Positions in Greek Education: Evidence of Inequality," *Education Policy Analysis Archives*, 10 (11), 19/3/2022, Available Online: Http://Epaa.Asu.Edu/Epaa/V10n11.Html/.
Avdela, E. (2009), "The Discovery of Precarious Work," *Avgi*, March 22. [In Greek]
Bacchi, C. (1996), *The Politics of Affirmative Action: "Women," Equality and Category Politics*, London: Sage.
Bagavos, C. (2001), "The Situation of Families in Greece," 11/7/2013, Available Online: Http://Www.Mmo.Gr/Pdf/Library/Greece/Gm_01_Greece_Bagavos.Pdf.
Bagavos, C. (2005), "Demographic Dimensions of Families and Households Changes in Greece: A First Approach." In L. Moussourou and M. Stratigaki (eds), *Issues of Family Policy*, 31–72, Athens: Gutenberg. [In Greek]
Bagilhole, B. and J. Goode (2001), "The Contradiction of the Myth of Individual Merit and the Reality of a Patriarchal Support System in Academic Careers: A Feminist Investigation," *European Journal of Women's Studies*, 8: 161–80.
Bakalbasi, E. and E. Fokas (2016), "Views of Primary and Secondary School Heads on the Selection System for Heads and Their Further Education on Leadership Matters," *Research on Education*, 2: 145–66. [In Greek]
Baker, P. S. (1991), "Metaphors of Mindful Engagement and a Vision of Better Schools," *Educational Leadership*, 48 (6): 32–5.
Bakhtin, M. (1984), *Rabelais and His World*, Bloomington: Indiana University Press.
Barlow, K. and B. L. Chapin (2010), "The Practice of Mothering: An Introduction," *Ethos*, 38 (4): 324–38.
Baron-Cohen, S. (2007), "Sex Differences in Mind: Keeping Science Distinct from Social Policy." In S. Seci and W. Williams (eds), *Why Aren't More Women in Science? Top Researchers Debate the Evidence*, 159–72, Washington, DC: American Psychological Association.
Bassow, S. A. (1992), *Gender Stereotypes and Roles*, Pacific Grove: Brooks/Cole Publishing Company.

Beaurain, G. and D. Masclet (2015), "Do Affirmative Action Policies Help Reducing Gender Discrimination and Enhance Efficiency? A New Experimental Evidence," *Paper Presented at the 6th Annual Meeting of the French Experimental Economics Association*, Paris, France, June 15–16, 2015.

Bechhofer, F. and L. Paterson (2000), *Principles of Research Design in the Social Sciences*, London: Routledge.

Bell, C. (1995), "If I Weren't Involved with Schools, I Might Be Radical. Gender Consciousness in Context." In D. Dunlap and P. Schmuck (eds), *Women Leading in Education*, 288–312, Albany: State University of New York Press.

Berman, J. (1982), "The Management Behavior of Female High School Principals," *Paper Presented at the Annual Meeting of the American Educational Research Association*, New York City, March 1982.

Bertrand, M. (2018), "Coarse Lecture—The Glass Ceiling," *Economica*, 85 (338): 205–31.

Beycioglu, K., N. Ozer and C. T. Ugurlu (2012), "Distributed Leadership and Organizational Trust: The Case of Elementary Schools," *Procedia-Social and Behavioral Sciences*, 46: 3316–19.

Biklen, S. K. and M. B. Brannigan (1981), *Women and Educational Leadership*, Lexington, DC: Heath & Company.

Birbili, M. (2000), "Translating from One Language to Another," *Social Research Update*, 32, 7/4/2021, Available Online: Http://Sru.Soc.Surrey.Ac.Uk/Sru31.Html.

Bjornberg, U. (1991), "Parenting in Transition: An Introduction and Summary." In U. Bjornberg (ed), *European Parents in the 1990s: Contradictions and Comparisons*, 1–44, New Jersey: Transaction Publishers.

Blackmore, J. (1989), "Educational Leadership: A Feminist Critique and Reconstruction." In J. Smyth (ed), *Critical Perspectives on Educational Leadership*, 93–130, London: The Falmer Press.

Blackmore, J. (1993), "'In the Shadow of Men': The Historical Construction of Administration as a 'Masculinist' Enterprise." In J. Blackmore and J. Kenway (eds), *Gender Matters in Educational Administration and Policy: A Feminist Introduction*, 27–48, London: Falmer.

Blackmore, J. (1999), *Troubling Women: Feminism, Leadership and Educational Change*, Buckingham: Open University Press.

Blackmore, J. and J. Sachs (2007), *Performing and Reforming Leaders: Gender, Educational Restructuring, and Organizational Change*, Albany, NY: State University of New York Press.

Blackmore, J., P. Thomson and K. Barty (2006), "Principal Selection: Homosociability, the Search for Security and the Production of Normalised Principal Identities," *Educational Management Administration and Leadership*, 34 (3): 297–317.

Blasé, J. and G. Anderson (1995), *The Micropolitics of Educational Leadership: From Control to Empowerment*, London: Cassell.

Blasé, J. R. and J. Blasé (1998), *Handbook of Instructional Leadership: How Effective Principals Promote Teaching and Learning*, Thousand Oaks, Ca: Corwin.

Blinkenstaff, J. (2005), "Women and Science Careers: Leaky Pipeline or Gender Filter?," *Gender and Education*, 17 (4): 369–86.

Blount, J. M. (2003), "Homosexuality and the School Superintendents: A Brief History," *Journal of School Leadership*, 13 (1): 7–26.

Boatwright, K., M. Gilbert, L. Forrest and K. Ketzenberger (1996), "Impact of Identity Development upon Career Trajectory: Listening to the Voices of Lesbian Women," *Journal of Vocational Behavior*, 48: 210–28.

Bodalina, K. N. and R. Mestry (2022), "A Case Study of the Experiences of Women Leaders in Senior Leadership Positions in the Education District Offices," *Educational Management Administration and Leadership*, 50 (3): 452–68.

Bogacki, D. F., D. J. Armstrong and K. J. Weiss (2005), "Reading School Violence: The Corporal Punishment Scale and Its Relationship to Authoritarianism," *The Journal of Psychiatry and Law*, 33 (3): 367–86.

Bogdan, R. and Biklen, S. (2007), *Qualitative Research for Education: An Introduction to Theories and Method*, Boston: Pearson international edition.

Botaiti, A. (2010), "Gender Representations during Tv Advertisements at Morning- 'Kids' Zone," MA Dissertation, Aristotel University of Thessaloniki, Thessaloniki. [In Greek]

Bradbury, L. and H. M. Gunter (2006), "Dialogic Identities: The Experiences of Women Who Are Headteachers and Mothers in English Primary Schools," *School Leadership and Management*, 26 (5): 489–504.

Bradley, H. (1996), *Fractured Identities*, Cambridge: Polity.

Bradley, H. (1999), *Gender and Power in the Workplace: Analysing the Impact of Economic Change*, Basingstoke: Macmillan.

Brezinski, M. (2011), *Knowing Your Value: Women, Money, and Getting What You're Worth*, New York: Weinstein Books.

Brinia, V. (2012), "Men vs Women; Educational Leadership in Primary Schools in Greece: An Empirical Study," *International Journal of Educational Management*, 6 (2): 175–91.

Brown, M. and S. Ralph (1996), "Barriers to Women Managers' Advancement in Education in Uganda," *International Journal of Educational Management*, 10 (6): 18–23.

Brunner, C. C. and M. Grogan (2007), *Women Leading School Systems: Uncommon Roads to Fulfillment*, Lanham, Md: Rowman & Littlefield.

Bryman, A. and E. Bell (2007), *Business Research Methods*, Oxford: Oxford University Press.

Bryson, V. (2003), *Feminist Political Theory: An Introduction*, Basingstoke: Palgrave Macmillan.

Burgess, R. G. (1984), *In the Field. An Introduction to Field Research*, London: George Allen and Unwin.

Burman, E. (1994), *Deconstructing Developmental Psychology*, East Sussex: Routledge.

Burn, E. (2005), "'Working with the Ankle Biters': Constructing the Male Early Years Teacher." In *CTRIP Seminar Series*, London: King's College.

Burr, V. (2003), *The Social Constructionism*, Hove: Routledge.
Bush, T. (1998), "The National Professional Qualification for Headship: The Key to Effective School Leadership?," *School Leadership and Management*, 18 (3): 321–34.
Bush, T. (2011), *Theories of Educational Leadership and Management*, London: Sage.
Businessdaily.Gr (June 25, 2020), The Espa Fiasco, 14/4/2023, Available Online: Https://Www.Businessdaily.Gr/Oikonomia/20784_Fiasko-Me-Espa-Limnazan-Anaxiopoiita-Kondylia-135-Dis. [In Greek]
Butler, J. (1990), *Gender Trouble*, London: Routledge.
Cambell, M. and G. D. Cambell-Whatley (2020), "Strategies and Barriers: Career Advancement for Women Administrators," *Journal of Applied Education and Policy Research*, 5 (1): 1–26.
Cammack, J. C. and D. K. Phillips (2002), "Discourses and Subjectivities of the Gendered Teacher," *Gender and Education*, 14 (2): 123–33.
Cassia, S. P. and C. Bada (2006), *The Making of the Modern Greek Family: Marriage and Exchange in Nineteenth Century Athens*, Cambridge: Cambridge University Press.
Celikten, M. (2009), "Portraying Women Administrators: Turkish Cases." In H. Sobehart (ed), *Women Leading Education across the Continents: Sharing the Spirit, Fanning the Flame,* 168–74, Plymouth: Rowman and Littlefield Education.
Chard, R. (2013), "A Study of Current Male Educational Leaders, Their Careers and Next Steps," *Management in Education*, 27 (4): 170–5.
Charlebois, J. (2011), *Gender and the Construction of Hegemonic and Oppositional Femininities*, Plymouth: Lexington Publishers.
Charlebois, J. (2012), *The Construction of Masculinities and Femininities in Beverly Hills, 90210*, New York: University Press of America.
Charlesworth, K. (1997), *A Question of Balance? A Survey of Managers' Changing Professional and Personal Roles*, London: The Institute of Management.
Chewning, L. V. and M. L. Doerfel (2013), "Integrating Crisis into the Organizational Lifecycle through Transitional Networks," *International Journal of Humanities and Social Science*, 3 (21): 39–52.
Christensen, A. and J. E. Larsen (2008), "Gender, Class and Family: Men and Gender Equality in a Danish Context," *Social Politics: International Studies in Gender, State and Society*, 15 (1): 53–78.
Christianopoulos, D. (2004), *The Rembetes of the World*, Thessaloniki: Ianos. [In Greek]
Christidou, V. and A. Kouvatas (2013), "Visual Self-Images of Statistics and Science in Greece," *Public Understanding of Science*, 22 (1): 91–109.
Christofides, L. N., A. Polycarpou and K. Vrachimis (2013), "Gender Wage Gaps, 'Sticky Floors' and 'Glass Ceilings' in Europe," *Labour Economics*, 21: 86–102.
Clarke, S. and J. Popay (1998), "I'm Just a Bloke Who's Had Kids: Men and Women on Parenthood," In J. Popay, J. Hearn and J. Edwards (eds), *Men, Gender Divisions and Welfare*, 196–230, London: Routledge.
Cleveland, J. N., M. Stockdale and K. R. Murphy (2000), *Women and Men in Organizations: Sex and Gender Issues at Work*, Mahwah, NJ: Erlbaum.

Cocciara, F. K., E. Kwesiga, M. P. Bell and Y. Baruch (2010), "Influences on Perceived Career Success: Findings from US Graduate Business Degree Alumni," *Career Development International*, 5 (1): 39–58.

Coffey, A. and S. Delamont (2000), *Feminism and the Classroom Teacher*, London: Routledge Falmer.

Coleman, M. (1996), "The Management Style of Female Headteachers," *Educational Management and Administration*, 24 (2): 163–74.

Coleman, M. (2001), "Achievement against the Odds: The Female Secondary Headteachers in England and Wales," *School Leadership and Management*, 21 (1): 75–100.

Coleman, M. (2002), *Women as Headteachers: Striking the Balance*, Stoke-on-Trent: Tretham Books Limited.

Coleman, M. (2005a), *Gender and Headship in the 21st Century*, Nottingham: Ncsl, 13/9/2022, Available Online: Https://Dera.Ioe.Ac.Uk/7260/1/Download%3fid%3d17191%26filename%3dgender-And-Headship-In-The-21st-Century.Pdf On.

Coleman, M. (2005b), "Theories and Practice of Leadership: An Introduction." In M. Coleman and P. Early (eds), *Leadership and Management in Education: Cultures, Change and Context*, 6–25, Oxford: Oxford University Press.

Coleman, M. (2007), "Gender and Educational Leadership in England: A Comparison of Secondary Head Teachers' Views Overtime," *School Leadership and Management*, 27 (4): 383–99.

Coleman, M. (2009), "Women in Educational Leadership in England." In H. Sobehart (ed), *Women Leading Education across the Continents: Sharing the Spirit, Fanning the Flame*, 13–20, Plymouth: Rowman and Littlefield Education.

Coleman, M. (2010), "Women-Only (Homophilous) Networks Supporting Women Leaders in Education," *Journal of Educational Administration*, 48 (6): 769–81.

Coleman, M. (2011), *Women at the Top: Challenges, Choices and Change*, Basingstoke: Palgrave Macmillan.

Coleman, M. (2022), "Gender and Career: Constraints and Facilitators for Women in Accessing Educational Leadership in the UK." In V. Showunmi, P. Moorosi, C. Shakeshaft and I. Oplatka (eds),*The Bloomsbury Handbook of Gender and Educational Leadership and Management*, 219–29, London: Bloomsbury Academic.

Coleman, M. and T. Fitzgerald (2008), "Gender and Leadership Development." In G. Crow, J. Lumby and P. Pashiardis (eds), *International Handbook on the Preparation and Development of School Leader*, 119–53, Thousand Oaks: Sage.

Collinson, D. and J. Hearn (2000), "Critical Research Studies on Men, Masculinities and Managements." In M. Davidson and R. Burke (eds), *Women in Management: Current Research Issues*, Vol. II, 363–78, London: Sage.

Collinson, D. and J. Hearn (eds) (2003), *Men, Masculinities and Management*, London: Sage.

Commission for Equality and Human Rights (2007), *Gender Equality Duty: Code of Practice for England and Wales*, 20/3/2015, Available Online: Http://Www2.Le.Ac.Uk/Offices/Equalities-Unit/Documents/Gender%20equalit%20duty%20cop.Pdf.

Connell, R. W. (1987), *Gender and Power: Society, the Person and Sexual Politics*, Sydney: Allen & Unwin.

Connell, R. W. (1995), *Masculinities*, Berkley: University of California Press.

Connell, R. W. (2000), *The Man and the Boys*, Cambridge: Polity Press.

Connell, R. W. (2002), *Gender*, Cambridge: Polity Press.

Connell, R. W. and J. W. Messerschmidt (2005), "Hegemonic Masculinity: Rethinking the Concept," *Gender and Society*, 19: 829–59.

Connolly, P. (1998), *Racism, Gender Identities and Young Children*, London: Routledge.

Cook, S. (2020), "Put Your Big Girl Knickers on! The Experiences of Two Female Leaders in New Zealand Primary Schools Turning Schools Around," K. Fuller, P. Moorosi, V. Showunmi and S. J. Shah (eds), *Ways of Seeing Women's Leadership in Education: Stories, Images, Metaphors, Methods and Theories. Frontiers in Education*, 5 (77): 36–54.

Court, M. (1994), "Removing Macho Management: Lessons from the Field of Education," *Gender, Work and Organization*, 1 (1): 33–49.

Cox, E. (1996), *Leading Women: Tactics for Making the Difference*, Sydney: Random House.

Cranston, N., C. Tromans and M. Reugebrink (2004), "Forgotten Leaders: What Do We Know about the Deputy Principalship in Secondary School?," *International Journal of Leadership in Education: Theory and Practice*, 7 (2): 225–42.

Crenshaw, K. C. (1991), "Mapping the Margins: Intersectionality, Identity Politics and Violence against Women of Color," *Stanford Law Review*, 43: 1241–99.

Crosby, F., A. Iyer and S. Sincharien (2006), "Understanding Affirmative Action," *Annual Review of Psychology*, 57: 585–611.

Cubillo, L. and M. Brown (2003), "Women into Leadership and Management: International Differences?," *Journal of Educational Administration*, 41 (3): 278–91.

D'Agostino, M., H. Levine, M. Sabharwal and A. C. Johnson-Manning (2022), "Organizational Practices and Second-Generation Gender Bias: A Qualitative Inquiry into the Career Progression of U.S. State-Level Managers," *The American Review of Public Administration*, 52 (5): 335–50.

Dana, J. A. and D. M. Bourisaw (2006), *Women in the Superintendency: Discarded Leadership*, Lanham: Rowman and Littlefield Education.

Daouli, J., M. Demoussis and N. Giannakopoulos (2004), "Child Care and Costs on Employment Decisions for Greek Women," *Behavioral and Experimental Economics*, N.Pag.

Daraki, E. (2007), *Educational Leadership and Gender*, Athens: Epikentro. [In Greek]

De Haan, M. and E. Elbers (2004), "Minority Status and Culture: Local Constructions of Diversity in a Classroom in the Netherlands," *Intercultural Education*, 15 (4): 441–53.

Dean, J. (2002), *Managing the Primary School*, New York: Routledge.

Delamont, S. (2001), *Changing Women, Unchanged Men? Sociological Perspectives on Gender in a Post-Industrial Society*, Buckingham: Open University Press.

Deligianni, V. and S. Ziogou (1993), *Education and Gender*, Thessaloniki: Vanias. [In Greek]

Denscombe, M. (2007), *The Good Research Guide: For Small-Scale Social Research projects*, Berkshire: Open University Press.

Denzin, N. K. and Y. S. Lincoln (eds) (2005), *The Sage Handbook of Qualitative Research*, Thousand Oaks: Sage.

Dey, I. (1993), *Creating Categories. Qualitative Data Analysis: A User Friendly Guide*, London: Routledge.

Dfes (2007), *Independent Study into School Leadership: Main Report*, 18/12/3013, Available Online: Http://Dera.Ioe.Ac.Uk/6366/1/Rr818a.Pdf.

Dimitrakopoulos, I. (2004), *Analytical Report of Education in Greece (2003)*, Athens: National Contact Point for Greece-Antigone, Information and Documentation Centre. [In Greek]

Dorwart, L. (2020), "Perspectives: Defining Sexual Harassment—For Myself." In M. D. Smith (ed), *Sexual Harassment: A Reference Handbook*, 125–8, Santa Barbara: Abc Clio.

Dougherty, C. J. (2009), "Foreword: For the Sake of Social Justice: Opening Remarks." In Shebehart, E. (ed), *Women Leading Education across the Continents: Sharing the Spirit, Fanning the Flame*, Xi–Xii, Lanham, Md: Rowman and Littlefield.

Drakopoulos, S. and I. Theodossiou (2006), *Gender Segregation at Work: A Theoretical and Literature Review*, 8/8/2022, Available Online: Http://Users.Uoa.Gr/~Drakop/Articles/Equeviewa.Doc. [In Greek]

Drever, E. (1997), *Using Semi-Structured Interviews in Small-Scale Research: A Teacher's Guide*, Glasgow: Scottish Council of Research in Education.

Drew, E. and E. Murtagh (2005), "Beyond the Glass Ceiling: Addressing Gender Imbalance in Corporate Leadership," *Paper Presented at the 4th European Conference on Research Methodology for Business and Management Studios*, April 21–22, 2005, University Paris-Dauphine, Paris, France.

Drosatos, D. B. (2020), *The Role of Gender in the Organization and Management of Primary Schools*, Athens: Attikos. [In Greek]

Du, Y., J. Nordell and K. Joseph (2022), "Insidious Nonetheless: How Small Effects and Hierarchical Norms Create and Maintain Gender Disparities in Organizations," *Scopus: A Sociological Research for a Dynamic World*, 8: 1–12.

Dustman, C. and T. Frattini (2013), "Immigration: The European Experience." In D. Card and S. Raphael (eds), *Immigration, Poverty, and Socioeconomic Inequality*, 423–56, New York: Russell Sage.

Duxbury, L. and C. Higgins (2013), *The 2011/12 National Study on Balancing Work, Life and Caregiving in Canada: The Situation for Alberta Teachers*, Edmonton, Alta: Ata.

DYPA (2022), *Unemployment Statistical Data: November 2022*, 20/12/2022, Available Online: Https://Www.Dypa.Gov.Gr/Statistika. [In Greek]

Eagly, A. and L. L. Carli (2003), "The Female Leadership Advantage: An Evaluation of Evidence," *The Leadership Quarterly*, 14: 807–34.

Eagly, A. H. and L. L. Carli (2007), *Through the Labyrinth: The Truth about How Women Become Leaders*, Cambridge, Ma: Harvard Business School Press.

Earl, L. and S. Katz (2006), *Leading Schools in a Data-Rich World*, Thousand Oaks: Corwin Press.

Edupame (2010), *Sanctions for Pregnant Women and for Mothers Are Increased*, 8/10/2021, Available Online: Http://Www.Edupame.Gr/Node/673. [In Greek]

Efimerida, Syntakton (September 1, 2022), *More than 84,000 Children out of Day Care, but D. Micailidou Is Cheering*, 23/3/2023, Available Online: Https://Www.Efsyn.Gr/Ellada/Koinonia/357584_Pano-Apo-84000-Paidia-Ektos-Paidikon-Stathmon-Alla-I-D-Mihailidoy. [In Greek]

Eleftherotypia (July 18, 2013), *Forthcoming....Pregnant Women Are Dismissed*. [In Greek]

Eliot, L. (2009), *Pink Brain, Blue Brain: How Small Differences Grow into Troublesome Gaps—And What We Can Do about It*, New York: Houghton Mifflin Harcourt.

Elson, D. and R. Pearson (1984), "The Subordination of Women and the Internationalization of Factory Production." In K. Young, C. Wolkowitz and R. Mccullagh (eds), *Of Marriage and the Market: Women's Subordination Internationally and Its Lessons*, 18–40, London: Routledge and Kegan Paul.

Endo, H., P. C. Reece-Miller and N. Santavicca (2010), "Surviving in the Trenches: A Narrative Inquiry into Queer Teachers' Experiences and Identity," *Teaching and Teacher Education*, 26 (4): 1023–30.

Eurobarometer (2007), *Discrimination in EU—Summary 2007. Special Eurobarometer 263/Wave 65.4—Tns Opinion and Social, European Commission*, 18/12/2013, Available Online: Http://Ec.Europa.Eu/Public_Opinion/Archives/Ebs/Ebs_263_Sum_En.Pdf.

European Commission (2019), *Report on Equality between Women and Men in the EU*, Publications Office, 25/3/2023, Available Online: Https://Data.Europa.Eu/Doi/10.2838/395144.

European Social Survey (2013), *Exploring Public Attitudes, Informing Public Policy: Selected Findings from the First Five Rounds*, 18/12/2013, Available Online: Http://Www.Europeansocialsurvey.Org/Docs/Findings/Ess1_5_Select_Findings.Pdf.

European Women's Lobby (2012), *The Price of Austerity—The Impact on Women's Rights and Gender Equality in Europe*, 8/8/2014, Available Online: Http://Www.Womenlobby.Org/Spip.Php?Action=Acceder_Document&Arg=2053&Cle=71883f01c9eac4e73e839bb512c87e564b5dc735&File=Pdf%2fthe_Price_Of_Austerity_-_Web_Edition.Pdf.

Eurostat (2020), *Gender Pay Gap Statistics—Statistics Explained*, 23/4/2023, Available Online: Https://Ec.Europa.Eu/Eurostat/Statisticsexplained/Index.Php/Gender_Pay_Gap_Statistics On.

Eurostat (2022a), *Employment Rate by Sex*, 4/1/2023, Available Online: Https://Ec.Europa.Eu/Eurostat/Databrowser/View/Tesem010/Default/Table?Lang=En().

Eurostat (2022b), *Pupils Enrolled in Early Childhood Education by Sex, Type of Institution and Intensity of Participation*, 16/4/2023, Available Online: Https://Ec.Europa.Eu/Eurostat/Databrowser/View/Educ_Uoe_Enrp01/Default/Table?Lang=En.

Eurydice (2019), *Teachers' and School Heads' Salaries and Allowances in Europe-2018/19*, Luxemburg: Publication Office of the European Union.

Eveline, J. (2004), *Ivory Basement Leadership. Power and Invisibility in the Changing University*, Perth: Uwa Press.

Evetts, J. (1994), *Becoming a Secondary Headteacher*, London: Cassell.

Fagan, C. and B. J. Burchell (2002), *Gender, Jobs and Working Conditions in the European Union*, Dublin: European Foundation for the Improvement of Living.

Fagan, C. and M. C. Gonzalez Menendez (2012), "Conclusions." In C. Fagan, M. C. Gonzalez and S. Anson (eds), *Women on Corporate Boards and in Top Management: European Trends and Policy*, 245–58, Basingstoke: Palgrave Macmillan.

Fagenson, E. A. (1994), "Women's Work Orientation: Something Old, Something New," *Group and Organization Studies*, 11 (1): 75–100.

Fennell, H. A. (1999), "Power in the Principalship: Four Women's Experiences," *Journal of Educational Administration*, 37: 23–49.

Ferfolja, T. (2007), "Teacher Negotiations of Sexual Subjectivities," *Gender and Education*, 19 (5): 569–86.

Ferguson, H. (2001), "Men and Masculinities in Late-Modern Ireland." In B. Pease and K. Pringle (eds), *A Man's World: Changing Men's Practices in a Globalised World*, 118–34, London: Zed Books.

Ferguson, K. (1984), *The Feminist Case against Bureaucracy*, Philadelphia: Temple University Press.

Ferrant, G., L. M. Pesando and K. Nowacka (2014), *Unpaid Care Work: The Missing Link in the Analysis of Gender Gaps in Labour Outcomes*, Oecd, Development Centre, 20/12/2022, Available Online: Https://Www.Oecd.Org/Dev/Development-Gender/Unpaid_Care_Work.Pdf.

Fine, C. (2010), *Delusions of Gender: How Our Minds, Society and Neurosexism Create Difference*, New York: WW Norton.

Flores, A. and C. M. Rodriguez (2006), "University Faculty Attitudes on Affirmative Action Principles towards Faculty and Students," *Equity and Excellence in Education*, 39: 303–12.

Fontana, A. (2003), *Psychology, Religion and Spirituality*, Leicester: Bps Blackwell.

Forbes, J. B., J. E. Piercy and T. L. Hayes (1988), "Women Executives: Breaking down the Barriers?," *Business Horizons*, 31 (6): 6–9.

Foucault, M. (1995), *Discipline and Punish: The Birth of the Prison*, New York: Vintage Book.

Francis, B. (2000), *Boys, Girls, and Achievement: Addressing the Classroom Issues*, London: Routledge.

Francis, B. (2002), "Relativism, Realism, and Reader-Response Criticism: An Analysis of Some Theoretical Tensions in Research on Gender Identity," *Journal of Gender Studies*, 11 (1): 39–54.

Francis, B. (2008), "'Teaching Manfully? Exploring Gendered Subjectivities and Power via Analysis of Men Teachers' Gender Performance," *Gender and Education*, 20 (2): 109–22.

Francis, B. (2010), "Re/Theorising Gender: Female Masculinity and Male Femininity in the Classroom?," *Gender and Education*, 22 (5): 477–90.

Friedman, N. (2006), "Nancy J. Hirschman on the Social Construction of Women's Freedom," *Hypatia*, 21 (4): 182–91.

Fuller, E. J., M. Lemay and A. Pendola (2018), "Who Should Be Our Leader? Examining the Representation in the Principalship across Geographic Locales in Texas Public Schools," E. Mchenry-Sorber and D. Hall (eds), *The Diversity of Rural Educational Leaders [Special Issue] Journal of Research in Rural Education*, 34 (4): 1–21.

Fuller, K. (2009), "Women Secondary Head Teachers: Alive and Well in Birmingham at the Beginning of the 21st Century," *Management in Education*, 23 (1): 19–31.

Fuller, K. (2014), "Gendered Educational Leadership: Beneath the Monoglossic Façade," *Gender and Education*, 26 (4): 321–37.

Fuller, K. (2015), "Learning Gendered Leadership: A Discursive Struggle." In E. Reilly and Q. Bauer (eds), *Women Leading Education across the Continents: Overcoming the Barriers*, 181–6, Lanham: Rowan & Littlefield.

Fuller, K. (2021), *Feminist Perspectives on Contemporary Educational Leadership*, London: Routledge.

Fuller, K. and J. Berry (2019), "#Womened: A Movement for Women Leaders in Education," University of Nottingham, 20/12/2022, Available Online: Https://Www.Nottingham.Ac.Uk/Research/Groups/Crelm/Documents/Womened-Report.Pdf.

Fuller, K. and J. Hartford (eds) (2016), *Gender and Leadership in Education: Women Achieving against the Odds*, Bern: Peter Lang.

Funk, C. (2010), "Female Leaders in Educational Administration: Sabotage within Our Own Ranks," *Advancing Women in Leadership Journal*, 17: 1–10.

Gaitanou, E. (2009), "Feminism in Times of Crisis: Women Struggle in Greece," *Paper Presented at the 9th Annual Conference Historical Materialism: Weighs Like a Nightmare*, 8–11, November, London.

Ganderton, P. S. (1991), "Subversion and the Organisation: Some Theoretical Considerations," *Educational Management and Administration*, 19 (1): 30–6.

Garret, V. (1999), "Preparation for Headship? The Role of the Deputy Head in the Primary School," *School Leadership and Management*, 19 (1): 67–81.

Gassouka, M. (2004), "Gender in the Family-School Relationship," *Parents' Counselling*, 46–57. [In Greek]

General Secretariat of Equality (2013), 20/11/2021, Available Online: Http://Www.Isotita.Gr/Var/Uploads/Press/Dt_Thlefonikh%20grammh%20sos%2015900_Martios%202012.Pdf. [In Greek]

Genz, S. (2009), *Postfemininities in Popular Culture*, Basingstoke: Palgrave Macmillan.

Gerson, G. M. and K. Peiss (1985), "Boundaries, Negotiation, Consciousness: Reconceptualising Gender Relations," *Social Problems*, 3 (4): 317–31.

Giannelos, G. (2000), "Statement." In Th. Papazizi, N. Chatzitrifon and Th. Ktenidis (eds), *Gender and Behaviour, Homosexuality-Homophobia. The Situation in*

Greece and Perspectives for Improvement. 9–10 October, Thessaloniki. Conference Proceedings, 1–10, Athens: Epikentro. [In Greek]

Gillborn, D. and H. Mirza (2000), *Educational Inequality—Mapping Race, Class and Gender: A Synthesis of Research Evidence*, London: Ofsted.

Gillborn, G. (2008), *Racism and Education: Coincidence or Conspiracy? Understanding Race Inequality in Education*, Oxon: Routledge.

Giorgi, A., C. Fisher and E. Murray (1975), *Duquesne Studies in Phenomenological Psychology*, Pittsburgh: Duquesne University Press.

Gipson, A. N., D. L. Pfaff, D. B. Mendelsohn, L. T. Catenacci and W. W. Burke (2017), "Women and Leadership: Selection, Development, Leadership Style and Performance," *Journal of Applied Behavioral Science*, 53: 32–65.

Gold, A. (1996), "Women into Educational Management," *European Journal of Education*, 31 (4): 419–33.

Goldin, D. C. (1991), "The Role of World War II in the Rise of Women's Employment," *The American Economic Review*, 81 (4): 741–56.

Gouli, C. and E. Kafkoula (2004), Education during the Era of Eleftherios Venizelos. *Paper Presented at the 3rd International Conference on History of Education*, October 1–3, University of Patra. [In Greek]

Grace, A. P. and F. J. Benson (2000), "Using Autobiographical Queer Life Narratives of Teachers to Connect Personal, Political and Pedagogical Spaces," *International Journal of Inclusive Education*, 4 (2): 89–109.

Gray, H. L. (1989), "Gender Considerations in School Management: Masculine and Feminine Leadership Styles." In C. Riches and C. Morgan (eds), *Human Resource Management in Education*, 38–47, Milton Keynes: Open University Press.

Gray, M. E. (2013), "Coming out as Lesbian, Gay or Bisexual Teacher: Negotiating Private and Professional Worlds," *Sex Education*, 13 (6): 702–71.

Greek Teachers Union (Doe) (2002), *Didaskaliko Vima*, 62–82. [In Greek]

Greek Teachers Union (Doe) (2012), "Announcement Regarding Violation of Workers,' Rights at the 2nd Primary School on Peania," 16/11/2014, Available Online: Http://Www.Doe.Gr/Index.Php?Categoryid=17&P2_Articleid=9501. [In Greek]

Greenfield, W. (1985), "Studies of the Assistant Principalship: Toward New Avenues of Enquiry," *Education and Urban Society*, 18 (1): 7–27.

Griffiths, V. (2002), "Crossing Boundaries: The Experiences of Mature Student Mothers in Initial Teacher Education," *International Journal of Inclusive Education*, 6 (3): 267–85.

Grogan, M. and C. C. Brunner (2005), "Women Superintendents and Role Conception: (Un)Troubling the Norms." In L. G. Bjork and T. J. Kowalski (eds), *The Contemporary Superintendent: Preparation, Practice and Development*, 227–50, Thousand Oaks: Corwin Press.

Grogan, M. and C. Shakeshaft (2011), *Women and Educational Leadership*, San Francisco: Jossey Bass.

Grummell, B., D. Devine and K. Lynch (2009), "The Care-Less Manager: Gender, Care and New Managerialism in Higher Education," *Gender and Education*, 21 (2): 191–208.

Gubrium, J. F. and J. A. Holstein (2003), "Postmodern Sensibilities." In J. F. Gubrium and J. A. Holstein (eds), *Postmodern Interviewing*, 3–18, London: Sage.

Guihen, L. (2019), "The Career Experiences and Aspirations of Women Deputy Head Teachers," *Educational Management Administration and Leadership*, 47 (4): 1–17.

Gunter, H. (1997), *Rethinking Education: The Consequences of Jurassic Management*, London: Cassell.

Gupton, S. L. (2009), *Women in Educational Leadership in the US: Reflections of a 50 Year Veteran*, 13/11/2014, Available Online: Http://Forumonpublicpolicy.Com/Summer09/Archivesummer09/Gupton.Pdf.

Gupton, S. L. and G. A. Slick (1996), *Highly Successful Women Administrators: The Inside Stories of How They Got There*, Thousand Oaks, Ca: Corwin.

Gurian, M., P. Henley and T. Trueman (2001), *Boys and Girls Learn Differently! A Guide for Teachers and Parents*, San Francisco, Ca: Jossey-Bass.

Gust, S. W. (2007), "'Look out for the Football Players and the Frat Boys': Autoethnographic Reflections of a Gay Teacher in a Gay Curricular Experience," *Educational Studies*, 41 (1): 43–60.

Hadjikyriakou, A. (2009), "'Exoticising Patriarchies': Rethinking the Anthropological Views on Gender in Post WWII Greece," *E-Pistime*, 2 (2): 17–29.

Hall, V. (1996), *Dancing on the Ceiling: A Study of Women Managers in Education*, London: Paul Chapman.

Hambidis, T. (2012), *Secondary Teachers' Beliefs about Gender Roles in the Educational Procedures*, Thessaloniki: Kyriakidis. [In Greek]

Hambidis, T. and E. Taratori (2008), "The Evolution of Co-Education in Greece," *Paper Presented at the 5th Interdisciplinary Conference "History of Education: Education and Social Justice,"* Historical Archives of Greek and International Education Laboratory, October 3–5, University of Patra. [In Greek]

Hanna, E., S. Robertson, J. Woodal and S. Rowlands (2018), "Women's Perspectives on the Value of the Father's Initiative in Shifting Practices within Families," *Journal of Gender Studies*, 27 (5): 562–73.

Haraway, D. (2013), *Simaons, Cyborgs and Women: The Reinvention of Nature*, New York: Routledge.

Hardalia, N. and A. Ioannidou (2008), *Gendered Social Representations in School Books: Annotated Bibliography*, Athens: Kethi. [In Greek]

Harding, S. (1991), *Whose Science? Whose Knowledge?*, Buckingham: Open University Press.

Harris, A., D. Muijs and M. Crawford (2003), *Deputy and Assistant Heads*, Warwick: National College for School Leadership.

Harris, I. M. (1995), *Messages Men Hear: Constructing Masculinities*, London: Taylor and Francis.

Harry, B. and J. Klinger (2006), *Why Are So Many Minority Students in Special Education: Understanding Race and Disability in Schools*, New York: Teachers College Press.

Hausman, C., A. Nebeker, J. Mccreary and G. Donaldson (2002), "The Worklife of the Assistant Principal," *Journal of Educational Administration*, 40 (2): 136–57.

Hays, S. (1996), *Cultural Contradictions of Motherhood*, New Haven: Yale University Press.

Haywood, C. and M. Mac An Ghail (2003), *Men and Masculinities: Theory, Research and Social Practice*, Buckingham: Open University Press.

Hellenic Statistical Authority (Has) (2010), *Teachers with Postgraduate or Other Studies*, 15/3/2022, Available Online: Http://Www.Statistics.Gr/Portal/Page/Portal/Esye/Bucket/A1401/Other/A1401_Sed11_Tb_An_00_2010_09l_F_Gr.Pdf. [In Greek]

Hellenic Statistical Authority (Has) (2013a), *Statistical Data for Primary Education 2013*, 4/9/2021, Available Online: Https://Www.Statistics.Gr/El/Statistics/-/Publication/Sed12/2013. [In Greek]

Hellenic Statistical Authority (Has) (2013b), *Teaching Personnel with Postgraduate or Other Additional Studies*, 10/12/2022, Available Online: Https://Www.Statistics.Gr/El/Statistics/-/Publication/Sed12/2013. [In Greek]

Hellenic Statistical Authority (Has) (2014a), *Statistical Data for Primary Education 2014*, 4/9/2021, Available Online: Https://Www.Statistics.Gr/El/Statistics/-/Publication/Sed12/2014. [In Greek]

Hellenic Statistical Authority (Has) (2014b), *Statistical Data for Tertiary Education*, 12/12/2022, Available Online: Https://Www.Statistics.Gr/El/Statistics/-/Publication/Sed33/2014. [In Greek]

Hellenic Statistical Authority (Has) (2015a), *Statistical Data for Primary Education 2015*, 4/9/2021, Available Online: Https://Www.Statistics.Gr/El/Statistics/-/Publication/Sed12/2015. [In Greek]

Hellenic Statistical Authority (Has) (2015b), *Employment and Workforce Survey*, 8/7/2015, Available Online: Http://Www.Statistics.Gr/Portal/Page/Portal/Esye/Bucket/A0101/Pressreleases/A0101_Sjo02_Dt_Mm_04_2015_01_F_Gr.Pdf. [In Greek]

Hellenic Statistical Authority (Has) (2016), *Statistical Data for Primary Education 2016*, 4/9/2021, Available Online: Https://Www.Statistics.Gr/El/Statistics/-/Publication/Sed12/2016. [In Greek]

Hellenic Statistical Authority (Has) (2017), *Statistical Data for Primary Education 2017*, 4/9/2021, Available Online: Https://Www.Statistics.Gr/El/Statistics/-/Publication/Sed12/2017. [In Greek]

Hellenic Statistical Authority (Has) (2018), *Statistical Data for Primary Education 2018*, 4/9/2021, Available Online: Https://Www.Statistics.Gr/El/Statistics/-/Publication/Sed12/2018. [In Greek]

Hellenic Statistical Authority (Has) (2019a), *Statistical Data for Primary Education 2019*, 4/9/2022, Available Online: Https://Www.Statistics.Gr/El/Statistics/-/Publication/Sed12/2019. [In Greek]

Hellenic Statistical Authority (Has) (2019b), *Teaching Personnel with Postgraduate or Other Additional Studies*, 10/12/2022, Available Online: Http://Www.Statistics.Gr/Portal/Page/Portal/Esye/Bucket/A1401/Other/A1401_Sed12_Tb_An_00_2019_09l_F_Gr.Xls. [In Greek]

Hellenic Statistical Authority (Has) (2020a), *Statistical Data for Primary Education 2020*, 4/9/2022, Available Online: Https://Www.Statistics.Gr/El/Statistics/-/Publication/Sed12/2020. [In Greek]

Hellenic Statistical Authority (Has) (2020b), *Statistical Data for Tertiary Education 2019*, 4/9/2022, Available Online: Https://Www.Statistics.Gr/El/Statistics/-/Publication/Sed34/2014. [In Greek]

Hellenic Statistical Authority (Has) (2020c), *Average Age of Women at First Child's Birth*, 13/3/2023, Available Online: Https://Www.Statistics.Gr/Demography/Bloc-2b.Html?Lang=El. [In Greek]

Hellenic Statistical Authority (Has) (2022), *Workforce (Three Month Period)*, 20/4/2023, Available Online: Https://Www.Statistics.Gr/El/Statistics/-/Publication/Sjo01/-. [In Greek]

Hellenic Statistical Authority (2023), *Employment and Workforce Survey*, 15/9/2023, Available Online: Https://www.statistics.gr/el/statistics/-/publication/SJO02/2023-M03.

Hesa (2022), *HE Student Enrolments by Personal Characteristics*, 14/12/2022, Available Online: Https://Www.Hesa.Ac.Uk/Data-And-Analysis/Students/Whos-In-He.

Hill, C., K. Miller, K. Benson and G. Handley (2016), *Barriers and Bias: The Status of Women in Leadership*, Washington, DC: American Association of University Women.

Hill Collins, P. (1990), *Black Feminist Thought: Knowledge, Consciousness and the Politics of Empowerment*, Boston, Ma: Unwin Hyman.

Hill Collins, P. (2004), "Learning from the Outsider within: The Sociological Significance of Black Feminist Thought." In S. G. Harding (ed), *The Feminist Standpoint Theory Reader: Intellectual and Political Controversies*, 103–26, New York: Routledge.

Hjalmarsson, M. and A. Lofdahl (2014), "Being Caring and Disciplinary—Male Primary School Teachers and Expectations from Others," *Gender and Education*, 26 (3): 280–92.

Hoff-Sommers, C. (2000), *The War against Boys (How Misguided Feminism Is Harming Our Young Men)*, New York: Simon and Schuster.

Holgersson, C. (2013), "Recruiting Managing Directors: Doing Homosociality," *Gender, Work and Organization*, 20 (4): 454–66.

Holzer, H. J. and D. Neumark (2006), "Affirmative Action: What Do We Know?," *The Journal of Policy Analysis and Management*, 26 (2): 463–90.

Home, A. L. (1998), "Predicting Role Conflict, Overload and Contagion in Adult Women University Students with Families and Jobs," *Adult Education Quarterly*, 48 (2): 85–97.

Hook, J. (2006), "Care in Context: Men's Unpaid Work in 20 Countries, 1965–2003," *American Sociological Review*, 71 (4): 639–60.

Hooks, B. (1981), *Ain't I a Woman: Black Women and Feminism*, Boston: South End Press.

Hooks, B. (2000), *Feminism Is for Everybody: Passionate Politics*, Cambridge, Ma: South End Press.

Hoshmand, L. T. (1994), *Orientation to Inquiry in a Reflexive Professional Psychology*, Albany: State University of New York.

Hsieh, C. L. and J. Shen (1998), "Teachers', Principals' and Superintendents' Conceptions of Leadership," *School Leadership and Management*, 18: 107–21.

Hughes, C. (N.D.), *Second Wave Feminism and beyond*, 20/12/2013, Available Online: Http://Www2.Warwick.Ac.Uk/Fac/Soc/Sociology/Staff/Academicstaff/Jonesc/Jonesc_Index/Teaching/Birth/Second_Wave_Feminism.Pdf.

Hughes, J. A. (1990), *The Philosophy of Social Research*, London: Longman.

Humm, M. (1995), *The Dictionary of Feminist Theory*, New York: Prentice Hall.

Hurty, K. S. (1995), "Women Principals—Leading With Power," In D. M. Dunlap and P. A. Schmuck (eds), *Women Leading in Education*, 380–406, New York: State University of New York Press.

Ibarra, H. and O. Obodaru (2009), "Women and the Vision Thing," *Harvard Business Review*, 87 (1): 62–70.

Ideological Library of White Women's Front (N.D.), *Woman's Place in People's Community*, 14/11/2014, Available Online: Www.Ideology-Studies.Blogspot.Com/2010/07/Blog-Post_17.Html.

Iefimerida.Gr (19/1/2017), *Gerasimos Giakoumatos: Homosexuality Is a Spreading Disease*, 20/12/2022, Available Online: Https://Www.Iefimerida.Gr/News/314172/Gerasimos-Giakoymatos-I-Omofylofilia-Einai-Kollitiki-Arrostia. [In Greek]

Jakobsh, D. R. (2004), "Barriers to Women's Leadership." In G. R. Goethals, G. J. Sorenson and J. Macgregor-Burns (eds), *Encyclopedia of Leadership. Vol. 4*, 77–81, Thousand Oaks: Sage.

Janta, B. (2014), *Caring for Children in Europe: How Childcare, Parental Leave and Flexible Working Arrangements Interact in Europe*, Brussels: European Union, 10/3/2023, Available Online: Https://Www.Rand.Org/Pubs/Research_Reports/Rr554.Html.

Jary, D. and J. Jary (2000), *Collins Dictionary of Sociology*, Glasgow: UK Harper Collins Publishing.

Johnson, N. N. and J. B. Fournillier (2022), "Increasing Diversity in Leadership: Perspectives of Four Black Women Educational Leaders in the Context of the US," *Journal of Educational Administration and History*, 54 (2): 174–92.

Jones, S. (2002), *Y: The Descent of Men*, London: Little, Brown.

Jones, S. (2013), "Nature, Nurture or Neither? What Do We Not Know about Genetics." *Lecture in Memoriam of Peter Lindsay*, London: Imperial College, February 27, 2013.

Kadartzi, E. and V. Pliogou (2007), "Gender Image in Primary School Books. The Case of Maths, Geography and Natural Sciences." In E. Dredogianni, F. Seroglou and E. Tressou (eds), *Gender and Education: Maths, Natural Sciences, New Technologies*, 421–37, Athens: Kaleidoskopio. [In Greek]

Kafiri, K. (2002), *Gender and Mass Media*, Athens: Centre for Women Studies and Research Panteion University. [In Greek].

Kakavoulia, M., V. Kappa and M. Liapi (2001), *Gender and Mass Media: Targeted Field Research*, Athens: Kethi. [In Greek]

Kallinikaki, T. (2010), "Gender, Children and Families in the Greek Welfare State." In M. Ajzenstandt and J. Gal (eds), *Children, Gender and Families in Mediterranean Welfare States*, 181–203, London: Springer.

Kambouri, N. (2013), *Gender Equality in the Greek Labour Market: The Gaps Narrow, Inequalities Persist*, Friedrich Ebert Stiftung, 17/8/2014, Available Online: Http://Library.Fes.De/Pdf-Files/Id/09822.Pdf.

Kanter, R. M. (1977), *Men and Women of the Corporation*, New York: Basic Books.

Kantzara, V. (2006), "Society." In T. Fitzpatrick, H. Kwon, N. Manning, J. Midgley, and G. Pascal (eds), *International Encyclopedia of Social Policy*, 563–5, London: Routledge.

Kaparou, M. and T. Bush (2007), "Invisible Barriers: The Career Progress of Women Secondary School Principals in Greece," *Compare*, 37 (2): 221–37.

Kapitsinis, N. (2023), "The 2007/8 Capitalist Crisis Evolution in Greece: A Geographical Political Economy Perspective," *Human Geography*, 16 (1): 3–16.

Karaiskaki, T. (2006), "Commentary: A Gloomy Future for Greek Women," *Kathimerini (English Edition)*, May 21–22.

Karamessini, M. (2011a), "Crisis, Women, Male Identity," *Avgi*, October 30. [In Greek]

Karamessini, M. (2011b), "Structural Crisis and Adjustment in Greece: Labour Market Effects by Gender and Changes in the Gendered Division of Paid Work," In *International Symposium "Women, Gender Equality and Economic Crisis,"* Athens, 1–2 December. [In Greek].

Karantonaki, A. (2021), "Female Representations on Greek Media and Greek Women's (Un)Employment before and after the Covid-19 Pandemic: Examining Whether and How Media Gender Stereotypes Can Affect Greek Women's Development in Light of a Crisis." In *Master Thesis*, Malmo: University of Malmo.

Karl, M. (1995), *Women and Empowerment: Participation and Decision Making*, London: Sed Books Ltd.

Kaufman, M. (1994), "Men, Feminism and Men's Contradictory Experiences of Power." In H. Bron and M. Kaufman (eds), *Research on Men and Masculinities Series: Theorizing Masculinities*, 142–65, Thousand Oaks: Sage.

Kedke-Eetaa (2005), "Study of Subsidies Distribution of Public Child and Infant Day Nurseries of the Local Authority Organizations." In *Unpublished Technical Report*, Athens: Ypesda-Kedke. [In Greek]

Keener, E., C. M. Mehta and K. E. Smirles (2017), "Contextualizing Bem: The Developmental Social Psychology of Masculinity and Femininity," *Advances in Gender Research*, 23: 1–18.

Kessler, J. S. and W. Mckenna (1978), *Gender: An Ethnomethodological Approach*, New York: Wiley.

Kethi (2001), *Women and Social Policy*, Athens: Kethi. [In Greek]

Kethi (2008), *Reports for Decision Making Centres and Politics*, Athens: Kethi. [In Greek]

Khanam, A., A. Kazi, A. Fakhra, S. Taj, A. Siddiqah, V. Showunmi and U. Quraishi (2022), "An Insight into the Professional Journey of Pakistani Women Academics." In V. Showunmi, P. Moorosi, C. Shakeshaft and I. Oplatka (eds), *The Bloomsbury Handbook of Gender and Educational Leadership and Management*, 306–18, London: Bloomsbury Academic.

Khattab, N. and J. Ibrahim (2006), "Why Are So Few Palestinian Women in Principalship Positions?" In I. Oplatka and R. Herz-Razarowitz (eds), *Women Principals in a Multicultural Society: New Insights into Feminist Educational Leadership*, 71–81, Rotterdam: Sense Publishers.

Khelan, E. (2010), "Gender Logic and (Un)Doing Gender at Work," *Gender, Work and Organization*, 17 (2): 174–94.

Khosravi, S. (2009), "Displaced Masculinity: Gender and Ethnicity among Iranian Men in Sweden," *Iranian Studies*, 42 (4): 591–609.

Kikilias, I. (2007), *Employment and Unemployment in Greece 2000–2005: Economic Growth and Social Reform*, Athens: Ekke. [In Greek]

Kimmel, M. (1994), "Masculinity as Homophobia: Fear Shame and Silence in the Construction of Gender Identity." In H. Brod and M. Kaufman (eds), *Theorizing Masculinities*, 213–19, London: Sage.

King, J. R. (1998), *Uncommon Caring Learning from Men Who Teach Young Children*, New York: Tcp.

Knouse, S. B. and S. C. Webb (2001), "Virtual Networking for Women and Minorities," *Career Development International*, 6 (4): 226–8.

Kodz, J., S. Davis, D. Lain, E. Sheppard, J. Rick, M. Strebler, P. Bates, J. Cummings, N. Meager, D. Anxo, S. Gineste and R. Trinczek (2003), *Working Long Hours in the UK: A Review of the Research Literature, Analysis of Survey Data and Cross-National Organizational Case Studies, Executive Summary*, London: Department of Trade and Industry.

Koenig, A. M., A. H. Eagly, A. A. Mitchell and T. Ristikari (2011), "Are Leader Stereotyped Masculine? A Meta-Analysis of Three Research Paradigms," *Psychological Bulletin*, 137: 616–42.

Kornrich, S., J. Brines and K. Leupp (2012), "Egalitarianism, Housework and Sexual Frequency in Marriage," *American Sociological Review*, 78 (1): 26–50.

Kousoulos, A., K. Bounias and G. Kambouridis (2004), "Participatory Leadership and the Decision-Making Process in Primary Education," *Education Matters Review*, 9: 33–41. [In Greek]

Krishnan, H., D. Park and L. Kilbourne (2006), "The Development of a Conceptual Model to Explain Turnover among Women in Top Management Teams," *International Journal of Management*, 23 (3): 470–7.

Kyriakidou, M. (2010), "'Another World Is Possible as long as It Is Feminist Too': Dissenting Discourses and Acts by Greek Leftish Feminists," *Interface: A Journal for and about Social Movements*, 2 (1): 214–20.

Kyriakousis, A. and A. Saiti (2006), "Underrepresentation of Women in Public Primary School Administration: The Experience of Greece," *International Electronic Journal for Leadership in Learning*, 10 (5).

Lad, K. (2000), "Two Women High School Principals: The Influence of Gender on Entry into Education and Their Professional Lives," *Journal of School Leadership*, 12: 663–89.

Lainas, A. (1993), "Administration in Education and Curricula," *Pedagogic Review*, 19: 254–94. [In Greek]

Lainas, A. (2000), "Administration and Planning in Schools: Scientific Approaches and Greek Reality," In Z. Papanaoum (ed), *Planning the Educational Process in the School Unit*, 23–39, Thessaloniki: Greek Pedagogical Institute and Aristotel University of Thessaloniki. [In Greek]

Lang, M. and B. Risman (2006), "Blending into Equality. Family Diversity and Gender Convergence." In D. K. Davis, M. Evans and J. Lorber (eds), *Handbook of Women's and Gender Studies*, 287–306, Thousand Oaks: Sage.

Langellier, K. and D. Hall (1989), "Interviewing Women: A Phenomenological Approach to Feminist Communication Research." In K. Carter and C. Spitzack (eds), *Doing Research on Women's Communication: Perspectives on Theory and Methods*, 193–220, Norwood, NJ: Ablex.

Lareau, A. and E. Weininger (2003), "Cultural Capital in Educational Research: A Critical Assessment," *Theory and Society*, 5/6: 567–606.

Laurie, N., C. Dwyer, S. Holloway and F. Smith (1999), *Geographies of New Femininities*, Harlow: Longman.

Law, S. and D. Glover (2000), *Educational Leadership and Learning: Practice, Policy and Research*, Buckingham: Open University Press.

Lazaridou, I. (2020), *Women's Leadership in Pre-Primary Education*, Athens: Bookstars—Giorgaras. [In Greek]

Leathwood, C. (2003), "Re/Presenting Intellectual Subjectivity: Gender and the Visual Imagery in the Field of Higher Education," *Gender and Education*, 25 (2): 1–22.

Leathwhood, C. and B. Read (2009), *Gender and the Changing Face of Higher Education: A Feminized Future?*, Berkshire: Open University Press.

Lee, C. (2023), "How Do Male and Female Head Teachers Evaluate Their Authenticity as School Leaders?," *Management in Education*, 37 (1): 46–55.

Lekule, C. (2018), "Overview: Factors Impacting Women's Leadership." In R. Mcnae and E. C. Reilly (eds), *Women Leading Education across Continents: Finding and Harnessing the Joy in Leadership*, 35–7, Lanham: Rowman and Littlefield.

Lewis, R. and K. Rake (2008), *Breaking the Mould for Women Leaders: Could Boardroom Quotas Hold the Key?*, London: Fawcett Society.

Lewis, S. (1994), "Role Tensions and Dual Career Couple." In M. Davidson and R. Burke (eds), *Women in Management: Current Research Issues. Vol. I*, 230–41, London: Paul Chapman.

Limerick, B. and C. Anderson (1999), "Female Administrators and School-Based Management," *Educational Management and Administration*, 27 (4): 401–14.

Lincoln, Y. S. and E. G. Guba (2005), "Paradigmatic Controversies, Contradictions and Emerging Confluences." In N. K. Denzin and Y. S. Lincoln (eds), *The Sage Handbook of Qualitative Research*, 163–88, Thousand Oaks: Sage.

Linehan, M. (2000), *Senior Female International Managers: Why So Few?*, Vermont: Ashgate Publishing.

Linehan, M. (2001), "Networking for Female Managers' Career Development," *Journal of Management Development*, 20 (10): 823–9.

Litosseliti, L. (2006), *Gender and Language: Theory and Practice*, New York: Routledge.

Liu, J. (2000), "Women Teachers' Role Conflict and Its Management," *Chinese Education and Society*, 33 (4): 68–74.

Livanos, I. and A. Zangelidis (2012), "Multiple Job-Holding among Male Workers in Greece," *Regional Studies*, 46 (1): 119–35.

Livanos, I. and E. Tzika (2022), *Precarious Employment in Greece: Economic Crisis, Labour Market Flexibilisation, and Vulnerable Workers. Paper No 171*. London, Lse: Hellenic Observatory Discussion Papers on Greece and S.E. Europe, 26/4/2023, Available Online: Https://Www.Lse.Ac.Uk/Hellenic-Observatory/Assets/Documents/Publications/Greese-Papers/Greese-171.Pdf.

Livanos, I. and K. Pouliakas (2012), "Educational Segregation and the Gender Wage Gap in Greece," *Journal of Economic Studies*, 39 (5): 554–75.

Logan, P. J. (1999), "An Educational Leadership Challenge: Refocusing Gender Equity Strategies," 25/2/2008, Available Online: Www.Aasa.Org/Publications/Tap/2000summer/Logan.Html.

Loizos, P. (2003), "A Broken Mirror: Masculine Sexuality in Greek Ethnography." In A. Cornwall and N. Lindisfarne (eds), *Dislocating Masculinity: Comparative Ethnographies*, 66–81, London: Routledge.

Lord, R. G. and K. J. Maher (1993), *Leadership and Information Processing: Linking Perceptions and Performance*, Boston: Unwin Hyman.

Loumbourdi, M. (2023), "Leadership Development Programmes: Part of the Solution or Part of the Problem of Women's Under-Representation on Leadership?," *Gender in Management: An International Journal*, 38 (5): 619–33.

Loutfi, M. F. (2001), *Women, Gender and Work: What Is Equality and How We Get There*, Washington, DC: International Labor Office.

Lumby, J. (2011), "Gender Representation and Social Justice: Ideology, Methodology and Smoke Screens," *Gender and Education*, 23 (7): 921–34.

Lumby, J. (2022), "Women's Way of Leading: Inappropriate Essentialism of Critical Question?" In V. Showunmi, P. Moorosi, C. Shakeshaft and I. Oplatka (eds), *The Bloomsbury Handbook of Gender and Educational Leadership and Management*, 202–11, London: Bloomsbury Academic.

Lumby, J. and M. C. Azaola (2014), "Women Principals in South Africa: Gender, Mothering and Leadership," *British Educational Research Journal*, 40 (1): 30–44.

Lynch, K. (1994), "Women Teach and Men Manage: Why Men Dominate Senior Posts in Irish Education?" In *Women for Leadership in Education*, Dublin: Education Commission of the Conference of Religious in Ireland.

Lynch, K. D. (2008), "Gender Roles and the American Academe: A Case Study of Graduate Student Mothers," *Gender and Education*, 20 (6): 585–605.

Macha, H. and Q. J. Bauer (2009), "The European Perspective on Women's Leadership," *Journal of Women in Educational Leadership*, 7 (1): 23–32.

Mackinnon, K. (2019), "'Boy, I Wish I Were a Man!': Navigating Principalship as a Woman," *Canadian Journal of Educational Administration and Policy*, 190: 18–25.

Magliveras, K. D. (2005), "The Regulation of Workplace Sexual Harassment in Greece: Legislation and Case Law Analysis," *International Journal of Discrimination and the Law*, 7 (1–4): 169–86.

Mahlioson, M. and M. Maxson (1998), "Metaphors as Structures for Elementary and Secondary Preservice Teachers' Thinking," *International Journal of Educational Research*, 29: 227–40.

Mahmood, A. (2018), "The Path of Leadership for Women in Pakistan." In R. Mcnae and E. C. Reilly (eds), *Women Leading Education across Continents: Finding and Harnessing the Joy in Leadership*, 171–7, Lanham: Rowman and Littlefield.

Mahoney, A. R. and C. Knudson-Martin (2009), "Gender Equality in Intimate Relationships." In C. Knudson-Martin and A. R. Mahoney (eds), *Couples, Gender and Power: Creating Change in Intimate Relationships*, 3–16, New York: Springer.

Malachias, R., L. A. Laudino and T. C. S. Balbino (2020), "Black Women Leading Education for Social Justice in the Region of Baixada Fluminense, Rio De Janeiro, Brazil," K. Fuller, P. Moorosi, V. Showunmi and S. J. Shah (eds), *Ways of Seeing Women's Leadership in Education: Stories, Images, Metaphors, Methods and Theories. Frontiers in Education*, 5 (77): 1–7.

Malleson, K. (2003), "Justifying Gender Equality on the Bench: Why Difference Won't Do," *Feminist Legal Studies*, 11: 1–24.

Manesi, D., S. Kanaouti, S. Gerakopoulou and A. Vouyioukas (2022), *Press/Preventing—Responding—Supporting—Young Survivors of Gbv: Sexual Harassment, Sexual and Cyberviolence*, 14/12/2022, Available Online: Https://Diotima.Org.Gr/Wp-Content/Uploads/2022/09/Del_2.1._State-Of-The-Art_Final_Long_Version_June_22.Pdf.

Maragoudaki, E. (2005), *Education and Genders: Children's Books in Pre-Primary Schools*, Athens: Odisseas. [In Greek]

Maratou-Aliprandi, L. (1995), *The Athenian Family: Family Examples and Spousal Practices*, Athens: National Centre for Social Research (Ekke). [In Greek]

Marland, M. (1982), "Staffing for Sexism: Educational Leadership and Role Models," *Westminster Studies in Education*, 5 (1): 11–26.

Martin, P. Y. (2006), "Practicing Gender at Work: Further Thoughts on Reflexivity," *Gender, Work and Organization*, 13 (3): 254–76.

Matsagianis, M. (2013), *The Greek Crisis: Social Impact and Policy Responses*, Berlin: Friedrich Ebert Stiftung.

McCracken, E. (1993), *Decoding Women's Magazines: From Mademoiselle to Ms*, New York: St Martin's Press.

McDonald, P. (2012), "Workplace Sexual Harassment 30 Years on: A Review of the Literature," *International Journal of Management Reviews*, 14 (1): 1–17.

McLay, M. (2008), "Headteacher Career Paths in UK Independent Secondary Coeducational Schools: Gender Issues," *Educational Management Administration and Leadership*, 36 (3): 353–72.

McMunn, A., L. Bird, E. Webb and A. Sacker (2020), "Gender Division of Paid and Unpaid Work in Contemporary UK Couples," *Work, Employment and Society*, 34 (2): 155–73.

McNae, R. (2022), "Women's Educational Leadership and the (Not So) Hidden Toll of Emotional Labour: The Vomit in My Handbag." In V. Showunmi, P. Moorosi, C. Shakeshaft and I. Oplatka (eds), *The Bloomsbury Handbook of Gender and Educational Leadership and Management*, 319–32, London: Bloomsbury Academic.

McNae, R. and E. C. Reilly (eds) (2018), *Women Leading Education across Continents: Finding and Harnessing the Joy in Leadership*, Lanham: Rowman and Littlefield.

McPherson, M., L. Smith-Lovin and J. M. Cook (2001), "Birds of a Feather: Homophily in Social Networks," *Annual Review of Sociology*, 27: 415–44.

Mencarini, L. and M. Sironi (2009), "Happiness and Gender Inequality in Europe," *Paper Presented at 1st International Conference on Labor Market and the Household*, November 6–7, Callegio Alberto, Moncalieri Torino.

Mencarini, L. and M. Sironi (2012), "Happiness, Household and Gender Inequality in Europe," *European Sociological Review*, 28 (2): 203–19.

Messerschmidt, J. W. (2011), "The Struggle for Heterofeminine Recognition: Bullying, Embodiment, and Reactive Sexual Offending by Adolescent Girls," *Feminist Criminology*, 6 (3): 203–33.

Meyers, H. (2002), "Men's View of Power in Women: A Woman's Perspective." In B. J. Seeling, R. A. Paul and C. B. Levy (eds), *Constructing and Deconstructing Woman's Power*, 123–30, London: Kanac.

Miles, M. B. and A. M. Huberman (1994), *Qualitative Data Analysis: An Expanded Source Book*, Thousand Oaks, Ca: Sage.

Mills, S. (1997), *Discourse*, London: Sage.

Mirza, H. (1992), *Young, Female and Black*, Buckingham: Open University Press.

Moi, T. (1988), "Feminist, Female, Feminine." In C. Besley and J. Moore (eds), *The Feminist Reader: Essays on Gender and Politics of Literary Criticism*, 117–32, New York: Blackwell.

Moore, B. and S. Webb (1998), "Equal Opportunity in the US Navy: Perceptions of Active-Duty African American Women," *Gender Issues*, 16 (3): 99–119.

Moore, H. L. (1994), *A Passion for Difference: Essays in Anthropology and Gender*, Cambridge: Polity Press.

Moorosi, P. (2014), "Constructing a Leader's Identity through a Leadership Development Programme: An Intersectional Analysis," *Educational Management Administration and Leadership*, 42 (6): 792–807.

Moorosi, P. (2022), "Gender, Career and Leadership Development." In V. Showunmi, P. Moorosi, C. Shakeshaft and I. Oplatka (eds), *The Bloomsbury Handbook of Gender and Educational Leadership and Management*, 213–17, London: Bloomsbury Academic.

Moreau, M., J. Osgood and A. Halsall (2007), "Making Sense of the Glass Ceiling in Schools: An Exploration of Women Teachers' Discourses," *Gender and Education*, 19 (2): 237–53.

Moreau, M.-P. (2019), *Teachers, Gender and the Feminisation Debate*, London: Routledge.

Moreau, M. P., J. Osgood and A. Halsall (2008), "Equal Opportunities Policies in English Schools: Towards Greater Gender Equality in the Teaching Workforce?," *Gender, Work and Organization*, 15 (6): 553–78.

Morgenroth, T., M. K. Ryan and K. Peters (2015), "The Motivational Theory of Role Modeling: How Role Models Influence Role Aspirants' Goals," *Review of General Psychology*, 19: 465–83.

Moussourou, L. (1985a), *Female Occupation and Family*, Athens: Estia. [In Greek]

Moussourou, L. (1985b), *Family and Children in Athens*, Athens: Estia. [In Greek]

Mudau, T. J. and D. Ncube (2017), "Leadership Qualities of Women in Educational Management Positions: Stakeholders' Perceptions of Selected Schools in Matabeleland South Region of Zimbabwe," *Gender and Behaviour*, 15 (4): 10595–608.

Mythili, N. (2022), "Mastering the Art of Fixing the Ethical Dilemma: Women Leading Schools in India." In V. Showunmi, P. Moorosi, C. Shakeshaft and I. Oplatka (eds), *The Bloomsbury Handbook of Gender and Educational Leadership and Management*, 175–89, London: Bloomsbury Academic.

Naht (2016), *The Balancing Act: Report on the Working Lives of Deputy and Assistant Head Teachers and Vice Principals*, National Association of Head Teachers, 11/6/2017, Available Online: Https://T.Co/Lrrfm0szbq.

Nater, C., M. E. Heilman and S. Sczesny (2023), "Footsteps I Would Like to Follow? How Gender Quotas Affect the Acceptance of Women Leaders as Role Models and Inspirations for Leadership," *European Journal of Social Psychology*, 53 (1): 129–46.

Nazou, D. (2002), *Women and Employment in Greece: Presentation and Comments of the Literature with an Emphasis on Social Sciences*, 8/8/2021, Available Online: Http://Www.Aegean.Gr/Gender-Postgraduate/Documents/%Ce%9c%Ce%B5%Ce%Bb%Ce%Ad%Cf%84%Ce%B7%20%Ce%9d%Ce%Ac%Ce%B6%Ce%Bf%Cf%85.Pdf. [In Greek]

Neary, A. (2013), "Lesbian and Gay Teachers' Experiences of 'Coming out' in Irish Schools," *British Journal of Sociology of Education*, 34 (4): 583–602.

Nikolaidou, M. (1981), *The Greek Woman: Work and Emancipation*, Athens: Kastaniotis. [In Greek]

Noddings, N. (2005), *The Challenge to Care in Schools: An Alternative Approach to Education*, New York: Teachers College Press.

Oakley, A. (1981), "Interviewing Women: A Contradiction in Terms." In H. Roberts (ed), *Doing Feminist Research*, 30–61, London: Routledge and Kegan Paul.

Odhiambo, G. (2011), "Women and Higher Education Leadership in Kenya: A Critical Analysis," *Journal of Higher Education Policy and Management*, 33 (6): 667–78.

Oecd (2001), *Employment Outlook 2001*, Paris: Oecd.

Oecd (2018), *Teachers' and School Heads' Statutory Salaries*, 8/7/2022, Available Online: Https://Stats.Oecd.Org/Index.Aspx?Datasetcode=Eag_Ts_Sta.

Oecd (2019), *Education at a Glance*, 15/3/2022, Available Online: Https://Www.Oecd-Ilibrary.Org/Sites/145d9f68-En/Index.Html?Itemid=/Content/Component/145d9f68-En.

Office for National Statistics (2020), *Birth Characteristics in England and Wales: 2020*, 20/12/2022, Available Online: Https://Www.Ons.Gov.Uk/Peoplepopulationandcommunity/Birthsdeathsandmarriages/Livebirths/Bulletins/Birthcharacteristicsinenglandandwales/2020.

Office for Students (2022), *Equality, Diversity and Students Characteristics Data. Students at English Higher Education Providers between 2010–11 and 2020–21*, 5/10/2022, Available Online: Https://Www.Officeforstudents.Org.Uk/Media/79a7bb57-83cf-4c50-A358-6bcfe80f165c/Ofs2022_29.Pdf.

Ognjenovic, K. (2022), "Multiple Job-Holding and Informality: May Pandemic Change Their Course?" In S. Redzepagic, A. P. Duarte, M. Sinicakova and D. Bodroza (eds), *Economic and Financial Implications of the Covid-19 Crisis*, 200–18, Universite Cote D' Azur, Nica: Balkan Institute of Science and Innovation (Bisi).

Oplatka, I. (2001), "'I Changed My Management Style': The Cross Gender Transition of Women Headteachers in Mid-Career," *School Leadership and Management*, 21: 219–33.

Oplatka, I. (2002), "Women Principals and the Concept of Burnout: An Alternative Voice?," *International Journal of Leadership in Education*, 5: 211–26.

Oplatka, I. (2003), "School Change and Self-Renewal: Some Reflections from Life Stories of Women Principals," *Journal of Educational Change*, 4: 25–43.

Oplatka, I. (2006), "Women in Educational Administration within Developing Countries. Towards a New International Research Agenda," *Journal of Educational Administration*, 44 (6): 604–24.

Oplatka, I. and R. Herzt-Lazarowitz (2006), *Women Principals in a Multicultural Society: New Insights into Feminist Educational Leadership*, Rotterdam: Sense Publishing.

Oplatka, I. and V. Tamir (2009), "'I Don't Want to Be a School Head': Women Deputy Heads' Insightful Constructions of Career Advancement and Retention," *Educational Management Administration and Leadership*, 37 (2): 216–38.

Oppenheim Mason, K. (1986), "The Status of Women: Conceptual and Methodological Issues in Demographic Studies," *Sociological Forum*, 1 (2): 284–300.

Ortiz, F. I. and C. Marshall (1988), "Women in Educational Administration." In N. Boyan (ed), *Handbook of Research in Educational Administration*, 123–42, New York: Longman.

Ozdogru, M. (2022), "School Administrators' Behaviors in the Professional Belonging of Teachers," *Education Quarterly Reviews*, 5 (2): 321–36.

Ozga, J. (1993), *Women in Educational Management*, Buckingham: Open University Press.

Paechter, C. (2001), "Using Poststructuralist Ideas in Gender Theory and Research." In B. Francis and C. Skelton (eds), *Investigating Gender: Contemporary Perspectives in Education*, 41–51, Buckingham: Open University Press.

Paechter, C. (2006), "Masculine Femininities/Feminine Masculinities: Power, Identities and Gender," *Gender and Education*, 18 (3): 253–63.

Pajares, F. and D. H. Schunk (2001), "Self-Beliefs and School Success: Self-Efficacy, Self-Concept and School Achievement." In R. Riding and S. Raynar (eds), *Self-Perception*, 239–66, Westport: Ablex.

Panagiotidou, A. (2013), "The On-Line Distance Training of Teachers on Gender Issues as a Factor of Blunting Gender-Defined Attitudes and Inequalities of the Educational System," *Education Cycle*, 1 (1): 119–29. [In Greek]

Panagiotopoulou, R. (2007), "Gender in Greek Media." In G. Papageorgiou (ed), *Gendering Transformations. Conference Proceedings*, 216–34, Rethymno: University of Crete. [In Greek]

Papadaki, V. and E. Papadaki (2011), "'So, What about Homosexuals?'—Views on Homosexuality among Social Work Students in Crete-Greece," *European Journal of Social Work*, 14 (2): 265–80.

Papadaki, V., K. Plotnikof and E. Papadaki (2013), "Social Work Students' Attitudes towards Lesbians and Gay Men: The Case of the Social Work Department in Crete, Greece," *Social Work Education: The International Journal*, 32 (4): 453–67.

Papanastasiou, E. (2009), "Gender and Head Teachers: What Is Happening in Greece?," *Paper Presented at a Research Students' Seminar at London Metropolitan University*, October 20, London Metropolitan University, London.

Papanastasiou, E. (2010), "Gender and School Management in Greece: The Under-Representation of Women," *Paper Presented at the 6th Biennial International Interdisciplinary Conference on Gender, Work and Organization*, June 21–23, Keele University, Staffordshire.

Papanastasiou, E. (2011), "Women Head Teachers in Greece: Constraints in Their Career Progression," *Paper Presented at the 8th International Gender and Education Conference: "Gender and Education: Past, Present and Future"*, April 27–30, Exeter University, Exeter.

Papanastasiou, E. (2013), "'Feminine' and 'Masculine' Educational Leadership Approaches: Fact or Fiction?," *Paper Presented at a Research Students' Seminar at*

London Metropolitan University. November 18, London Metropolitan University, London.

Papanastasiou, E. (2014), "Constructing Change: Women in Educational Leadership in Greece," *Paper Presented at the British Sociological Association Annual Conference, "Changing Society"*, April 23–25, University of Leeds, Leeds.

Papanastasiou, E. (2015), "Discursive Practices of Gender, Sexuality and Educational Leadership in Greek Primary Schools: A Case Study," *Paper Presented at the 10th International Gender and Education Conference: "Feminisms, Power and Pedagogy,"* June 24–26, University of Roehampton, Roehampton.

Papanastasiou, E. (2016), "Gender and Educational Leadership in Greek Primary Education," PhD Thesis. London: London Metropolitan University.

Papanastasiou, E. (2019), "Gender and Neo-Nazis: The Case of Golden Dawn in Greece," *Paper Presented at Nora 2019 Conference "Borders, Regimes, Territorial Discourses and Feminist Politics,"* May 22–24, Reykjavik.

Papanastasiou, E. (2020), "Discursive Practices of Gender and Teaching: A Case Study from Greece," *International Journal of Teaching and Education*, 8 (1): 47–63.

Papanastasiou, E. (2022), "How Children in Pre-Primary Education Understand the Financial Crisis." In Th. Thanos and A. Kyridis (eds), *Education and Society in Greece*, 359–74, Athens: Gutenberg. [In Greek]

Papataxiarchis, E. (1992), "The World of the Coffee Shop. Identity and Exchange in Male Conviviality." In E. Papataxiarchis and Th. Papadellis (eds), *Identities and Gender in Modern Greece*, 209–50, Athens: Kastaniotis. [In Greek]

Parkman, A. M. (2009), "Bargaining over Homework: The Frustrating Situation of Secondary Wage Earners," *The American Journal of Economics and Sociology*, 63: 765–95.

Paustian-Underdahl, S. C., L. S. Walter and D. J. Woehr (2014), "Gender and Perceptions of Leadership Effectiveness: A Meta-Analysis of Contextual Moderators," *Journal of Applied Psychology*, 99 (6): 1129–45.

Peeters, J. (2008), *The Construction of a New Profession. A European Perspective on Professionalism in Ecec*, Amsterdam: Swp.

Peters, J. K. (1997), *When Mothers Work: Loving Our Children without Sacrificing Our Selves*, Reading, Ma: Perseus.

Peterson, V. S. and A. S. Runyan (1999), *Global Gender Issues*, Colorado: Westview.

Phillips, A. (1995), *The Politics of Presence*, New York: Oxford University Press.

Phoenix, A. (2002), "Mapping Present Inequalities to Navigate Future Success: Racialisation and Education," *British Journal of Sociology of Education*, 23 (3): 505–15.

Piterman, H. (2013), "Diversity and Gender: Realities for Growth in the Global Economy." In *Women in Leadership: Understanding the Gender Gap*, 100–10, Melbourne: Committee for Economic Development of Australia, 25/3/2015, Available Online: Https://Sciencewomensforum.Files.Wordpress.Com/2014/08/Women_In_Leadership_2013.Pdf.

Porter, M. K. and C. Fahrenwald (2022), "Reframing Constructive Spaces for Women in Educational Leadership: A Transnational Study." In V. Showunmi, P. Moorosi, C. Shakeshaft and I. Oplatka (eds), *The Bloomsbury Handbook of Gender and Educational Leadership and Management*, 24–37, London: Bloomsbury Academic.

Powney, J., S. Hall, V. Wilson, J. Davidson, S. Kirk, S. Edward and H. Mirza (2003), *Teachers' Careers: The Impact of Age, Disability, Ethnicity, Gender and Sexual Orientation*, London: Dfes.

Pritchard, S. M. (1994), "Backlash, Backwater, or Back to the Drawing Board? Feminist Thinking and Librarianship in the 1990s," *Wilson Library Bulletin*, 68: 42–6.

Pyke, K. D. (1996), "Class-Based Masculinities: The Interdependence of Gender, Class and Interpersonal Power," *Gender and Society*, 10 (5): 527–49.

Ramazanoglu, C. (1989), *Feminism and the Contradictions of Oppression*, London: Routledge.

Ramazanoglu, C. and J. Holland (2002), *Feminist Methodology: Changes and Choices*. London: Sage.

Rammund-Mansingh, A. and M. Seedat-Khan (2020), "Understanding the Career Trajectories of Black Female Academics in South Africa: A Case Study of the University of Kwazulu—Natal," *Perspectives in Education*, 38 (2): 56–69.

Reay, D. and S. Ball (2000), "Essentials of Female Management: Women's Ways of Working in the Education Marketplace?," *Educational Management and Administration*, 28 (2): 145–59.

Regan, H. B. and G. H. Brooks (1995), *Out of Women's Experience: Creating Relational Leadership*, Thousand Oaks: Corwin Press.

Reilly, E. C. (2022), "Women in Educational Leadership in Afghanistan, Costa Rica, and Rwanda: Reifying Sociocultural Capital." In V. Showunmi, P. Moorosi, C. Shakeshaft and I. Oplatka (eds), *The Bloomsbury Handbook of Gender and Educational Leadership and Management*, 257–71, London: Bloomsbury Academic.

Reilly, E. C. and Q. J. Bauer (eds) (2015), *Women Leading across Continents: Overcoming the Barriers*, Lanham: Rowman and Littlefield.

Reskin, B. F. (2003), "Including Mechanisms in Our Models of a Scriptive Inequality," *American Sociological Review*, 65: 210–33.

Reynolds, C. (2008), "Women and Secondary School Principal Rotation/Succession: A Study of the Beliefs of Decision Makers in Four Provinces," *Canadian Journal of Education,* 31 (1): 32–54.

Reynolds, T. (2002), "Re-Thinking a Black Feminist Standpoint," *Ethnic and Racial Studies*, 26 (3): 591–606.

Richardson, D. (2008), "Conceptualising Gender." In D. Richardson and V. Robinson (eds), *Introducing Gender and Women's Studies*, 3–19, Basingstoke: Palgrave Macmillan.

Riehl, C., and M. A. Byrd (1997), "Gender Differences among New Recruits to School Administration," *Educational Evaluation and Policy Analysis*, 19: 45–64.

Rivera, L. A. (2012), "Hiring as Cultural Matching: The Case of Elite Professional Service Firms," *American Sociological Review*, 77 (6): 999–1022.

Rosario, H. A. (2018), "Barriers and Strategies: Stories of Women's Rise to Leadership in Higher Education in the Philippines," In R. Mcnae and E. C. Reilly (eds), *Women Leading Education across Continents: Finding and Harnessing the Joy in Leadership*, 52–9, Lanham: Rowman and Littlefield.

Rose, S. (2001), "Escaping Evolutionary Psychology." In H. Rose and S. Rose (eds), *Alas Poor Darwin: Arguments against Evolutionary Psychology*, 299–320, London: Vintage.

Rubin, H. and I. Rubin (1995), *Qualitative Interviewing: The Art of Hearing Data*, Thousand Oaks: Sage.

Ruijs, A. (1993), *Women Managers in Education: A Worldwide Progress Report*, Bristol: The Staff College, Coombe Lodge Report.

Runte, M. and A. J. Mills (2006), "Cold War, Chilly Climate: Exploring the Roots of Gendered Discourse in Organization and Management Theory," *Human Relations*, 59 (5): 695–720.

Ryan, M. K. and S. A. Haslam (2005), "The Glass Cliff: Evidence That Women Are Over-Represented in Precarious Leadership Positions," *British Journal of Management*, 16 (2): 81–90.

Rydstrom, H. (2006), "Masculinity and Punishment: Men's Upbringing of Boys in Rural Vietnam," *Childhood*, 13 (3): 329–48.

Saban, A., B. N. Kocbeker and A. Saban (2007), "Prospective Teachers' Conception of Teaching and Learning through Metaphor Analysis," *Learning and Instruction*, 17: 123–39.

Sachs, J. and J. Blackmore (1998), "You Never Show You Can't Cope: Women in School Leadership Roles Managing Their Emotions," *Gender and Education*, 10 (3): 265–80.

Sadker, M. and D. Sadker (1994), *Failing at Fairness: How America's Schools Cheat Girls*, New York: Charles Scribner's Sons.

Saitis, C. (2002), *The Head Teacher in the Modern School*, Athens: Self Publication. [In Greek]

Salvati, L. (2018), "Populations Structure and Economic Cycles in Greece: A Multidimensional Regional Analysis (1988–2016)," *Journal of Urban and Regional Analysis*, X (1): 61–78.

Sam, F. K., A. M. Amartei, B. Osei-Owusu and O. O. Antrobe (2013), "Female Leadership Stereotypes: The Perception of the Leadership of Female Heads of Senior High Schools in Ashanti Region," *Educational Research*, 4 (10): 702–9.

Samman, E., E. Presler-Marchal, N. Jones, T. Bhatkal, C. Melamed, M. S. Tavropoulou and J. Wallace (2016), *Women's Work: Mothers, Children and the Global Childcare Crisis*, London: Overseas Development Institute.

Sandilands, C. (2004), "Sexual Politics and Environmental Justice: Lesbian Separatists in Rural Oregon." In R. Stein (ed), *New Perspectives on Environmental Justice: Gender, Sexuality and Activism*, 109–26, New Jersey: Rutgers.

Sandoval, C. (1990), "Women Respond to Racism: A Report of the 1981 National Women's Studies Association Conference." In G. Anzalua (ed), *Making Face, Making*

Soul: Creative and Critical Perspectives by Feminists-of-Color, 55–71, San Francisco: Spinsters/Aunt Lane.

Schein, V. (1994), "Managerial Sex Typing: A Persistent and Pervasive Barrier to Women's Opportunities." In M. Davidson and R. Burke (eds), *Women in Management. Current Research Issues*, Vol. I, 41–52, London: Paul Chapman Publishing.

Schmuck, P. A. (1980), "Changing Women's Representation in School Management: A Systems Perspective." In S. K. Biklen and M. Brannigan (eds), *Women and Educational Leadership*, 239–59, Lexington: Lexington.

Sergiovanni, T. J. (1991), *The Principalship: A Reflective Practice Perspective*, Boston: Allyn and Bacon.

Shah, S. (2009), "Women and Educational Leadership in a Muslim Society: A Study of Women College Heads in Pakistan." In H. Sobehart (ed), *Women Leading Education across the Continents: Sharing the Spirit, Fanning the Flame*, 128–42, Plymouth: Rowman and Littlefield Education.

Shah, S. (2018), "'We Are Equals': Datum or Delusion: Perception of Muslim Women Academics in Three Malaysian Universities," *British Journal of Sociology of Education*, 39 (3): 299–315.

Shah, S. (2022), "Gender, Leadership and Positional Power." In V. Showunmi, P. Moorosi, C. Shakeshaft and I. Oplatka (eds), *The Bloomsbury Handbook of Gender and Educational Leadership and Management*, 56–65, London: Bloomsbury Academic.

Shakeshaft, C. (1985), "Strategies for Overcoming Barrier to Women Administrators." In S. S. Klein (ed), *Handbook of Achieving Sex Equity through Education*, 122–44, Baltimore: The Johns Hopkins University Press.

Shakeshaft, C. (1989), *Women in Educational Administration*, Newbury Park, Ca: Sage.

Shakeshaft, C. (2006), "Gender and Educational Management." In C. Skelton, B. Francis and L. Smulyan (eds), *The Sage Handbook of Gender in Education*, 408–512, London: Sage.

Shakeshaft, C., G. Brown, B. I. Irby, M. Grogan and J. Ballenger (2010), "Increasing Gender Equity in Educational Leadership." In S. S. Klein (ed), *Handbook for Achieving Gender Equity through Education. Second Edition*, 103–29, New York: Routledge.

Sherman, W. H., A. J. Muñoz and A. Pankake (2008), "The Great Divide: Women's Experiences with Mentoring," *Journal of Women in Educational Leadership*, 6 (4): 239–59.

Showunmi, V. (2018), "Black and White Women's Leadership: Disadvantage and Privilege." In J. S. Brooks and G. Theoharis (eds), *White Education: Privilege, Power, and Prejudice in School and Society*, 62–78, Abingdon: Routledge.

Showunmi, V., D. Atewologun, and D. Beddington (2016), "Ethnic, Gender and Class Intersections in British Women's Leadership Experience," *Educational Management Administration and Leadership*, 44 (6): 917–35.

Showunmi, V., P. Moorosi, C. Shakeshaft, and I. Oplatka (eds) (2022), *The Bloomsbury Handbook of Gender and Educational Leadership and Management*, London: Bloomsbury.

Sikes, P. (1997), *Parents Who Teach: Stories from School and from Home*, London: Cassell.

Silverman, D. (2009), *Doing Qualitative Research*, London: Sage.

Sinclair, A. (2004), "Journey around Leadership," *Discourse: Studies in the Cultural Politics of Education*, 25 (1): 7–19.

Sinclair, A. (2013), "Not Just 'Adding Women' in: Women Re-Making Leadership." In R. Francis, P. Grimshaw and P. Standish (eds), *Seizing the Initiative: Australian Women Leaders in Politics, Workplaces and Communities*, 15–34, Melbourne: University of Melbourne Press.

Sinclair, A. and V. Wilson (2002), *New Faces of Leadership*, Melbourne: Melbourne University Press.

Singh, V., S. Terjesen and S. Vinnicombe (2008), "Newly Appointed Directors in the Boardroom: How Do Women and Men Differ?," *European Management Journal*, 26 (1): 48–58.

Singleton, C. (1993), "Women Deputy Headteachers in Educational Management." In M. Preedy (ed), *Managing the Effective School*, 163–76, London: Paul Chapman Publishing.

Skelton, C. (2002), "The 'Feminisation of Schooling' or 'Remasculinising Primary Education'?," *International Studies in Sociology of Education*, 12: 77–96.

Smith, J. (2016), "Motherhood and Women Teachers' Career Decisions: A Constant Battle." In K. Fuller and J. Hartford (eds), *Gender and Leadership in Education: Women Achieving against the Odds*, 83–114, Oxford: Peter Lang.

Sowell, T. (2005), *Affirmative Action around the World: An Empirical Analysis*, New Haven, Ct: Yale University Press.

Speer, S. (2005), "The Interactional Organization of the Gender Attribution Process," *Sociology*, 39 (1): 67–87.

Stanley, L. (1990), *Feminist Praxis*, London: Routledge.

Stark, O. and W. Hyll (2014), "Socially Gainful Gender Quotas." In *Zef-Discussion Papers on Development Policy No 190*, Bonn: Center for Development Research.

Steed, K., J. De Nobile and M. Waniganayake (2021), "Promotion to Leadership, Not Just Merit, but Insider Knowledge: What Do School Principals Say?," *Journal of Educational Leadership, Policy and Practice*, 36 (1): 1–21.

Stevens, P. (2007), "Researching Race/Ethnicity and Educational Inequality in English Secondary Schools: A Critical Review of the Research Literature between 1980 and 2005," *Review of Educational Research*, 77 (2): 147–85.

Stevens, P. (2008), "Exploring Pupils' Perceptions of Teacher Racism in Their Context: A Case Study of Turkish and Belgian Vocational Education Pupils in a Belgian School," *British Journal of Sociology of Education*, 29 (2): 175–87.

Stobo-Gaskell, J. (1995), *Secondary Schools in Canada: The National Report of the Exemplary Schools Project*, Toronto: Canadian Education Association.

Strachan, J. (1999), "Feminist Educational Leadership: Locating the Concepts in Practice," *Gender and Education*, 11 (3): 309–22.
Stratigaki, M. (N.D.), *Annotated Bibliography on Gender Issues. Lab for Gender Studies and Equality*, Athens: Panteion University, 11/3/2012, Available Online: Http://Www.Genderpanteion.Gr/Gr/Didaktiko_Pdf/Spiridaki.Pdf. [In Greek]
Sullivan, O. (2006), *Changing Gender Relations, Changing Families: Tracing the Pace of Change over Time*, Lanham: Rowman and Littlefield Publishers.
Surgue, C. and C. Furlong (2002), "The Cosmologies of Irish Primary Principals' Identities. Between the Modern and the Postmodern?," *International Journal of Leadership in Education*, 5 (3): 189–210.
Svensson, A. M. and A. Gunnarsson (2012), "Gender Equality on the Swedish Welfare State," *Feminists@Law*, 2 (1).
Swann, W. B., J. H. Langlois and L. A. Gilbert (1999), "Introduction." In W. B. Swann, J. H. Langlois and L. A. Gilbert (eds), *Sexism and Stereotypes in Modern Society. The Gender Science of Janet Tayler Spence*, 3–7, Washington, DC: Apa.
Taki, V. (2009), *Gendered Absence: Women in Educational Management—An Alternative Model*, Athens: Epikentro. [In Greek]
Tamale, S. (1997), "When Hens Begin to Crow: Gender and Parliamentary Politics in Contemporary Uganda," PhD Thesis, University of Minnesota.
Tangonyire, R., G. Nyame, K. B. Assare and A. J. Alhassan (2022), "The Experiences of Female Headteschers of Boys' Senior High Schools in Ghana," *Educational Management Administration and Leadership*, 0 (0): 1–22.
Taylor, E. (2021), "'No Fear': Privilege and the Navigation of Hierarchy at an Elite Boys' School in England," *British Journal of Sociology of Education*, 42 (7): 935–50.
Taylor, L. E. (1995), "Joining the Old Boys' Club," *Canada and the World Backgrounder*, 60 (4): 12–15.
Taylor, V. (1998), "Feminist Methodology in Social Movements Research," *Qualitative Sociology*, 21 (4): 357–79.
The Guardian (July 16, 2014), *Greece's Golden Dawn Party Describes Hitler as "Great Personality,"* 20/9/2014, Available Online: Http://Www.Theguardian.Com/World/2014/Apr/16/Greece-Golden-Dawn-Hitler.
Thomas, D. (2006), "A General Inductive Approach for Analysing Qualitative Evaluation Data," *American Journal of Evaluation*, 27 (2): 237–46.
Thornton, M. and P. Bricheno (2006), *Missing Men in Education*, Stoke-on-Trent: Trentham.
Thylefors, I., O. Persson, M. Thylefors, J. O. Agak and D. T. Kipchirchir Serem (2007), "Same but Different: Head Teachers' Perceptions of Leadership in Kenya and Sweden," *Education Review*, 4 (2): 42–59.
To Vima (July 24, 2011), *Taxman in the Mornings, Shepherd in the Afternoons*. [In Greek]
Tronto, J. (2002), "Care as the Work of Citizens: A Modest Proposal." In M. Friedman (ed), *Women and Citizenship*, 130–45, Oxford: Oxford University Press.

Tsoulea, R., and M. Kaitanidi (2005), "Lottery Ticket Is to Find a Place in a Day Nursery," *Ta Nea*, June 13. [In Greek]

Turkel, R. A. (1988), "Money as a Mirror of Marriage," *Journal of the American Academy of Psychoanalysis*, 16: 525–35.

Tzamalouka, G. (2000), "Social Representations of Homosexuality in Modern Greece." In Th. Papazizi, N. Chatzitrifon and Th. Ktenidis (eds), *Gender and Behaviour, Homosexuality-Homophobia. The Situation in Greece and Perspectives for Improvement. 9–10 October, Thessaloniki. Conference Proceedings*, 133–44, Athens: Epikentro. [In Greek]

Tzamalouka, G. (2002), "Social Representations and Attributional Attitudes of Homesexuality in Modern Greece," PhD Thesis Panteion University: Faculty of Political and Social Sciences.

UNESCO (1953), *Progress of Literacy in Various Countries: A Preliminary Statistical Study of Available Census Data since 1900*, Paris: UNESCO.

US Bureau of Labor Statistics (2021), 19/3/2023, Available Online: Https://Www.Dol.Gov/Agencies/Wb/Data/Mothers-Families/Laborforceparticipationrates-Mothers-Father-Agechild.

Van Der Boon, M. (2003), "Women in International Management: An International Perspective on Women's Ways of Leadership," *Women in Management Review*, 18 (3): 132–46.

Van Helden, D. L., L. Den Dulk, B. Seijn and M. W. Vernooij (2021), "Gender, Networks and Academic Leadership: A Systematic Review," *Educational Management Administration and Leadership*, 0 (0): 1–18.

Van Veelen, R., B. Derks and M. D. Endedijk (2019), "Double Trouble: How Being Outnumbered and Negatively Stereotyped Threatens Career Outcomes of Women in Stem," *Frontiers in Psychology*, 10: 40–57.

Varikas, E. (2004), "National and Gender Identity in Turn-Off the Century Greece." In S. Paletschek and B. Pietrow-Ennker (eds), *Women's Emancipation Movements in the Nineteenth Century*, 263–79, Stanford: Stanford University Press.

Vella, R. (2022), "Leadership and Women: The Space between Us. Narrating the Stories of Senior Female Academic Leaders in Malta," *Educational Management Administration and Leadership*, 50 (1): 121–39.

Vincovic, M. (2023), "Leading or Breeding: Looking Ahead: Gender Segregation in the Labour Market and the Equal Distribution of Family Responsibilities." In F. G. Caparezz, L. Kovacevic and E. Kristoffersson (eds), *Gender Perspectives in Private Law. Gender Perspectives in Law, Vol. 4*, 129–51, Cambridge: Springer.

Voulgaridis, E. (2018), "Critical Approach to Qualifications and the System of Choice of School Unit Managers from Secondary School Teachers in Pieria," MA Dissertation, Alexander Tei of Thessaloniki, Thessaloniki. [In Greek]

Wahl, A. (2010), "The Impact of Gender Equality on the Management and Leadership: Reflections on Change and Resistance." In L. Huusu, J. Hearn, A.-M. Lamsa and S. Vanhala (eds), *Leadership through the Gender Lens: Women and Men in Organizations*, 1–20, Helsinki: Hanken School of Economics Reports.

Wajcman, J. (1998), *Managing Like a Man: Women and Men in Corporate Management*, Cambridge: Polity Press.
Walby, S. (1990), *Theorizing Patriarchy*, Oxford: Blackwell.
Walby, S. (1997), *Gender Transformations*, London: Routledge.
Walby, S. (2007), "Theorizing the Gendering of the Knowledge Economy: Comparative Perspectives." In S. Walby, H. Gottfried, K. Gottschall and M. Osawa (eds), *Gendering the Knowledge Economy: Comparative Perspectives*, 3–50, London: Palgrave.
Walby, S. (2009), "Gender and the Financial Crisis," *Paper for UNESCO Project on "Gender and the Financial Crisis*," 20/8/2022, Available Online: Http://Www.Lancaster.Ac.Uk/Fass/Doc_Library/Sociology/Gender_And_Financial_Crisis_Sylvia_Walby.Pdf.
Walker, A. and P. Kwan (2012), "Principal Selection Panels: Strategies, Preferences and Perceptions," *Journal of Educational Administration*, 50 (2): 188–205.
Walkerdine, V. (1990), *Schoolgirl Fictions*, London: Verso.
Ware, V. (1991), *Beyond the Pale: White Women, Racism and History*, London: Verso.
Warin, J. and E. Gannerud (2014), "Gender, Teaching and Care: A Comparative Conversation," *Gender and Education*, 26 (3): 193–200.
Warning, R. and F. R. Buchanan (2009), "An Exploration of Unspoken Bias: Women Who Work for Woman," *Gender in Management: An International Journal*, 24 (2): 131–45.
Warsal, D. (2015), "The Impact of Culture on Women's Leadership in Vanuatu Secondary Schools." In R. Mcnae Mcnae and E. C. Reilly (eds), *Women Leading Education across Continents: Finding and Harnessing the Joy in Leadership*, 22–6, Lanham: Rowman and Littlefield.
Weitzman, E. A. (2000), "Software and Qualitative Research." In N. K. Denzin and Y. S. Lincoln (eds), *The Sage Handbook of Qualitative Research*, 803–20, Thousand Oaks: Sage.
West, C. and D. H. Zimmerman (1987), "Doing Gender," *Gender and Society*, 1: 125–51.
White, K. (2001), "Women in the Professorate in Australia," *International Journal of Organizational Behavior*, 3 (2): 64–76.
White, K. (2018), "If It Ain't Broke, Don't Fix It [Book Review]," *The Australian Universities' Review*, 60 (2): 88–9.
Whitehead, K. (2013), "Worklife Balance and Wellbeing, and the Un/Changing Nature of Teachers' Work," *Education Research and Perspectives*, 40: 255–75.
Whitehead, S. M. (2002), *Men and Masculinities: Key Themes and New Directions*, Cambridge: Polity Press.
Wigfield, A., J. S. Eccles and P. R. Pintrich (1996), "Development between the Ages of 11 and 25." In D. C. Berliner and R. C. Calfee (eds), *Handbook of Educational Psychology*, 148–85, New York: Macmillan.
Wilkinson, J. (1991), "Perceived Barriers of Women Who Aspire to the Principalship," PhD Thesis, Ohio: The Ohio State University.
Wilkinson, J. and K. Macdonald (2022), "Gender, Educational Leadership and Social Justice." In V. Showunmi, P. Moorosi, C. Shakeshaft and I. Oplatka (eds), *The*

Bloomsbury Handbook of Gender and Educational Leadership and Management, 90–100, London: Bloomsbury Academic.

Williams, C. L. (1992), "The Glass Escalator: Hidden Advantages for Men in the 'Female' Professions," *Social Problems*, 39 (3): 253–67.

Wilson, M. (ed) (1997), *Women in Educational Management: A European Perspective*, London: Paul Chapman.

Wimmer, A. and K. Lewis (2010), "Beyond and below Racial Homophily," *American Journal of Sociology*, 116: 583–642.

Witt, S. D. (2000), "The Influence of Television on Children's Gender Socialization: A Review of the Literature," *Childhood Education*, 76 (5): 322–4.

Witz, A. (1992), *Professions and Patriarchy*, London: Routledge.

Wolf-Wendel, L. and K. Wark (2006), "Academic Life and Motherhood: Variations by Institutional Type," *Higher Education*, 52 (3): 487–521.

Women of Syriza Network Declaration (2008), "For Syriza for Both Genders," 15/5/2012, Available Online: Www.Syriza.Gr/Taytotita/Epitropes-Syriza/Dysktio-Gynaikon-Syriza/Gia-Ton-Syriza-Ton-Dyo-Fylon.

Wood, M. (1997), "Gender Differences in Mentoring: A Biographical Reflection," *Educational Management and Administration*, 25 (1): 25–34.

Woodhouse, J. and L. Guihen (2022), "The Missing Statistics in Initial Teachers Education: Experiences and Support Needs of Student Teachers Who Are Mothers." In V. Showunmi, P. Moorosi, C. Shakeshaft and I. Oplatka (eds), *The Bloomsbury Handbook of Gender and Educational Leadership and Management*, 291–304, London: Bloomsbury Academic.

World Economic Forum (2022), "Global Gender Gap Report," 20/3/2023, Available Online: Https://Www.Weforum.Org/Reports/Global-Gender-Gap-Report-2022/.

Worlddata.Info (2021), "Cost of Living and Purchasing Power Related to Average Income," 27/9/2022, Available Online: Https://Www.Worlddata.Info/Cost-Of-Living.Php.

You, M. H. and P. S. Ko (2004), "Gender and Career Development: An Analysis of the Promotion of Elementary School Principles in Taiwan," *Bulletin of Educational Research*, 50 (4): 45–77.

Zehnter, K. M. and E. Kirchler (2020), "Women Quotas vs Men Quotas in Academia: Students Perceive Favoring Women as Less Fair than Favoring Men," *Frontiers in Psychology*, 11: 700.

Zembylas, M., V. Bozalek and T. Shefer (2014), "Tronto's Notion of *Privileged Responsibility* and the Reconceptualisation of Care: Implications for Critical Pedagogies of Emotion in Higher Education," *Gender and Education*, 26 (3): 200–14.

Zimianitis, K. (2007), "The Role of Television in Shaping Children's Social Behavior," *Scientific Debate*, N.P. [In Greek]

Index

ability 6, 39, 45, 59, 67, 73, 94, 100
actions 7, 17, 74, 75, 76, 77, 91
administration 3, 43, 109, 110, 111
administrative 1, 31, 33, 47, 55, 97, 107, 114, 115
    post 33
administrator 4, 57, 58, 81
androgynous 34
approach 3, 4, 7, 12, 13, 14, 17, 18, 19, 34, 39, 40, 43, 72, 73, 76, 77, 78, 79, 80, 81, 93, 106, 109, 122, 130, 132, 133
    gendered 3, 77, 132
    general inductive 41, 130
    grounded theory 33
    leadership 14, 17, 18, 19, 32, 33, 34, 35, 64, 71, 72, 76, 77, 78, 79, 80, 81, 90, 92, 93, 99, 100, 106, 110, 131, 132
    multidimensional 18
    social constructionist 4
    theoretical 38, 71, 101
aspirations 19, 21, 47, 107
    career. *see career aspirations*
authoritative 72, 76, 79, 81, 86, 87, 88, 89, 97
authority 11, 27, 37, 43, 54, 73, 74, 76, 77, 79, 80, 84, 86, 100, 110
autocratic 32, 33, 76, 77, 78, 79, 92

Bakhtin 9
balance 22, 50, 52, 63, 65, 94, 100, 114, 116, 132
barriers 19, 20, 37, 52, 53, 98, 104, 106, 107, 108, 128
    cultural 19
    internal 37, 105, 106, 107
    societal 106
    structural 19
binary 6, 10, 34, 71, 81, 99, 106
    gender 4, 87, 98
biological 4, 6, 7, 71, 72
    differences 7
Blackmore 3, 44, 46, 47, 53, 61, 65, 89, 100, 103

blame the victim 19, 102, 106
bureaucracy 4, 55, 93
bureaucratic 7, 32
Burr 4, 8, 38, 82, 88, 106, 129

capable 21, 48, 49, 65, 67, 70, 81, 82, 84
career 3, 14, 17, 18, 19, 20, 22, 33, 34, 37, 41, 42, 44, 46, 48, 50, 51, 52, 53, 61, 62, 65, 67, 70, 71, 72, 73, 94, 95, 96, 98, 100, 101, 102, 107, 109, 123, 125, 128, 131, 132
    aspirations 46, 70, 100, 132
    development 20, 33, 94
    plan 41, 46
    progress 57, 59, 70
    progression 20, 42, 47, 64, 94, 95, 131
    trajectories 46
caring 8, 17, 21, 26, 47, 50, 51, 64, 65, 68, 69, 78, 81, 82, 83, 86, 87, 88, 89, 90, 99, 100, 103, 104, 127, 132
    profession 27
    responsibilities 50, 67
    roles 66, 72, 79, 88, 126
changes 11, 16, 84, 100, 108, 112, 114, 115, 116, 118, 119, 121, 122, 127, 128, 129, 132
childcare 53, 70, 114, 116, 117, 119, 128, 132
    provision 115, 116, 117, 118
Coleman 3, 18, 20, 21, 22, 25, 26, 27, 33, 42, 44, 45, 48, 50, 52, 61, 62, 63, 64, 65, 66, 73, 90, 93, 94, 96, 101, 110, 115, 130, 131
colleagues 1, 15, 20, 29, 31, 46, 47, 48, 49, 52, 55, 58, 64, 65, 73, 78, 80, 82, 83, 85, 88, 96, 104, 130, 131
combining 14, 21, 33, 37, 50, 53, 73, 107
confidence 19, 45, 46, 47, 48, 49, 70, 101, 104, 108, 131
Connell 8, 9, 10, 47, 66, 68, 74, 81, 91, 128
constructed 5, 7, 10, 18, 21, 27, 34, 37, 45, 47, 50, 53, 57, 61, 67, 68, 72, 73, 74, 77, 81, 83, 84, 85, 86, 87, 89, 91, 92,

170 *Index*

93, 94, 97, 99, 101, 108, 121, 123, 124, 125, 126, 127, 129, 131, 132
construction 7, 10
constructionism 8
   social 2, 5, 6, 8, 38, 129
constructions 3, 4, 5, 8, 11, 14, 19, 21, 38, 45, 53, 65, 66, 67, 68, 69, 72, 73, 75, 78, 80, 81, 82, 83, 85, 90, 92, 94, 99, 100, 104, 105, 108, 114, 115, 120, 124, 125, 129, 130, 131, 132, 133
   feminine 47, 49, 80
   femininities 8, 104
   femininity 23, 53, 54, 57, 61, 69, 70, 83, 99, 104, 106, 108, 120, 121, 125, 127, 128, 132
   gender 13, 21, 34, 59, 66, 73, 78, 80, 81, 86, 87, 122, 126, 127, 128, 132
   gendered. *see gendered constructions*
   homogeneous 104
   identities 2
   leadership 14, 31
   masculine 35, 47, 53, 64, 76, 80, 103, 107, 110, 119
   masculinities 9
   masculinity 49, 54, 57, 69, 70, 99, 106, 121, 125, 128, 132
   motherhood 82, 83
   traditional 10, 23, 54, 61, 66, 67, 83, 99, 106, 114, 121, 123, 126, 128
context 4, 5, 7, 8, 9, 14, 17, 18, 19, 22, 33, 35, 38, 53, 57, 68, 69, 71, 79, 85, 87, 88, 90, 97, 100, 101, 105, 106, 113, 130, 133
corporal punishment 74, 75, 76
criticized 8, 56, 113
critique 3, 6, 7, 11, 12, 39, 71
culture 7, 11, 12, 20, 26, 103, 106, 129
   heteronormative 56
   heterosexism 55, 56
   masculine. *see masculine culture*
   organizational 20, 37
   school 18

democratic 17, 18, 33, 57, 69, 76, 77
deputy 26, 30, 31, 42, 43, 130
deputy head teachers. *see deputy*
dichotomy 17, 18, 68, 81
differences 3, 6, 7, 8, 9, 12, 15, 17, 18, 19, 21, 23, 34, 35, 39, 41, 71, 79, 90, 92, 103, 104, 106, 133

biological. *see biological differences*
   gender 99
difficulties 14, 15, 21, 52, 70, 89, 96, 99, 119
directive 7, 18
discipline 32, 34, 54, 73, 74, 76, 77, 81, 86, 90, 100
discrimination 20, 58, 63, 66, 109, 113, 114
   covert 131
   reverse 112
domestic work 51, 52, 61, 70, 96, 97, 120, 126
domesticity 23, 65, 103
dominance 9, 23, 91, 113
drift 96
drifting 46

effective 17, 31, 54, 62, 74, 90, 130
encouragement 20
England 20, 21, 26, 66, 75, 91, 115
equal 15, 25, 29, 65, 79, 88, 100, 110, 111, 112, 127, 128
equality 25, 91, 109, 111, 112, 118, 123, 124, 133
essentialism 2, 98
   gender 6
essentialist 6, 7, 8, 18
   dualisms 18
essentialized 104, 108, 127
EU 16, 21, 26, 50, 111, 117
European Parliament 26
European Union 115
events
   monoglossic 10
exclusion 11, 20, 33, 56, 62, 63
experiences 2, 3, 5, 6, 7, 10, 13, 14, 15, 17, 18, 19, 21, 27, 29, 35, 37, 38, 39, 40, 41, 44, 47, 54, 58, 60, 62, 70, 87, 94, 99, 104, 107, 110, 119, 129, 130, 131, 133

family 11, 14, 21, 23, 26, 27, 33, 51, 52, 53, 61, 65, 66, 67, 70, 72, 73, 75, 76, 79, 95, 96, 97, 99, 100, 107, 110, 115, 116, 120, 121, 122, 123, 125, 126, 127, 128, 130, 131, 132, 133
   commitment 34, 94, 116
   responsibilities. *see responsibilities family*

father 1, 23, 25, 53, 67, 72, 74, 79, 81, 82, 85, 86, 87
fatherhood 86, 96
female activities 121
feminine 6, 7, 8, 9, 10, 13, 14, 17, 18, 26, 28, 29, 33, 34, 35, 39, 47, 48, 49, 62, 66, 69, 71, 72, 76, 77, 79, 80, 81, 82, 88, 89, 91, 92, 93, 94, 97, 98, 100, 104, 106, 124, 125, 128, 131
  constructions. *see constructions feminine*
femininities 2, 8, 9, 18, 68, 78
  construction of. *see constructions femininities*
  dominant 124
femininity 8, 9, 10, 18, 29, 47, 50, 54, 57, 61, 66, 68, 69, 70, 72, 78, 83, 85, 86, 87, 89, 99, 103, 104, 106, 108, 113, 114, 120, 121, 125, 126, 127, 128, 132
  constructions of. *see constructions of femininity*
  traditional notions of 10, 47
feminist 3, 5, 6, 10, 38, 39, 72, 119, 129, 130
  perspectives 3, 75
flexible 12, 17, 64, 92
fluid 7, 10, 11, 12, 34, 71, 79, 86, 105, 106, 131
Foucault 56
framework 5, 38, 41, 91, 125
  legal 25, 43, 50, 91, 94, 111
  legislative 61
  methodological 70, 72
  social constructionist 3, 5, 9
  theoretical 10, 18, 37, 38, 70, 72, 129
Francis 9, 10, 71, 75, 76, 81, 100, 106, 129, 132

gender 6, 7, 8, 9, 10, 11, 12, 13, 14, 15, 17, 18, 19, 22, 23, 24, 25, 26, 27, 28, 29, 33, 34, 35, 37, 38, 39, 40, 41, 44, 45, 49, 53, 58, 60, 61, 65, 66, 67, 68, 70, 71, 72, 73, 78, 81, 82, 86, 87, 89, 97, 99, 101, 104, 106, 109, 110, 111, 112, 113, 118, 119, 120, 121, 122, 123, 124, 125, 126, 129, 130, 131, 133
  binary. *see binary gender*
  constructions. *see constructions gender*
  differences. *see differences gender*
  essentialism. *see essentialism gender*
  heteroglossia 10, 100
  identities 6, 7, 8, 10, 34, 129, 131
  identity 8, 10, 72
  monoglossia 10
  relations. *see relations gender*
  theory 6
gendered 6, 7, 10, 27, 39, 61, 71, 72, 73, 75, 101, 105, 107, 123, 126, 129, 131
  approach. *see approach gendered*
  constructions 33, 130
  identities. *see identities gendered*
  relations. *see relations gendered*
Greece 2, 6, 11, 13, 14, 22, 23, 24, 25, 26, 27, 29, 30, 31, 32, 33, 34, 37, 39, 40, 42, 43, 44, 45, 47, 49, 50, 51, 52, 53, 55, 58, 59, 60, 61, 62, 63, 74, 89, 91, 94, 95, 96, 97, 98, 101, 102, 105, 108, 109, 111, 113, 114, 115, 116, 117, 118, 119, 120, 121, 123, 124, 130, 131, 133
Greek 1, 2, 4, 9, 11, 13, 14, 22, 23, 24, 25, 26, 27, 29, 30, 31, 32, 33, 34, 35, 37, 40, 43, 44, 48, 49, 53, 56, 58, 61, 65, 75, 76, 77, 82, 84, 91, 92, 97, 100, 107, 111, 113, 114, 115, 118, 119, 120, 121, 122, 123, 124, 125, 126, 128, 129, 130, 133
Greeks 9, 23, 60, 75, 128

harassment 56
  sexual 27, 91, 112
hegemonic masculinity 68, 99
Hellenic Statistical Authority 26, 27, 28, 29, 30, 31, 44, 96, 118, 124
heteroglossia 9
heteroglossic
  events 10
heterosexual 57, 58, 66, 129
heterosexuality 56, 125
hierarchical 26, 30, 32, 77, 79
  relationship. *see relationship hierarchical*
Higher Education Statistics Agency 45
hindrance 66, 98, 107
homogeneous 68, 75, 104
  constructions. *see constructions homogeneous*
  groups 18, 34, 35
homophily 48

household 1, 11, 12, 22, 24, 99, 119
  responsibilities 21, 22, 52, 120
housework 22

identities 4, 6, 7, 8, 10, 12, 18, 22, 35, 48, 49, 56, 67, 73, 78, 86, 88, 89, 90, 97, 99, 104, 113, 125, 127, 132
  constructions. *see constructions identities*
  gender. *see gender identities*
  gendered 17, 71, 131
  multiple 21, 35, 37
  social 52, 67
identity 7, 8, 19, 21, 56, 57, 75, 78, 79, 83, 85, 86, 87, 88, 89, 90, 99, 104, 127, 131
  gender. *see gender identity*
  professional 56
inequalities 6, 10, 11, 25, 39, 66, 84, 105, 109, 119
inferior 21, 23, 24, 37, 45
informal 17, 93, 131
Intersectionality 39
interviews 5, 40, 41, 55, 57, 58, 59, 61, 64, 65, 67, 69, 76, 80, 90, 101, 108, 110, 111, 113, 115, 126, 127, 130, 131
  in-depth 34
  panel 20, 131
  semi-structured 39, 72

LEA. *see Local Educational Authorities*
leadership 2, 3, 4, 6, 7, 8, 10, 13, 15, 16, 18, 19, 20, 21, 22, 27, 29, 30, 33, 35, 37, 39, 44, 48, 53, 54, 59, 62, 65, 66, 68, 69, 71, 78, 79, 81, 82, 83, 85, 89, 90, 92, 93, 95, 98, 101, 102, 103, 104, 105, 106, 107, 108, 109, 111, 113, 114, 116, 118, 123, 126, 128, 129, 130, 131, 132, 133
  approach. *see approach leadership*
  constructions. *see constructions leadership*
  diversity 3, 10, 62, 72
  style 13, 17, 34, 44
  theory 7
Local Educational Authorities 31, 33, 45, 48, 59, 64, 78, 79

male femininities 10
management 3, 18, 31, 43, 47, 49, 54, 55, 59, 62, 85, 99, 102, 109, 115, 127
  educational 2, 6, 11, 33, 39, 60, 120

masculine 6, 7, 9, 10, 13, 14, 17, 18, 19, 20, 26, 29, 31, 34, 35, 39, 44, 47, 48, 49, 54, 57, 63, 65, 66, 68, 69, 71, 72, 76, 77, 79, 80, 81, 82, 86, 87, 89, 90, 92, 93, 94, 98, 99, 100, 106, 108, 110, 111, 115, 121, 125, 128, 129, 131
  constructions. *see constructions masculine*
  culture 19, 35, 102
masculine femininity 81
masculinities
  dominant 124
  multiple 2, 8, 9, 99, 124
masculinity 9, 10, 23, 47, 49, 50, 54, 57, 62, 66, 67, 68, 69, 70, 72, 74, 78, 80, 81, 83, 85, 86, 87, 91, 99, 103, 106, 113, 114, 121, 125, 126, 127, 128, 132
  constructions of. *see constructions masculinity*
  dominant 69, 81
  hegemonic 66, 81, 91
  paternalistic 67
  traditional notions of 10
mentors 20, 63
methodology 14, 37
Ministry of Education and Religious Affairs 25
Ministry of Education, Research and Religious Affairs 25, 28, 32, 107, 117
monoglossia 9
monoglossic
  events 10
mother 1, 21, 22, 23, 24, 25, 51, 52, 53, 72, 79, 83, 85, 86, 88, 89, 90, 96, 115, 118, 123, 124, 125, 126, 127
motherhood 53, 82, 83, 86, 89, 96, 99, 103

network 19, 20, 21, 38, 48, 59, 61, 62, 63, 109, 110, 118, 131
  good old boys 62
  informal 62
  old boys 20
  old boys' 61, 62, 63
  political 60, 61
  professional. *see professional networks*
  women's 21
networking 20, 21, 48, 61, 62, 63, 66, 70, 105
nurturant 50, 80, 83, 88, 89
nurturing 8, 21, 23, 81, 83, 90, 99, 104

obstacles 19, 20, 33, 35, 70, 94, 130
    external 20
OECD 15, 16, 32, 61
oppressed 12, 23, 54, 84
oppression 6, 54

participant 5, 38, 55, 68, 90, 95, 98, 102, 108, 120, 127, 132, 133
participation 6, 19, 35, 37, 39, 50, 68, 101, 103, 104, 107, 108, 109, 110, 111, 112, 113, 114, 116, 118, 120, 123, 127, 129, 130, 132, 133
passive 23, 78, 86, 104, 126
patriarchal 23, 25, 63, 84, 89, 99, 111, 117, 119, 124
    power. *see power patriarchal*
    society 11, 13, 104
patriarchy 2, 11, 12, 13, 23, 122
    private 11, 12
    public 11, 12, 104
pipeline 123
policies 4, 6, 28, 39, 108, 111, 113, 114, 123
policy-makers 2, 6, 39
political beliefs 24, 59, 60, 61, 110
power 2, 3, 8, 9, 11, 12, 13, 17, 20, 21, 27, 30, 32, 34, 35, 37, 38, 48, 62, 69, 73, 74, 77, 78, 79, 80, 84, 85, 86, 87, 91, 99, 100, 103, 105, 110, 113, 120, 124, 127, 129
    patriarchal 84
    relations 12, 68, 73, 113
    relationships. *see relationship power*
powerful 25, 48, 57, 69, 77, 79, 80, 86, 88, 89, 90, 104, 105, 127
powerless 57, 69, 77, 84, 86, 125
primary education 1, 2, 13, 14, 27, 28, 29, 30, 33, 44, 63, 130, 131
primary schools 1, 9, 27, 37, 113, 121, 129, 130, 133
principals 20, 45, 54, 94, 130
private 3, 17, 21, 24, 26, 27, 62, 110
    patriarchy. *see patriarchy private*
    sphere. *see sphere private*
professional 13, 17, 24, 27, 45, 50, 51, 56, 62, 69, 71, 79, 81, 90, 92, 94, 101, 120, 123
    identity. *see identity professional*
    networks 15
    responsibilities. *see responsibilities professional*

promotion 20, 22, 34, 37, 52, 53, 61, 63, 66, 95, 131
psychological 6, 105, 106

qualifications 39, 43, 44, 45, 46, 49, 59, 63, 102, 110, 111, 131
qualified 44, 45, 46, 67, 109, 110, 111, 112, 123
qualitative 33, 34, 39, 58, 113, 130, 133
quantitative 29, 34
quota 109, 111, 112, 113, 114, 128
    system 108, 109, 112, 113, 114

Reay and Ball 3, 18, 35, 47, 53, 57, 65, 68, 69, 71, 78, 83, 86, 87, 88, 89, 103, 104, 127, 130, 132, 133
recruitment 20, 62, 112
relations
    gender 6, 9, 11, 12, 39, 73, 122, 124, 125, 129
    gendered 68
    power. *see power relations*
relationship 3, 7, 8, 9, 17, 23, 39, 40, 46, 47, 74, 78, 79, 80, 81, 89, 91, 92, 100, 103, 104, 115
    hierarchical 2, 9, 79, 91
    power 6, 73, 79
representation 22, 26, 29, 35, 83, 105, 111, 114, 119, 120, 124, 125, 126, 129, 131
resistance 16, 56
responsibilities 2, 31, 32, 43, 50, 51, 52, 53, 55, 59, 61, 67, 70, 72, 77, 81, 82, 83, 86, 87, 94, 96, 97, 98, 99, 101, 103, 107, 108, 113, 115, 116, 117, 120, 121, 124, 126, 127, 128, 132
    caring. *see caring responsibilities*
    child 95
    domestic 51, 72, 94, 114, 120
    family 22, 37, 41, 46, 52, 53, 67, 94, 95, 103
    household. *see household responsibilities*
    professional 94
roles 115
    multiple 8, 9, 11, 18, 24, 25, 27, 35, 53, 61, 66, 68, 72, 79, 84, 86, 99, 106, 119, 120, 121, 123, 126, 127, 128, 131
    traditional 118

salaries 15, 20, 24, 32, 33, 63
selection procedures 37, 38, 41, 59, 60, 68, 70, 107, 131
self-esteem 19, 45, 104, 106
sexes 7, 8, 20, 70
sexual orientation 6, 39, 55, 58
sexuality 8, 11, 13, 55, 56, 57, 66, 69
Shakeshaft 2, 3, 16, 17, 19, 22, 27, 45, 58, 62, 92, 101, 102, 105, 106, 107, 116, 131
social constructionist 4, 10, 38, 72, 130
social justice 3
social process 7
social structures 8, 11
sphere 6, 116
   domestic 61
   private 13, 23, 61
   public 11, 12, 13, 61, 104
status 5, 6, 8, 22, 23, 28, 30, 39, 43, 48, 51, 66, 68, 80, 94, 97, 98, 99, 105, 120
stereotypes 7, 11, 20, 24, 35, 49, 53, 65, 66, 67, 68, 70, 75, 81, 83, 94, 104, 105, 109, 113, 124, 126, 128, 131, 132
stereotypical 9, 21, 25, 29, 68, 121
stereotyping 45, 66, 70
style 17, 34, 78
subordinate 21, 22, 23, 78, 84, 86, 99, 103, 105, 120, 124, 125, 126, 127, 128, 133

subordination 11, 12, 91, 104, 128
suitable 33, 37, 48, 66, 67, 83, 84, 90, 98, 113, 130
superintendents 20, 53
superiors 15, 49, 55, 58, 74, 112
support 15, 18, 20, 21, 24, 25, 37, 43, 52, 62, 63, 64, 75, 98, 100, 113, 117, 132

the God trick 5, 38
theoretical 1, 2, 3, 6, 10, 14, 70, 71, 72, 76, 130, 133
   approach. *see approach theoretical*
   framework. *see framework theoretical*

UK 2, 3, 17, 22, 24, 25, 26, 29, 31, 32, 33, 42, 43, 44, 45, 49, 51, 52, 56, 58, 61, 63, 65, 66, 91, 94, 96, 109, 110, 125, 131
underrepresentation 2, 3, 12, 13, 14, 15, 16, 19, 20, 21, 27, 33, 37, 44, 53, 105, 106, 110
unemployment 52, 118, 124
United States 21, 33, 44, 45, 46, 52, 53, 58, 75, 91, 105, 107, 110, 115, 120, 122

Walby 11, 12, 104
women leaders 17, 20, 54, 63, 96, 116, 133
workload 46, 65, 95, 128

www.ingramcontent.com/pod-product-compliance
Lightning Source LLC
Chambersburg PA
CBHW071847230426
43671CB00012B/2087